THIS STRANGER, MY HUSBAND

Dolores Clark thought she knew the man she had married. Bob Clark. A widower who had been shattered by the death of his wife. A kind and gentle suitor who had overcome her reluctance to wed. A hardworking breadwinner. And a deeply God-fearing man.

Everyone else was sure they knew Bob Clark as well. His neighbors, his friends, his employers. A good, decent, generous man, without an ounce of evil in him.

They were wrong. Terribly wrong.

DEATH SENTENCE

The true-crime story that tells the truth about mass murderer John List and the perfectly planned lie he lived.

DEATH SENTENCE

The Inside Story
of the John List Murders

JOE SHARKEY

A SIGNET BOOK

SIGNET
Published by the Penguin Group
Penguin Books USA Inc., 375 Hudson Street,
New York, New York 10014, U.S.A.
Penguin Books Ltd, 27 Wrights Lane,
London W8 5TZ, England
Penguin Books Australia Ltd, Ringwood,
Victoria, Australia
Penguin Books Canada Ltd, 2801 John Street,
Markham, Ontario, Canada L3R 1B4
Penguin Books (N.Z.) Ltd, 182–190 Wairau Road,
Auckland 10, New Zealand

Penguin Books Ltd, Registered Offices:
Harmondsworth, Middlesex, England

First published by Signet, an imprint of New American Library, a division of
Penguin Books USA Inc.

First Printing, August, 1990
10 9 8 7 6 5 4 3 2 1

 REGISTERED TRADEMARK—MARCA REGISTRADA

Printed in the United States of America
Designed by Nissa Knuth-Cassidy

For Nancy

Z 8354

KEY NO FOR READERS
DIGEST

2ND NO ON RIGHT

Acknowledgments

The material in this book was derived from interviews with people directly involved in the story, and from my own reporting across the country tracing the long and secretive odyssey of John Emil List. Where conversation is rendered, it is based on the recollection of at least one party who was involved. No characters have been invented; all of the names are real. I have tried to avoid going beyond known facts in presenting dramatic events; to the best of my knowledge, this is how it happened.

I am very grateful to Jean Syfert, of Midwest City, Oklahoma, and to Edwin A. Illiano, of Elizabeth, New Jersey, for the long hours they spent with me over many months discussing a very painful part of their separate lives.

I also wish to express my thanks to others who, for no reason other than a willingness to help a sometimes confounded reporter get the facts straight, contributed to this project. Among them are Betty Garter Lane, of Richmond, Virginia, and Gary Morrison and Bob Wetmore, both of Denver. In addition, John J. Henderson, of New York, offered early insight that subsequently proved to be most valuable. I want to commend the excellent facilities and helpful staffs of the public libraries of Westfield and Bloomfield, New Jersey, and of the Bay City and Frankenmuth, Michigan, historical societies.

A note of thanks to newspaper friends who provided important encouragement and assistance: Steve Chambers, of the Asbury Park (N.J.) Press; Fred Brock and Jeffrey

A. Trachtenberg of the *Wall Street Journal*; Frank Scandale, of the Elizabeth, New Jersey, *Daily Journal*; Mark Johnson, of the Richmond, Virginia, *Times Dispatch*; Don Hecker of the New York *Daily News*, and Janet Piorko of *The New York Times*. Ed Gravely, of *The New York Times* technology department, kindly and expertly got me out of computer trouble a couple of important times.

Many thanks to the multitalented Carolyn Albaugh, who worked long and hard on the photographs, in some cases miraculously coaxing faded snapshots back to life and, on several occasions, stepping behind the lens herself. More than once, Judson K. Albaugh, M.D., sagely navigated me from the perilous channels of speculative psychology and onto firm ground. Thanks also to Lisa Sharkey, Caroline Sharkey, and Christopher Sharkey for their encouragement and understanding, and for those long walks in the city. I also want to thank my parents, Joseph and Marcella Sharkey, of Cape Coral, Florida, who proved that a good marriage, well and honestly lived, is the real pot of gold at the end of a rainbow.

My agent, Jane Dystel, was a teacher and a friend; my editor, Michaela Hamilton, was patient and supportive when it counted most. Her guidance is greatly appreciated.

Nancy Albaugh Sharkey, the finest journalist I know, selflessly took out an oar and helped to paddle through the white water on a couple of memorable occasions during this endeavor. I am most grateful for her help. It is to my wife's standards of accuracy and empathy that this book aspires.

O Jerusalem, wash your heart from
        wickedness
    that you may be saved
How long shall your evil thoughts
    lodge within you?

Like keepers of a field are they
    against her round about,
because she has rebelled against me,
        says the Lord.

Your ways and your doings
    have brought this upon you.
This is your doom, and it is bitter;
    it has reached your very heart.
My anguish, my anguish! I writhe in
        pain!
My heart is beating wildly;
    I cannot keep silent;
for I hear the sound of the trumpet,
    the alarm of war.
Disaster follows hard on disaster,
    the whole land is laid waste.
Suddenly my tents are destroyed,
    my curtains in a moment.
How long must I see the standard
    and hear the sound of the trumpet?
For my people are foolish,
    they know me not;
they are stupid children,
    they have no understanding.
They are skilled in doing evil,
    but how to do good they know not.
                                    —Jeremiah

PART ONE

Descent into Hell

Prologue

ON TWO OCCASIONS IN 1971, JOHN LIST CAME TO THE Westfield, New Jersey, police station—once at the behest of the police, and once on his own initiative.

The first time was at two-thirty in the morning on a sultry late summer's day. His daughter, sixteen-year-old Patricia List, a pretty and vivacious girl who was called Patty by her family and Pat by her friends, had been stopped by a Westfield patrol car and brought in to headquarters in the municipal building beside the park. She was accompanied by a girlfriend. The girls' only offense had been to be out walking on the dark streets after midnight, smoking cigarettes and giggling as they strolled. But in small towns such as Westfield, walking the sidewalks after the shops have closed is an activity looked upon with some suspicion, and so the girls found themselves in custody, in tears, waiting for their fathers to come down in the middle of the night and pick them up.

The father of Pat's friend showed up somewhat annoyed, both at his daughter for slipping out of the house and at the police for taking her into custody.

Pat's father, on the other hand, showed up in a red-faced, tight-lipped rage that was directed at his daughter.

But that isn't what the police found most remarkable about John List when they had cause to recall the man four months later. Many fathers would be furious under such circumstances.

3

What they really remembered about John was that the man, who had clearly been asleep when the night sergeant phoned, showed up in a suit and tie, smelling faintly of after-shave lotion.

"Who gets up and puts on a suit, with a white shirt and tie, at two-thirty in the morning?" the police chief at the time, James Moran, recalled wondering the next morning when an officer mentioned it to him casually.

"Oh, I know the guy," put in another cop, a man who drove a patrol car. "The guy lives in a big house up on Hillside Avenue. I've seen him out there mowing his lawn in a suit and tie."

Four months later, when Chief Moran arrived at the grisly crime scene where the bodies lay on the ballroom floor, that was what he recalled about the head of the List household: The guy in the suit and tie did this.

The memory of the night at the police station troubled the teenaged girl for what little time she had left to live. Although Pat seldom mentioned her family life to friends— "We were preoccupied with being hip," one of them, Eileen Livesey, recalled. "It just wasn't hip to talk about your family"—Pat did tell another friend about being brought in by the police and brought home by her father.

John didn't speak to his daughter in the old Chevy that night as he drove the mile back to the house on Hillside Avenue, in the most affluent section of town. That wasn't a surprise, however. John had almost completely stopped speaking to his daughter several months earlier, after he had told her he strongly disapproved of her friends, whom he regarded as hippies; her attitude, which he decided had become rebellious; and her aspiration to have a career in the theater, which he considered beneath contempt.

Despite the hour, John slammed the car door loudly when he parked in the drive that curved behind the big Victorian house. Once inside, he made enough of a commotion to wake the entire household, which, besides John and his daughter, consisted on that night of Helen List, John's wife; John and Fred List, their two younger teenaged sons; Alma List, John's aged mother; and Eva Morris, Helen's mother, who was on an extended visit and would depart for North Carolina by the end of the month.

John, a taciturn man who seldom raised his voice, even when severely provoked, began berating his daughter in the center hall that dominated the interior of the nineteen-room house.

"You are out of control!" he shouted at the girl.

"But Daddy, we were only—"

"You are going straight to hell, and there is nothing I can do about it!"

For a second, she told her friend later, she was afraid he would slap her across her face, although John had never raised a hand to any of his children. Pat held her ground silently, without defiance.

"There is *nothing* I can do!" John said loudly, with a note of finality in his voice.

On either side of the center hall was a grand staircase that curled up to landings on the second and third floors. A large amber chandelier hung from the ceiling high above the hall. On the second floor, the noise had drawn Helen from her bedroom to the railing, where she stood in her nightgown. Down the hall, the fifteen-year-old, John, and his thirteen-year-old brother, Fred, huddled with their grandmother, Eva. Above, on the landing outside her apartment on the third floor, John's mother also was awake, lingering quietly in the shadows.

"I'm sorry, Daddy," Pat was pleading downstairs. As she started up the steps, Helen moved more into the light to wait for her.

"Slut!" John shouted at the girl, who had never heard him use such a word before and was stunned by the insult.

Helen, who had been seriously ill, put her arms around Pat as the girl reached the top of the stairs.

"Sluts!" John raged from below, pointing a finger of accusation now at both his daughter and his wife. "Sluts! Sluts!"

John did not sleep upstairs that night. Instead he retired, as he often did in those days, to a room that he insisted on calling the "billiard room," even though it hadn't seen a billiard table for many years before the Lists bought the house six years earlier.

The room, which was situated just under the ballroom in a wing on the left side of the house, was furnished meagerly, with a cot, a table and lamp, some chairs, and a number of bookshelves on which John stored some of the things that gave him comfort as his troubles reached the point in 1971 when he decided to deal with them decisively.

These comforts included books, the most important of which was the Bible which he read every night, often with his mother in the solace of her apartment. There also was a collection of murder mysteries and books on unsolved crimes.

There were some framed photographs: John and the boys in their Cub Scout uniforms; Mother pushing the infant Patty in a stroller in a long-gone happier time; Helen, beautiful and alluring, in the years before she became ill.

He also had a large collection of military strategy board games, which were stacked like books on the shelves. When he got out of the army after the Korean War, John began developing an avid interest in these complex board games, which demanded progressive degrees of skill and cunning over many hours of play. Many of the games had World War II themes, with names like Third Reich and Russian Front. John, when he played with an opponent, always took the German side in these. Others were based on the Civil War, including one of his favorites, Bull Run, which required tactical skill in re-creating the First Battle of Bull Run.

In that battle, according to the manufacturer's description of the game, "Both armies had the strange and fascinating task of defending on one flank while attacking on the other."

There was one other item in the room worthy of note, a calendar. John had recently scrawled a thick red circle around a date in November. In the summer of 1971, John had decided, the time had come to augment his ongoing defense against a tormenting world with a surprise attack.

But John played by the rules. This accounts for his second visit to the Westfield police station, less than two months later, in October. He came to be fingerprinted for a firearms registration application. "Home protection" was the reason he gave.

Three weeks after that, John would confront his wife and daughter once again. This time, he would have a gun in his hand. And when it was done, he would take no prisoners. Except for John List himself, there wouldn't be any survivors.

Chapter One

ALONG WITH ALL OF THE TERRIBLE THINGS, BRENDA remembered some good ones, such as ice fishing on the Saginaw River with the man she called Daddy.

Like most happy childhood memories, this one undoubtedly benefits from a degree of melancholy hindsight. But it says something about the kind of father John List once had tried to be that the one child who did not die at his hands—actually, she was a stepdaughter, and she was grown and married by the time of the murders—could summon a loving picture of him, despite what happened.

John was no fisherman. An occasional stroll down the block or a Saturday trip to the zoo was the closest the man usually got to nature. But he understood the role of father and, in the early years at least, he worked diligently at playing it, even if it meant sitting on a frozen river with a line in his hands, not knowing what he would do if he pulled it up with a fish on the hook. John didn't even like to eat cooked fish. He was quite certain he wouldn't want to touch a living one.

Yet on regular winter visits with his wife, Brenda, and infant Patty to his widowed mother in Bay City, Michigan, a town beside the frozen river that widens into Saginaw Bay a few miles downstream, he would bundle the girl up and take her to a place where, for a couple of dollars, they would rent tackle and a couple of folding chairs beside a hole cut through the ice.

Before they left the house, both John and Brenda would
be subject to the inspection of John's mother, Alma, a tall,
white-haired woman with formal bearing who would make
sure their scarves were tucked in and boots were laced up
before sending them off with an exasperated admonition
delivered in a German-accented voice: "You vill catch your
death of cold!"

On these occasions, while John and Brenda were out
fishing, Helen, a North Carolina girl who had no love of
the cold, would stay behind in Alma's house on Wenona
Avenue. But they wouldn't spend the day together. From
the day John first brought his wife back home to meet
Mother during Christmas of 1951, Alma had regarded her
daughter-in-law with a disdain that her frosty manner
scarcely concealed.

When John and Brenda would return (without fish) in
the late afternoon after a few hours on the river, Alma
would be bustling in the kitchen, preparing the sort of
heavy German dinner that she insisted could ward off winter illnesses. Patty, whom the grandmother adored, would
be amusing herself contentedly nearby in the playpen.
Helen would be upstairs in the guest room, reading a book.

"That woman is on the remake," Alma once said of
Helen to a close friend. She meant "rebound." Rolling her
eyes, she added, "and with a ten-year-old child from a
previous marriage!

"With his education, the intelligence he has, my
Chonny," Alma lamented, "could have done so much
better."

Helen, a woman always sensitive to a slight, responded
to her mother-in-law's disapproval by shutting the old
woman out of her life as much as was possible for someone
married to a man who was referred to all of his life as a
"mama's boy." Within a few years, after the two other
children, John and Frederick, were born, Helen would
consider herself sufficiently estranged from Alma that she

didn't feel compelled to exchange more than a few civil words with the woman. After a while, Helen simply refused to accompany John, or to let him take the children, on his visits to his mother.

As a result, early in his marriage, John was already finding himself torn between these two women—a protective mother whose approval he had basked in all of his life and a resentful wife whose approval he couldn't seem to get, no matter how he tried to win it, or even to buy it.

It was one of the many conflicts that he would ultimately settle, over the course of one long and bloody day, with a stunning finality that would cause those who knew him, or thought they did, to wonder which clues they had missed that might have indicated just how deep and dangerous was the anger that raged below the calm, well-mannered surface of John List.

In fact, there no apparent clues at all.

No one could have guessed, because no one alive really got close enough to see how tightly the spring was coiling.

John Emil List was born in Bay City, Michigan, on September 17, 1925, to John Frederick and Alma Marie List. At sixty-four, John's father was twenty-six years older than Alma, whom he had married one year earlier, after his first wife died of cancer. With his first wife, John Frederick had had a son, William George, who happened to be the same age as Alma. John Frederick had met Alma when he hired her as a live-in registered nurse to care for his terminally ill first wife.

John List's parents were descended along parallel branches of the same family, whose roots in Michigan had been established by two enterprising brothers who shared the same first name, Johann List and Johann Adam List. The brothers emigrated to America from Bavaria in 1845 and 1846 respectively, at the behest of the fledgling U.S. German Lutheran church.

The Lutherans were seeking missionaries to proselytize the Chippewa Indians in a section of Michigan near Bay City, a hundred miles north of Detroit. Along with the missionaries came Bavarian farmers and craftsmen who helped to hack out a new life in the hardwood wilderness along the banks of the Cass River.

The community they founded was called Frankenmuth, and for almost a hundred years it remained an enclave of German-speaking farmers and tradesmen, all of whom belonged to the conservative Missouri Synod branch of the Lutheran church. In the rural isolation of Frankenmuth, lives traditionally centered, with little deviation permitted, on God, family, obedience, hard work, and thrift.

Both of the immigrant List brothers figure prominently in the history of the town and the church that was its center. But of the two, the older, Johann Adam, was the more renowned—a master carpenter who designed and built many of the community's houses, farm buildings, and wooden bridges. He was also a folk artist whose drawings would be displayed in the local museum more than a hundred years after his death. More important, he became a towering pillar of his church and community, serving many terms as a treasurer of both.

This man was Alma's grandfather. Her father, Michael Johann, followed in his footsteps as a master carpenter. Michael was one of the designers and builders of the pride of Frankenmuth, the church of St. Lorenz, constructed on the site of the log cabin where the settlers first worshipped.

It was her grandfather and her father who Alma held up to her son John as role models.

It wasn't that the other side of the family were slouchers. It was just that they had ventured more boldly into a world outside the security of Frankenmuth, a world that Alma saw as morally perilous, even though she lived in it. It is a small indication of the dichotomy that Alma now lies buried in Frankenmuth and her husband in Bay City.

Alma's husband, John Frederick, was the son of the younger immigrant brother, Johann. As a young man, John Frederick struck out from Frankenmuth for a more exciting and prosperous life, which he found less than twenty miles away, in Bay City, where the Saginaw River enters the bay.

In the late 1870s, when John Frederick came to town, Bay City was far removed from the austerity of his native Frankenmuth. Once an Indian trading village, Bay City had developed rapidly after the Civil War into the commercial and shipping center for a regional lumber industry that was expanding wildly to meet the needs of the growing population along the Great Lakes. When the burly young man arrived, there were thirty-six sawmills along the banks of the Saginaw. "Some of them," according to a 1941 Federal Writers' Project history of the era, "were among the largest in the country. The settlements constituted a one-industry town; the whine of saws biting into logs was heard ten hours a day, and the smell of fresh lumber was strong enough to flavor food. The lumber lined the banks of the river so solidly that the Saginaw appeared to flow between wooden walls."

Yet John Frederick avoided the commercial district on the east bank of the Saginaw, where whiskey-swilling lumberjacks caroused till dawn, and settled instead on the west bank, in a small German community called Salzburg. There, he worked diligently, in a general store and later a planing mill, and saved his money. By the turn of the century, he had married and fathered a son, and was prosperous enough not only to purchase fifty-six acres of good farmland just outside of town but also to start his own dry-goods business in a brick building on Salzburg Avenue with the name "LIST" chiseled in stone at the cornice.

By 1925, John Frederick was comfortably into his sixties,

a man well able to look back on his accomplishments and not particularly disposed to look forward, even with a new wife and an infant son at home.

The house on Wenona Avenue that John Emil List grew up in was a substantial Victorian dwelling. During the early years of the Depression, his father had remodeled the upper floor into an apartment. Thrift, not pressing financial need, prompted John Frederick to become a landlord.

With tenants upstairs, the Lists lived on the ground floor, which had a large kitchen, where Alma spent most of her time; one large bedroom; a bathroom; and a formal parlor.

All of the time he lived at home, the boy had to sleep on the couch in the parlor, which had no door. In the daytime, before he hurried off to the Lutheran elementary school a few blocks away, or public high school in later years, young John had to put his sheets and blanket away, along with books, clothes, and other personal effects. The boy grew up with the understanding that he was not to leave a trace of his tenancy behind.

"He was the neatest little boy I ever saw," said Laura Werner, a woman who rented the apartment in the List house with her husband for many years when John was growing up. "You never knew he was around."

It was an ability, or perhaps an affliction, that many people remarked on when they discussed John List. "He was there, but he just blended into the background," said a school classmate.

John Frederick, a stern old German, usually dealt with his son, whom he always referred to as "the boy," through his wife. The boy was expected to be seen when necessary, and not heard unless invited. He was expected to excel in school and to reflect the family dignity in church. Aside from that, a largely disinterested John Frederick went about his business and left it to his wife to bring up their child.

People who knew the family when John was growing up do not recall images of the boy and his father together, except at church services, which were conducted in High German.

Beyond his industry, his deep booming voice, and bristling black mustache, there are few things people alive today remember about John Frederick, except for the Halloween incident.

This occurred shortly before young John went to high school, on a Halloween night, when a couple of neighborhood boys, unhappy at the fact that treats weren't being passed out at the List house, rang the doorbell and ran away to hide and laugh in the bushes. After this happened several times, John Frederick, a man who despised Halloween as a celebration of evil, flew out the door in a fury and gave chase with such determination that one of the boys, his bravado in hasty retreat, stumbled into a gully and sprained an ankle. His wails of pain brought the neighbors out.

As boys will do when misfortune follows a prank, they tried to convince their parents that old List, then in his seventies but still in robust health, had stormed violently out after trick-or-treaters who came innocently to his door. Since John Frederick was already regarded as something of a neighborhood crank—he was known for hollering at any youth who happened to cross his property line—there was talk of bringing assault charges against him. It required the intercession of the Lutheran minister to dissuade the injured boy's outraged parents from having John Frederick arrested.

The incident aroused enough bad will that it was remembered even fifty years later in the old neighborhood. One of the things people recall is that John Frederick's son, who was never allowed out on Halloween night, bore the brunt of the residual resentment. For years afterward, other neighborhood boys taunted him with the nickname "Trick-or-Treat Johnny."

John grew up in a cocoon protected by his mother, whose warmth was in sharp contrast to her husband's coldness. Where John Frederick went to work early in the morning and came home late, and liked to spend his scant leisure time in solitude, Alma had friends and liked to spend time with them, even if only to pass the time of day at the bakery or the butcher shops on Salzburg Avenue, a short walk from her house.

As it would be for her son, the Lutheran church was the center of her social life. In Bay City, this was Zion Lutheran, affiliated with the strict Missouri Synod, whose traditions stressed the "inspiration, inerrancy and infallability" of the Bible against the creeping liberalism of the modern world. Obedience to God and other responsible authority was stressed with clarion clarity. So firm is the bulwark against liberalism that even today men and women at Zion Lutheran give different responses to the pastor's invocation during services.

When John was growing up, his father, continuing in the family tradition that Alma insisted her son eventually emulate, was the parish treasurer and a trustee of the church.

A picture many remember of mother and son together is their arrival with John Frederick at church. Usually, the boy and his mother, hand in hand, followed a few steps behind the father. On Sunday afternoons after church, Alma always cooked a hearty meal, which often would be attended by a few of her relatives or friends from church. As she cooked, John would sit in the steamy kitchen, reading. He wasn't encouraged to go out and play with other children. Most nights, he and his mother read the Bible together.

Said a relative, "His mother was afraid he would get a

cold, or even get his hands dirty. She watched him like a hawk. After a while, as I recall, no one even asked him out to play." One picture that persists is that of a boy bundled in layers of winter clothing with a wool scarf and shiny black galoshes, standing on the schoolyard sidelines with his arms dangling and eyeglasses slightly fogged, looking as if his protective bulk would prevent him from getting up again if he ever fell over.

"She was careful of him," said Laura Werner, the tenant, who would become a lifelong friend of Alma's. "There were children in the neighborhood that she didn't approve of for John. She didn't let him go in the street, and she made sure he stayed away from the railroad tracks" even as an adolescent.

In fact, the neighborhood was a commercial area and trains shrieked by on the Michigan Central tracks a half block away, so there was reason for a degree of caution. But those who knew him all describe John as a boy who seemed smothered by his mother's protectiveness, a boy whose idea of the world was defined by his mother as a place of peril and disorder, unworthy of more than a passing nod.

"Mrs. List reminded me of a queen," said a former neighbor who is John's age. "She stood very erect, with her chin up, and spoke precisely, like she was addressing a group even when it was only just you. It didn't matter that she would say things like 'chust' instead of 'just' with that German accent. We thought she was like a queen. And Johnny, he sure was her little prince."

Nevertheless, John is also recalled as a quiet, likable boy, with delicate, almost girlish features, with cupid's-bow lips and soft, watchful brown eyes that projected, as did the submissive tilt of his head when being directly addressed, an eagerness to please, to be liked, to be of assistance.

High school provided John with his first small taste of

independence. Much to his mother's consternation, it required a daily trip out of the neighborhood, across the Lafayette Street bridge over the Saginaw River and into downtown Bay City. For a boy who was never allowed to venture far from the front porch, John figured out his bus connections easily.

The bus took him along Center Avenue, the city's finest street, where lumber barons and shipping magnates had built their mansions during the boom days. While in high school, John took a part-time job at the Sage Library, housed in what had once been a lumberman's French Provincial mansion, with grounds shaded by towering trees. It was just the sort of elegant house, John told a high school classmate, that he wished to live in someday.

At Bay City's Central High School, despite his eagerness to please, John barely made an impression on his classmates, even though he would become the most famous graduate of the class of 1943. He had few male friends, and no girlfriends, and those people who vaguely remembered him recalled a tall, bookish, deeply religious boy, always snappily dressed, who never participated in group activities. The record shows he was a member of the school's chapter of the National Honor Society. The yearbook had a section called "class prophesy," but amid all the wisecracks, no one apparently was able to come up with anything amusing to say about John. It was merely predicted that he would wind up in the army supply corps.

Twenty-eight years later, when John's mild countenance appeared on television and in the newspapers identified as a fugitive wanted for what the FBI flier termed "multiple murders involving members of his family," stunned classmates had to dig out their high school yearbooks just to make the connection.

"John List just blended into the scenery," said Ann Hachtel, a high school classmate who briefly dated him in college and *even then* did not recall him from her high school class.

The class of 1943 had more on its mind than socializing, however. By the time John graduated in June, almost half of the boys in his senior class had already opted for early graduation to join the service.

Always intensely patriotic, John itched to get to the action, and only his mother's importuning prevented him from dropping out of high school early to enlist. Soon after graduation, he was in the service.

But so were sixteen million others as the war entered its final stages. With well-trained troops poised for major assaults in Europe and Asia, the immediate demand for cannon fodder had abated, and Private List unhappily spent his first year in the army in unglorious Louisiana. In his letters home, he made it clear that army life, where the rules were almost as clear and inflexible as they were at Zion Lutheran Church, suited him fine.

On August 30, 1944, the base chaplain called him in to inform John that his father had died. He was given emergency leave to attend the funeral.

"John came home all proud in his uniform," said a relative. "But he seemed a little embarrassed about not being overseas."

The funeral was one of the first occasions that would prompt people to remark on how cold and impassive John could be. Laura Werner, who had lived with her husband in the apartment in the List house until 1941, recalled that Alma sent John over in his father's car to pick her up for the funeral.

"John was as nice as could be," said the woman, who had just had her first child. "He held the baby." But she noticed with a slight chill that John showed no sign whatsoever of grief. "It was as if nothing happened," she said.

* * *

Soon after the funeral, John was finally shipped overseas to Europe, where Allied forces were well on their way into Germany. With the Nazi surrender imminent in early 1945, John and hundreds of thousands of other servicemen suddenly found themselves bound for the other side of the world, for the Pacific theater. But no sooner had that great wave of troops rolled in than the war with Japan was over, too. It took the bloated military bureaucracy almost as long to disgorge millions of homesick and now superfluous troops as it had to process them into war in the first place. On April 22, 1946, eight months after the end of the war, Private First Class John List returned home to his widowed mother.

Back in mufti, John made a point of not discussing his overseas service, as if he were healing from a dark and painful experience. The truth is, John never saw much action. As one older relative noted, he spent a total of only eleven months overseas, and a good portion of that in transit, or in waiting to be transferred. On both fronts, by the time John got to war it was almost over.

Like most soldiers, John came back from the war with a handful of routine campaign medals. Less routine, for a boy who had been so sheltered, was a new interest in firearms and in the strategy of war. Among the war souvenirs that John displayed proudly were two that would cast a chilling shadow toward the future. One was an Army sharpshooter's badge. The other was a pistol, a classic Austrian Steyr that he had purchased in 1944 and used to qualify for the sharpshooter's badge.

He wouldn't fire the pistol again for twenty-seven years.

Chapter Two

JOHN'S FATHER HAD ALWAYS SALTED HIS MONEY AWAY. The general store on Salzburg Avenue had prospered with the regional economy; by World War I, when the lumber boom was largely spent, the speculators began fleeing Bay City. Across the river, Salzburg's business district began a slow decline. But the thrifty people stayed and rebuilt an economy based on mining, fishing, and beet-sugar farming.

The fifty-six acres of farmland the old man had bought for $900 in 1901 lay just to the west of town, precisely the area that came under cultivation for beet sugar with the waning of the lumber industry. Later, after World War II, the same area would be in demand for suburban development. Thanks to her husband's prudence, Alma was able to live with a comfortable nest egg for almost the rest of her life.

Home from the war and eager to set out on a career, John began making plans with his mother for college. Alma edged him into accounting, a field more suited to the sensibilities of her branch of the List family tree than to the entrepreneurial bent of her late husband's. Accounting was stable. Given hard work and careful planning, an accountant had respect, position, an office with a name on the door and a receptionist out front, not like some dry-goods store with a screen door that anybody off the street could bang through.

Because of its respected business administration master's program and its proximity, Alma and her son decided on the University of Michigan in Ann Arbor, a hundred miles south of Bay City. Tuition, room, and board were about $900 a year, easily covered by GI Bill benefits of $65 a month, augmented by savings from the Army.

John joined millions of other former servicemen in the trek to the campuses in 1946, where their arrival was marked by two phenomena: Being older and, given the long deprivations of the war, more motivated, they tended to be serious students with little time for college frivolities. And, with their sheer overwhelming numbers, they effected a dramatic transformation of the American campus itself, especially at the state and other land-grant universities, where students on the G.I. Bill were flocking. Campuses reverberated with the roar of bulldozers and the clanging of hammers as new buildings—dorms to house them, classrooms to educate them, dining halls to feed them—rose in a profusion that would forever change the physical and even academic structures of most American colleges.

"They were purposeful, serious-minded young men, and I say men deliberately. One occasionally looked over the class rosters at the beginning of the year and saw a woman's name, but most of the students, the large majority, were men," recalled Paul W. McCracken, who came to Ann Arbor as a young professor of economics in those postwar years, and who later would serve as chairman of the President's Council of Economic Advisers.

At Michigan, as at other business schools of the time, the teaching method was geared toward creating analytical ability. Case studies were the main tool—"solving a problem at Podunk Paper Company," McCracken said. "Students were prepared to suggest ways of solving specific problems at companies, but were not prepared for interdisciplinary thinking and a good grounding in other, related fields."

Assessments like this, ironically, would be applied to John List throughout his later career. John, employers would later decide, was fine at solving problems step by step in a structured environment. But in the management environment he aspired to in a changing American workplace, John would later get poor grades from employers for his inability to adapt and move beyond the structures.

In college, John's continued the aloofness that had characterized him in high school. But while they were barely noticing him, he seemed to pay careful attention to his classmates. In many letters from college to his mother and to a few other older people like Laura Werner who had gained his trust, he referred often to classmates by name, as though they were close chums. Yet most of these people later had a difficult time remembering him. Indeed, one of them, a classmate named Robert Clark, whose name John would adopt as his own in a later life, couldn't recall ever meeting the man.

At least once a month, Alma visited her son for the weekend, making the three-hour bus trip from Bay City to Ann Arbor on a Friday night. She stayed at a rooming house recommended by the campus Lutheran organization. On those weekends, mother and son spent all of their time together, usually going out for dinner on Saturday nights and always attending church services at the Lutheran center on Sundays. While together, they invariably found a quiet spot—in the student union when it was cold, on a bench outside in nice weather—to read and discuss the Bible.

Like all unmarried students who didn't commute, John was required to live in a dorm, in this case Wenley House in the West Quad. Still, his group activity was confined to the university's Lutheran student organization, Gamma Delta. There, at least, John was well remembered, as a willing volunteer who was always on hand early to help set the tables and serve food for the weekly Sunday suppers, which began at five-thirty and were followed by a religious program. As many as a hundred students attended, and John was always among the first arrivals, to help set up tables. Moreover, when the volunteer work list was posted for cleanups and other chores, John's name was always near the top.

In his senior year, John joined the fraternity for business majors, Delta Sigma Pi, which had about fifty members. It wasn't a social fraternity; most of its efforts were centered on corporate recruiting and on what, thirty years later, would come to be known as "networking." Throughout college, John also belonged to the Army Reserve Officer Training Corps, in which students trained in uniform several times a week and spent an intensified period of summer training before senior year.

In June 1950, John, a solid B student, graduated with a bachelor's degree in business administration. Because of the ROTC, he was also commissioned as a second lieutenant in the army reserve. In early September, thanks to an accelerated master's program in business at Michigan and the awarding of certain credits for Army service experience, John and his mother stood beaming as he was awarded his M.B.A.

Meanwhile, his networking at Delta Sigma Pi paid off. Ernst & Ernst, the prestigious accounting firm, hired him as a junior auditor in its Detroit office. The starting pay was $56.25 a week, a respectable salary for the time. Energetic and ambitious, he quickly qualified as a certified public accountant.

But there was a sudden career delay. In June 1950, North Korean tanks rumbled across the 38th parallel; by the time John moved to Detroit, U.S. forces were being rapidly mobilized. He knew it was only a matter of time before his army reserve unit was called up.

This occurred in November. With a leave of absence

from Ernst & Ernst, burning once more with patriotism, John was back in uniform full time. But this time he had a status that he and Alma found more appropriate. He was an officer.

To his chagrin, he didn't see action in Korea, either. Instead, he spent most of the Korean War in Virginia, eventually winding up at the large army base at Fort Eustis, situated among the jumble of military installations that sprawl along the peninsula of southern Virginia between the James River and Chesapeake Bay.

This time, army life was significantly more pleasant than it was in World War II. Korea was officially described not as a war but as a "police action," waged entirely within the confines of one small country. Since the drastic de-mobilization that had followed World War II (the troop strength of the army alone plummeted from a 1945 peak of 8.3 million to a mere 591,000 at the beginning of 1950), the generals and admirals had been aghast at how ema-ciated their bureaucracies had become. Korea afforded a perfect opportunity to quickly fatten up the ranks well beyond the immediate needs of a fierce but limited military conflict.

For young stateside officers such as John, this translated into ample time to pursue their own interests. As a ded-icated number cruncher, John took advantage of various specialized army schools on the strategy and logistics of transporting people and material under both peacetime and wartime conditions. Off the base, he passed up the sur-rounding towns with their noisy bars and credit jewelry shops in favor of touring the Civil War battlefields and other outposts of the Old Confederacy that dotted the Rich-mond area. An avid history buff, he often whiled away whole Saturdays poring over historical archives.

Not that he was a recluse. He had began to date women occasionally in college, usually at parties and outings spon-sored by the Lutheran group. But in a military area swarm-

ing with hordes of lonely men in uniform, it was difficult
to meet women who didn't make their living in bars. So
when he did socialize, it was usually with a small group
of male friends from the post.

On one such occasion, on Saturday night, October 13,
1951, John and two other junior officers went bowling in
nearby Newport News. One of them, whose name was
Ted, soon began teasing two attractive young women bowling in the adjoining lane. The women were not good bowl-
ers. Many of the balls they rolled wobbled down the gutter,
giving the soldiers in the next lane ample opportunity to
show off.

Before long, Ted was paying great attention to one of
the women, a thin and pretty woman who told him her
name was Helen Taylor.

Helen had reluctantly gone out that night with her sister, Jean Syfert. Just the day before, Helen had buried her
husband, Marvin Taylor, a soldier who had been killed in
Korea a full six months earlier and whose body had only
recently been returned to the States. Widowed at twenty-
six, with a nine-year-old daughter, the distraught Helen
was living with her parents, Eva and Edward Morris, in
Newport News.

The funeral, of course, had reopened a wound that had
begun to heal. After the services Helen cried all day and
all night. The next night, Jean took her bowling to help
her get her mind off her misery.

While Ted worked on winning Helen's attention, John
struck up a conversation with her younger sister, Jean,
who quickly warned him that she was married and had a
child. This seemed to relax John rather than put him off.
Sensing that he was only looking for a friendly chat, Jean
returned his friendliness. She liked him right off. She was
impressed at how gentlemanly he was, and wondered to
herself if he might be someone Helen would find in-

teresting. They seemed so *opposite*, she thought. But still . . .

It was too late. Ted had already managed to make a date with Helen.

Ted and Helen saw each other two or three times, but then Ted let slip that he had a wife somewhere. Helen dropped him like a hot coal.

The next thing she knew, John was calling.

"To be truthful with you, I think the first time we met, John was interested in me," Jean said many years later. "But I wasn't available."

John began enthusiastically courting Helen, who seemed to welcome the attention.

Helen's nine-year-old daughter, Brenda, recalled in a 1971 interview with the New York *Daily News* that her mother "was in bad shape then, really destroyed over my real dad's death, and she had been seeing a lot of men. I guess she just settled on John."

John's inexperience with women was actually a plus as far as Helen was concerned. Having left high school at sixteen to marry her first husband and knowing nothing else as an adult except marriage, she was anxious to find a new husband. So John List wasn't terribly exciting. So he had those quirky little mannerisms and seemed a little . . . well, prim. He was steady, well educated, kind, and obviously ambitious, with a future ahead of him after the army. He obviously was infatuated with her. John was as good a prospect as was likely to emerge anytime soon in Newport News, and Helen used his naiveté to her advantage. They were quickly in bed together.

Jean and her husband, Gene, didn't think much of him, and for differing reasons. Gene, then a young officer in the air force, simply disliked John. He didn't make any bones about it within the family then—and he didn't need much prompting forty years later. "I didn't like him," said Gene, a pleasant, soft-spoken man who would spend twenty years in the air force and then retire to a second career as an Oklahoma schoolteacher. "He wasn't one of my favorite people. He had feminine tendencies, you see. I considered him a mama's boy." He thought that over briefly and added flatly: "I thought they had a loser from the word go."

His wife had a different problem. She liked John just fine. He clearly had a kind nature, and seemed intelligent in most ways. But he was *timid*, which was the last thing anyone would ever call her impetuous older sister Helen. And what's worse, he already seemed to be deliriously in love, spending most of his weekly paycheck on a woman he had just met. This didn't strike Jean as a propitious sign. Helen, she thought, needed a firmer partner, someone tough like Marvin, who had been able to keep a lid on Helen's excesses—not the least of which was her propensity, in Jean's estimation, to "spend money like it was going to be out of style by tomorrow." She wondered how John, whom she had already seen as being unable to manage his money, would ever be able to deal with Helen.

Helen, for her part, was already pressing hard for marriage. Finally, John got nervous, especially after talking over the situation by phone with his mother in Bay City and realizing that she strongly disapproved of his liaison with the woman he described.

Casting about, he solicited other opinions. Ann Hachtel, the Bay City classmate, remembered thinking how odd it was that John would write from Virginia to ask her for advice on marriage, years after they had last seen each other. "He was uncertain," she recalled. Her reply was that if he really believed Helen was the right one for him, he should marry her.

Sensing her boyfriend's waffling, Helen promptly announced to anyone who would listen that she was pregnant. For his part, John didn't make any more of a secret about this than Helen did. In fact, he seemed proud to let others know that he had scored.

"Helen is pregnant, we've been intimate several times. What in the world can I do?" John told an army acquaintance one night back at the post. "We have to get married."

On December 1, 1951, with Jean and Gene Syfert acting as witnesses, John and Helen were married in a Lutheran church in Baltimore. It was eight months after Helen's first husband had been killed in action, and less than two months since the newlyweds had met at the bowling alley. Helen wore a smart wool suit that her sister had helped her to choose, and John wore his army uniform. Before the wedding, Helen, a Methodist, agreed to John's only condition, that she join him in belonging to the Lutheran church.

In order to allow time for a visit to Bay City to introduce his new bride to his mother, John took only a few days leave for the honeymoon. They spent it in nearby Washington, D.C., with the Syferts along for the trip. One night, at Helen's insistence, the four of them went to a swank nightclub and had a grand time eating and drinking, laughing and dancing. Gene Syfert ended up with the bill— he didn't complain about it, but he never forgot how much it was, either: seventy-four dollars, about a month's salary for a young officer.

Then, leaving Brenda in Newport News with Helen's mother, John and Helen borrowed the Syferts' car and drove up to Bay City, where Alma was polite but cool toward her new daughter-in-law. But she told a friend afterward that she was devastated at her son's choice in a wife.

John didn't seem fazed when, shortly after the wedding, Helen told him that she had been wrong about being pregnant. He was, in fact, delighted to be married to such an attractive woman. In January 1952, after having been promoted to first lieutenant, the new husband wrote proudly

to his boss back at Ernst & Ernst: "I spent three months
at Fort Eustis, Va., attending transportation school. That
is also where I met my wife. We were married before I
left Virginia. I feel very well adjusted to the Army regi-
men."

The military being regarded an institution that liked
nothing less than to see its troops in stationary position for
any length of time, John received orders soon after his
marriage transferring him to an army accounting center
near San Francisco, where preparations were being made
to process back into civilian life the hundreds of thousands
of returning troops who would begin flooding West Coast
military facilities once the impending cease-fire took hold
in Korea. John and Helen, setting off for what they knew
would be a fairly short time in California, left Brenda
behind in the care of Helen's mother. But at the last minute, John decided to invite his own mother along for the
trip. Mother, he explained, had never seen California and
might never again have the opportunity.

Helen didn't especially care whether Alma got to see
California or not. At the time, though, she kept her sentiments largely to herself, not fully aware yet that Alma
would be a close presence in the List household throughout
the remainder of her life as John List's wife.

Born on January 1, 1925, Helen was nine months older
than her new husband and far more experienced. The third
of five children, she grew up in Greensboro, North Carolina, where her father worked in a cotton mill and her
mother rode herd on the household. One of the things
Helen's sister was most reluctant to discuss was this:
"Helen was an abused child," is all Jean would say. "Physically abused."

Helen had been agitating to get away from home when
she married Marvin Everett Taylor, a twenty-three-year-
old soldier stationed nearby who managed to overwhelm

her with his brash charm and self-confidence. In 1941, when they were married, Marvin was about to be shipped overseas; he planned to make a career of the army, and Helen, wide-eyed with the dream of travel and adventure, was thrilled to be a part of it.

It was a happy and well-balanced marriage, marred chiefly by several unfortunate occurrences that befell Helen. The first happened during Brenda's birth in 1942, when an attending military physician accidentally splashed ether into Helen's right eye, severely damaging the cornea.

Helen was shattered by the accident, which not only affected her appearance, giving her a slightly walleyed look in one eye because it had lost some muscle control, but also seriously limited her peripheral vision. "On her right side, she wouldn't be able to tell you were there," Jean said. Yet there was no liability compensation, Jean recalled with a shrug. "With the military then," she said succinctly, "if they cut your leg off by accident, you'd be just one leg short."

After the war, during which Helen and Brenda stayed in North Carolina with her parents, Marvin was transferred to a base in Alabama. There, another child, Kenneth Everett, was born. But the infant died six months later from complications that were attributed to an Rh blood factor of Helen's. The following year, she had a miscarriage, and several more would follow in succeeding years.

When Marvin was transferred to Korea in 1947, peacetime conditions allowed him to bring his wife and small daughter along, although that did not prevent Marvin from engaging in a favorite pastime of carousing in bars at night while Helen stayed home with Brenda. At the time, venereal diseases were rampant among the bar girls of Seoul. Eighteen months after their arrival, Helen became seriously ill, jaundiced from a condition that was diagnosed as hepatitis. Accompanied by Brenda, she was rushed back to the States by emergency airlift.

Helen was at home recovering from the initial assault of this illness when the war in Korea began in 1950, just before Marvin had been scheduled to be transferred back to the States. She and Brenda would never see him alive again.

In the spring of 1951, she got a terse army telegram that told her Marvin had been killed in action. In a later message from the army, she was informed that Marvin had died heroically and had been posthumously awarded the Silver Star, the nation's highest award for valor after the Medal of Honor.

The citation the grieving young widow received with her notice of Marvin's award said that while serving with the 24th Infantry Division in Kun Jong Dong, Korea, on April 16, 1951, Second Lieutenant Marvin E. Taylor, seeing that forward elements of the troops were pinned down as his company attacked Hill 404, "left his platoon and joined the lead elements, which were without a leader. Exposing himself to enemy fire, he completely took over the situation. . . . His continuing exposure to enemy fire was an inspiration to all his men."

Even after she remarried, Helen kept a photo of Marvin in a bureau drawer and always kept that letter close to her. Over the years, she would take it out on occasion and read it aloud. Sometimes, in the later years, and with malicious intent, she would read it aloud to John.

As they had expected, John's presence on the West Coast wasn't required for long; the army discharged him in April. He and Helen made the long trip back, picking Brenda up first at her grandmother's in North Carolina, and then, with Alma still in tow, heading up to Michigan, where John's old job at Ernst & Ernst was waiting.

Brenda was not happy about her mother remarrying so soon after her father's funeral. Brenda would always cherish her fleeting memories of the three of them, of Marvin in his uniform and she and her mother nestling beside him. So she naturally resented and mistrusted the intruder who came into her mother's life, a life that Brenda had begun to notice was now filled with sorrow and an anger that occasionally flared toward her child for no apparent good reason.

But John quickly won her over. A smart child, she quickly developed certain survival instincts that allowed her to discern in John a potential ally. John's overanxiousness to be liked, a trait that many adults found repellent, appealed greatly to the preadolescent Brenda. Unlike others, who went pointedly unnamed, "he would never cut you down," she said in 1971.

After a brief stay in Bay City, John and Helen found an apartment near Detroit. John returned happily to Ernst & Ernst, to a good job with a future, at a prestigious firm where he had proudly written on his personnel form, under the heading "Hobbies": "Going to plays and listening to classical music."

To John and Helen List, as to millions of other newlyweds holding hands at the edge of a new decade ripe with promise in 1952, with the Depression and two wars finally behind them, with bouncy songs on the Hit Parade expounding the joys of a happy little house and a family with a child, or two, or three or more, the long-delayed American dream lay at last within their grasp.

Chapter Three

IN 1954, JOHN AND HELEN MOVED INTO A SMALL RENTED house in Inkster, a suburb of Detroit.

Their first child, Patricia Marie, was born on January 8, 1955, in a Detroit hospital. She was a pretty baby, a delightful child who came into the world with a smile on her face.

Patty's birth heralded the happiest times the Lists would ever know. They were a merry little group. Helen, proud and happy to be a new mother once again, was doted on by her own mother, who came to visit, and even Alma's chilly nature melted into effusive German warmth once she held the baby in her arms. She even kissed Helen, for the first time.

Brenda, just turned thirteen, bubbled with delight over the baby. And John, who read Dr. Spock and other authors of the child-rearing books that had sprung up for the parents of the Baby Boom, made a concerted effort to gather Brenda firmly into the fold. Among Brenda's happiest childhood memories are of trips to the city zoo and the circus, and of her stepfather making pizza for the family on Saturday nights. John also spent hours a week coaching Brenda in the Lutheran religious instructions he insisted on. These were the years of the winter visits to Alma and the ice fishing, the time when Brenda first recalled being comfortable calling her new father Daddy.

The networking techniques John had learned at Mich-

igan, meanwhile, paid an unexpected dividend. An Ernst
& Ernst executive John had known and liked, Bernard
White, had recently left to become comptroller of Sutherland Paper Company, a producer of paper packaging
based in Kalamazoo, Michigan. Throwaway packaging was
starting on a period of phenomenal growth as the fifties
gathered momentum. White suggested that an ambitious
young man with a growing family like John List might
want to break away from the hidebound atmosphere of an
accounting firm, where promotions were limited.

Initially wary, for he was proud of working for one of
the most prestigious accounting firms in the country, John
did not decide to come to Kalamazoo to have a look until
late in 1955, just before Patty's first birthday. He was
impressed. The people at Sutherland seemed to be on the
ball. What's more, they seemed to genuinely like him as
a person, not just an M.B.A. on a résumé. Kalamazoo was
a fine town to raise a family, 165 miles removed from the
gritty outskirts of Detroit. Elated, John drove back to Inkster to think over the offer from Sutherland.

Strategically—and John always thought strategically—
a move to the packaging business made sense. In the years
after being freed from the constraints imposed by the demands of World War II, American consumers were buying
with a vengeance. Industry was going on an unprecedented
spree of production driven by the twin engines of advertising and marketing. Literally millions of young families,
with millions and millions of new babies, were breaking
free from shackles put in place by the Depression of the
1930s and kept there by the war. Materially acquisitive,
a generation of new Americans was practically giddy with
the awareness that it was now quite possible to have a
piece of the good life. All over the nation, they were fleeing
the cities for newly developed suburbs, where an explosion
of home building, highway construction, and automobile
production, all of it illuminated by the new domination of

television, was effecting the biggest change in American
society since the Industrial Revolution. In the America of
the fifties, optimism blazed into the sky like a searchlight
outside a new car dealership.

John realized what these new settlers demanded to go
with their split-level homes with the big V-8 cars in the
driveway next to well-tended lawns. More convenience to
enjoy it all! Throwaway packaging was clearly a wave of
the future.

He had brought back from Kalamazoo a handsome
twelve-page recruitment booklet that Sutherland's personnel office handed out to prospective employees. To a man
of thirty at a crossroads in his career, the brochure made
a persuasive case.

The brochure proudly listed the company's products,
among them "butter and margarine cartons, cigarette cartons, soap boxes, packages for baked goods, soft drink and
beer carry-outs, sanitary napkin cartons, shirt boxes and
shirt protectors, lard and shortening packages, frozen food
containers and egg and cereal cartons" as well as "paper
plates and cups, both plastic-coated and plain, meat boards
for prepackaging, butter chips, produce and fruit trays."
Not to mention "Plasta-Plate, the best plastic-coated paper
plate on the market."

Sutherland boasted of its tradition. One of the two men
who had founded it in 1917 was still chairman of the board.
It was one of the largest employers in Kalamazoo, with
thirty-five hundred people on the payroll. The brochure
practically begged for "young, well-trained men ready to
step into sales, production and administrative positions."
Sutherland stressed that it was more than a company, it
was a corporate family, happily located in a municipality,
Kalamazoo, that called itself the "Debt-Free City."

"If the Company is to grow successfully, the management team must grow too," Sutherland's president, William Race, noted in the brochure that John avidly read. "I

believe that there is a good future in the Company for the right men, and the future of Sutherland Paper Company will be in the hands of those right men. Perhaps you can be one of them."

Perhaps? John List was sold. He jumped at the opportunity to join the Sutherland corporate family.

Early in 1956, John started in Sutherland's costs division at $7,200 a year, a handsome salary for a thirty-year-old at a time when a new home cost little more than that.

The Lists didn't have enough for the down payment on a house when they arrived. They rented an apartment, and John began putting aside money for a house.

Initially, Sutherland was everything it had promised. And John got good marks there from the start, when a personnel officer who interviewed him made this note about the new employee: "A very good appearance, seems to be well-adjusted, a very capable person with a good personality."

Erwin Slesdet, an accountant whose desk was adjacent to John's, remembered a "neatly dressed man, a polite man. He always wore a hat, walked erect, and kept his clothes pressed and his shoes shined."

At first Helen seemed happy in Kalamazoo. Always an avid reader, she now seemed to find in books a refuge from the demands of being a mother to children, both of whom were at particularly demanding ages: one and fourteen.

"Helen was very proud of the fact that in Kalamazoo she belonged to three book clubs," said her sister Jean, who was living with her husband and their young son then in Illinois. The families visited each other regularly. "I've seen her in a day's time go through two books," Jean said with a laugh. "She would rather read than do housework and things like that. She read anything she could get her hands on."

Helen became pregnant again shortly after the move to Kalamazoo, and because of her history of miscarriages, she

was advised by her doctor to stay in bed as much as possible.
Not especially happy at the prospect of another baby anyway, she welcomed the excuse to do little but read. When
she wasn't in school, Brenda was saddled with the hands-
on supervision of little Patty, who had only been walking
for a few months.

The baby, named John Frederick after John's own father, was born on October 21, 1956. The infant was an
amiable, extraordinarily engaging, and active child, but
one who, even as an infant, could show a temper.

Helen's mother came up from North Carolina for a few
weeks to help after the baby was born; when Eva left,
Alma, who was becoming a frequent visitor, was on the
next bus down from Bay City. Helen was glad to see the
last of both of them. While the Lists had moved to a bigger
apartment, it was still too small during the day for two
babies, an increasingly rambunctious teenager, and an unhappy new mother who only wanted to be left in peace.

One of the first things John had done upon arriving in
Kalamazoo, of course, was to enroll the family in a Lutheran church affiliated with the Missouri Synod. There
he was proud to be seen at Sunday services with his attractive wife—and Helen could look stunning when she
was in the mood—and two pretty daughters.

And a year later, in recognition both of his accounting
skills and of his respect as a new pillar of his church, John
was elected treasurer of the parish. Proudly, he phoned
his mother with the news that he was keeping the family
tradition alive.

But the afterglow faded sooner than John would have
liked. Though Helen was proud of her husband's new
status at church, she never quite shared the fervor John
always seemed to experience in a church. She had converted to John's religion to make him happy, but she wasn't
prepared to devote much of her week to it. Indeed, after
spending hours dressing the babies and tugging the in-

creasingly resistant Brenda along to church, it seemed that they were only there to sit on display beside John as the model family, always in the same pew and always in place early as the congregation filed in around them. A busy mother exhausted by three children who kept her going all the time, Helen began begging off attending church every Sunday. She would rather sleep late and, a terrific cook who genuinely enjoyed being in the kitchen, make a great breakfast for her family.

Since she was certain the God she knew didn't mind, Helen had difficulty understanding why her husband so evidently did. John had his own way of letting her know. As usual, he didn't say anything overtly. Balefully, he would get up and go about dressing the babies. He would hustle Brenda along and then wordlessly slump off to church, where everyone could see—she knew he wanted her to realize that *everyone saw*—that his wife once again had not cared to come to church with that handsome family. After a while, Brenda took the cue from her mother. She began sleeping late on Sundays, too. Then it was just John, juggling two toddlers on his knee, feeling exposed and abandoned.

John couldn't understand what was going wrong. He catered to Helen's whims. Money that would otherwise have been going into the bank for the down payment on a house went toward presents that he showered on her, including expensive jewelry. He was a model father, a good provider. But Helen wanted something more than what she had taken to calling John on those increasing occasions when she drank too much at night and gave voice to her resentment: a "goody two-shoes." John didn't engage with her on these occasions. Instead, he began a period of sulking that would last for many years.

Around Christmas, Helen got pregnant again. Deeply depressed, she began spending long periods of time in bed, as advised by her doctor.

By now the family had moved to larger quarters, a rented
duplex on Coy Avenue in Kalamazoo. Brenda, now sixteen,
was miserable leaving her old neighborhood friends behind.
What's more, she was beginning to feel like a permanent
babysitter and nursemaid. She began looking forward to
leaving home. More and more, she and her mother seemed
to be shouting at each other.

Money was one of the irritants. As the child of a ser-
viceman who had been killed in action, Brenda was to
receive until age eighteen a monthly pension, which she
was beginning to regard as her potential ticket out of that
household.

John and Helen were required to file regular reports
with the government showing how the pension money—
Jean Syfert said she believed it was a total of about five
hundred dollars a month—was being spent. Brenda complained that the money should be hers to do with as she
pleased. The dispute caused a rift that never really healed.
"I know without a doubt that that's why they had their
falling out," Jean said of Brenda's growing estrangement
from her mother and her stepfather.

John and Helen's last child, Frederick Michael, was
born on August 26, 1958. After the initial phase of cooing
and fawning over a new infant, Helen became despondent
again. With a screaming infant—for little Frederick was
not as mild-mannered as his siblings—and two whining
toddlers, with a teenage daughter threatening to run away
from home, Helen began drinking regularly. Helen had
always liked a drink, but in Kalamazoo, cooped up with
four children, she began liking her scotch rather more.

Worse, she added chemical depressants to the mix. This
was the era of the Wonder Drug, the prescription tran-
quilizer. Helen, recovering from postpartum depression,
under extra scrutiny because of her history of miscarriages
and the illness that had sent her back from Korea, was

now seeing a psychiatrist regularly. She began a dependency on various medications, primarily Doriden, that, off and on, would continue for the rest of her life. Combined with even moderate nighttime drinking, the medication left her lethargic on many days.

John, meanwhile, was too caught up in the demands of his job, where he was obviously on the right career track, to pay much attention. He did bristle a bit on those nights, which occurred more frequently now than before, when he would come home from work and find Helen curled up on the couch with a book and a glass of scotch. All the same, he kept his anger inside. He simply changed the badly soiled diapers of the two boys, looked after Patty, and ascertained Brenda's whereabouts. Then he made dinner himself.

Though a growing family was a significant drain on even a comfortable income like John's, and though both John and Helen were the sort of people who bought on impulse, they had enough money by 1959 for the down payment on a house, which they purchased on April 14 with a mortgage of $17,300.

This money hadn't accrued through any sort of prudent financial planning, however. As usual, John had come to his mother with his problems. Shortly before John and Helen made settlement on their new home in Kalamazoo, Alma went to Bay County Probate Court to petition for an amendment to her late husband's 1943 will, the terms of which left the entire estate to her; upon her death, half of the estate would go to the deceased's first son, William G., who was the same age as Alma, then seventy-one, and the other half to John. What Alma's petition asked the court to do was to accelerate certain terms and allow the sale of the old general store on Salzburg Avenue.

On December 2, the store was sold to cousins for a price listed as $1 plus "other consideration"—a common accounting practice in Michigan at the time to avoid a tax assessment. The property was estimated to be worth about $20,000 at the time it was sold. John and Helen had their one-third share of the proceeds in plenty of time to use it for the down payment on their first home.

The house was a three-year-old redwood-hued split-level with four bedrooms and a fireplace, on a wooded lot on a street called Lovers Lane in a pleasant suburban setting about two miles from downtown Kalamazoo. Despite the winsome street name, it was not a happy home.

All too soon, the neighbors were talking. One reported that upon returning from a trip very late one night, she happened to glance into the brightly lit List house and see Helen was doing the vacuum cleaning, at three o'clock in the morning! No wonder she was seldom seen outside during the day, and even when she was, she wouldn't stop to talk.

"She wasn't very neighborly," said Ruth Snow, who lived next door. "He was nice, but not her."

And Helen spent money as if it grew on trees, another said. Those children didn't seem to have a mother, but they had the most expensive clothes in the neighborhood. The playpen alone must have cost more than a hundred dollars.

The playpen was something of a scandal itself. Ruth Snow was always shocked to see it out there in the driveway, with Frederick inside, unattended but apparently otherwise fine in the fresh air. "In the morning, she'd put the playpen out there in the driveway, where it goes up along the wall in front of the garage," the neighbor recalled. "And when that little baby was just a few months old, she'd put him out there in that playpen, and she wouldn't come near him much before noon.

"She didn't pay attention to the poor little fellow. She was no mama."

John, on the other hand, was both mother and father, she decided. He always seemed to let people know. She liked John very well, though she did think he had some odd ways.

"I'd be doing my yardwork, and we'd both be outside. We'd talk back and forth. He never talked about her to me. I never gave it a thought, that there was any problem between them," she said.

"After they moved away, he wrote to me several times, nice letters. I thought then that not many men, after they moved, would have bothered to write to some old lady who was just a neighbor. I don't know of anyone who would do that."

Left up to her neck in babies and housework, a depressed Helen began directing her resentment at the most appropriate person, her husband, and in the two places, his office and his church, where it seemed to her he was spending a lot of extra time that could be better spent helping out at home.

After baby John had grown into a toddler, John would arrive at the office on some mornings and find an embarrassing message such as this sitting in the middle of his desk: "Your wife called and said your son messed in his pants. If you want them changed, come home and do it."

On more than one occasion, coworkers noticed, John did just that.

A paternalistic company that prided itself on giving its employees free rein, Sutherland had liberal policies about doing errands during the work day, so dashing home from time to time during the day didn't cause a serious work problem for John. It was more of a social problem. He was mortified by the fact that his coworkers were aware his wife had so little respect for him.

Erwin Slesdet, who worked beside John, said he was unaware of these diaper messages. But he did notice that Helen was on the phone a lot asking for help. "She would call about problems with the children that she couldn't seem to handle," he said. "On occasion, he would go home, and he would be gone for maybe an hour. At that time, the company was very generous with its employees, and if you had any kind of a situation at home and you had to leave, why no one ever said anything. Other people did the same thing from time to time, but on a more limited basis than John."

Still, Slesdet said, John never complained. In fact, John never said much of anything about his life outside the office. Although he knew John for four years and considered himself a friend, he never met Helen.

Helen's animosity reached a point that she even phoned the church after John had left for services one Sunday and left a similar message about changing a diaper.

"Mom was really boozing it up then," Brenda said. "She kept saying she couldn't forget Marvin, that John was nothing compared to him. She was on heavy doses of medication. Daddy couldn't control her."

When she wasn't in bed, Helen seemed to spend most of her time cooking, the only pastime besides reading that she engaged in with enthusiasm anymore.

At church, John's fellow parishoners sympathized with his predicament and rallied to the cause. On several occasions, women from the church made personal calls to the List house on Lovers Lane. Helen wanted nothing to do with them.

"We tried desperately to get her into the parish life," sighed the Reverend Louis Grother. The pastor, who had been counseling John about his marital problems, had noticed a habit that had by now become full-blown: Unable to win Helen's respect and affection with his own personality, John lavished gifts on her, small and large. But it was Grother's impression that Helen had simply decided that John would never measure up to her late husband Marvin, the war hero.

"So John tried to throw money at his memory," the

minister said. "And he was starting to get himself in over his head in debt." Included in the mounting financial pressure were the bills from Helen's psychotherapy.

Brenda, who was by now making plans to elope with a boyfriend, noticed the growing rift between her mother and her stepfather. In a 1971 interview with the New York *Daily News*, she recalled the only time she ever saw John lose his temper:

"One night, he was reading at the table and she kept nagging at him to get a butch haircut like the other men were wearing those days," Brenda said, referring to the stubby crewcut hairstyle that was popular with some men in the late 1950s. John had always worn his hair with a precise part on the side and a modest pompadour in front.

"He just sat there reading, and she kept on teasing him. Finally, he just stood up, his face got all blotchy, and he threw the table and all the dishes to the floor," said Brenda, who remembered being terrified by the incident.

It was also around this time that the few friends who had ever been to John's house were invited to play one of his collection of military-strategy games. John could spend hour after hour matching wits with any opponent who cared to take him on in these games, which required cunning and stealth, as well considerable attention to detail and strategical analysis. No one among the few with the ability or the patience to take him on can recall John ever losing.

"The guy was something of a military nut anyway," one former coworker said. "You never wanted to get him talking about politics, especially in an election year. He thought Democrats were Communists. Playing one of those games, he'd sit perfectly straight in his chair and concentrate on nothing else. It was exhausting. After a while, I stopped coming over."

*   *   *

Brenda decided that she wanted out sometime in the middle of 1959, when she and her boyfriend, Richard Wayne Herndon, drove across the state line to Indiana, where they tried to get married. They were rebuffed, however, because Brenda wasn't yet eighteen. On their way from the courthouse, they were involved in a traffic accident that caused the young man to be hospitalized with minor injuries.

John and Helen were distraught when they got a call from the police asking them to come to pick up Brenda in Indiana. For a while, they forgot their problems and focused on Brenda. They had hoped she would go to college and make something of herself, and instead she had run away from home with a boy John strongly disapproved of. John had always treated Brenda as his own daughter. If nothing else, the crisis reconciled John and Helen for a while.

They lectured Brenda and brought the two teenagers back to Kalamazoo. But Brenda wasn't happy about it. As she saw it, her mother had another family, the three children of her own with John. Brenda didn't feel a part of it, except as a convenient babysitter. She even had to call John's mother Mother List while the real kids got to call her Grandma.

When Brenda turned eighteen, she left home and married her boyfriend the same day they got the license.

Despite the tensions at home, John seemed to be forging ahead at work. In January 1959, he had been promoted to supervisor of general accounting, with a raise to $9,300 a year.

The company was thriving on the fast-growing demand for disposable packaging and poised for rapid expansion into new markets across the country. However, it was still a family-run business, and the Sutherlands were members of the old-line Kalamazoo establishment that had prided itself on the town's hard-earned reputation as the "debt-free" city. This attitude extended to business as well as municipal government: If you didn't have, you didn't spend it.

One of John's first major projects at Sutherland was a long-range study done jointly with Slesdet to determine whether the company should construct a plant in Alabama to facilitate a market expansion for one of Sutherland's top products, ice cream cartons. "We spent quite a lot of time working on the cost and the return on investment on that operation, but it never materialized," Slesdet recalled. "We just didn't have the money to put into it.

"In its beginnings, the company was pretty much Kalamazoo-financed. It later became national and traded on the New York Stock Exchange, but many people in Kalamazoo were the stockholders, and at this time it was a pretty conservative town. They were not really willing for us to go out on a limb and have tremendous indebtedness. They would go for the short term, but they didn't like the twenty-year payback.

"We never had any trouble paying our bills. But when we expanded, when we built new plants, those were all paid for out of earnings. Maybe that wasn't the smart way to go, but that was the way it was."

Smart or not, it was certainly the old way of doing business. And as American industry entered the 1960s and began consolidating its gains from the boom decade, debt was no longer a dirty word. Growth needed to be bold, it needed to be acquisitive. There was other people's money around, and it was cheaper in the long run to buy an industry than to create one.

Short on capital, hurting for cash flow, Sutherland found itself unexpectedly dead in the water, almost without notice, at the edge of this new era, which would totally transform the nation's corporate structure in the next two decades.

On October 8, 1959, Sutherland was suddenly acquired

by KVP Company, which merged it into a new corporation with the name KVP Sutherland Paper Company.

For many of the former employees of Sutherland, some of whom, like John List, had signed on fairly recently in the belief that they were joining a corporate family, not just a company, the merger was a stunning setback for their plans for the future. All of a sudden, all deals were off.

"After the merger, of course, we suddenly had two accounting departments, two financial people in practically all areas," said Slesdet. The company seemed to have two of everything. The new and the old.

As it happened, Sutherland was also top-heavy with executives whose background was in accounting. The merger brought still more on board, and the new ones were now in charge of the ship. "We had a treasurer, we had an assistant treasurer, in both companies. We obviously didn't need all of those people." It was clear who would be tossed overboard.

John, while well-liked and admired for his industry and good nature, was nevertheless not the kind of manager that a new organization looking to trim away fat could honestly encourage. Even his old, easygoing superiors hadn't been impressed with the management skills John had been called on to demonstrate more forcefully in the year before the merger.

So John was politely told that this would be a good time to explore his options elsewhere.

He threw himself into his job hunt with a sense of urgency and betrayal despite the new regime's assurance that he would receive an excellent recommendation and all the time he needed, within reason, of course, to find something suitable. John bought every business classified publication he could find in Kalamazoo. Working feverishly, he sent out nearly a hundred résumés.

One of them attracted the attention of a company in Rochester, New York, that was about to embark on one of the most remarkable expansions in corporate history. The company was Xerox, and it was desperate for people like John List.

Chapter Four

Until the early 1960s, few outside of Rochester had heard of Xerox; then, almost overnight, it was one of the hottest new companies ever listed on the New York Stock Exchange. After years of floundering, Xerox had finally come up with an office photocopier—its revolutionary model 914—that not only worked but was relatively dependable, affordable, and compact. The office would never be the same.

Suddenly, Xerox needed lots of people not only to help manufacture, market, and service its new copiers but also to help manage its phenomenal growth. And it needed them fast. This was a company whose operating revenues were $37 million in 1960—and $528 million in 1966. In 1960, it employed about 2,000 people; within ten years, Xerox would have 55,000 employees.

John List couldn't have picked a better time to show up with his eager manner and his impressive résumé. Sutherland, only too happy to see him go, sent him off with an inflated job title and a glowing recommendation. The Xerox personnel office, with its voracious appetite at the time, was delighted to hear from him.

These were heady days indeed. Xerox offered him $12,000 a year—to start. Neither he nor Helen could believe it. That was almost $3,000 more than he had been making in Kalamazoo. On the phone, he said he'd have to think about it. Helen smacked him playfully, hard, on the arm. In the next breath, he said he'd thought about it.

Rochester, located east of Buffalo and just south of Lake Ontario, lies in a part of New York State that manages to deftly combine cultural elements both of the Midwest and the East Coast. Helen, who had loathed Michigan, liked Rochester immediately. And John, who distrusted the liberal influence of the eastern megalopolis, soon decided it was enough like Michigan to relax.

In any case, his new job quickly began consuming most of his time. Unlike Sutherland, Xerox was a company moving fast, a company where a junior executive was expected to remain in the office long after subordinates went home to dinner. This was a quite different corporate culture; there would be no opportunities to dash off and answer a diaper call at Xerox.

In the summer of 1961, John and Helen bought a ranch house at 149 Clearbrook Drive in Irondequoit, a suburb. As before, Helen stayed home with the children, but the move had improved her outlook. Patty, who had become a little chatterbox, would start first grade in September. It was summer, the time Helen liked best. John seemed on the verge of success at last. Alma was back in Michigan. There was a new president in the White House, John Kennedy, a man she admired (and her husband despised). Overall, there seemed to be a new spirit about. Some weekends, they even hired a babysitter and went out together to parties, to dinner, to the movies. At Helen's prompting, John did something his staunch father would have considered unthinkable and his mother was not told about: Helen would not have to endure another pregnancy. He had a vasectomy.

He enrolled the family in a Lutheran church, of course. For a time, Helen even resumed attending Sunday services.

But that new resolve faded fast. The truth was, Helen just did not care for church.

John conveyed his concerns about his wife to the pastor of Faith Lutheran Church in Rochester, the Reverend Edward Saresky, "Helen expected great things of him," he said. John gave the strong impression that he feared he wasn't managing to live up to her expectations.

In Rochester, certain conditions of their marriage had become quite clear. Helen was willing to be an active partner, so long as John ensured her of a good time and material comforts. This coincided well enough with John's own strong desire to honor the List family name through success in his career. So long as that condition prevailed, a semblance of a smooth marriage could be maintained. But it had become a marriage built on a very shaky foundation. And in Rochester, the ground would start to tremble underneath.

But not right away. Again, John was riding high in a new job. After he accrued enough vacation time at Xerox, he and Helen took their first real vacation together. Leaving the children in Rochester in the care of Helen's mother, the Lists made the grand tour, Helen's first visit to Europe and John's first as a civilian—to Ireland, England, and Germany, where John made a tearful pilgrimage to the List family redoubt in Rosstal, Mittel Franken, in what had once been the kingdom of Bavaria.

One of the gifts the Lists brought back for Helen's sister Jean, reflected John's interest in genealogy. It was a plaque John had bought in Ireland, and on it was the name "Morris" and the family coat of arms, under which John had an engraver inscribe these words:

"Si Deus nobiscum, qui contra nos." If God is for us, who can be against us?

Jean thought the plaque was beautiful. But she didn't have a clue as to what the Latin quote meant. The line was familiar to John, given his interest in classical music, especially German composers, as the title of a soprano aria, No. 52, from Handel's *Messiah*. Handel had taken it from a scriptural source, the Letter of Paul to the Romans. The entire passage, which John was very familiar with, was eerily prophetic:

"What then shall we say to this? If God is for us, who can be against us? He who did not spare his own son but gave him up for us all, will he not also give us all things with him? . . . Who shall separate us from the love of Christ? Shall tribulation, or distress, or persecution, or famine, or nakedness, or peril, or sword? As it is written:

> *'For thy sake we are being killed all*
> *   the day long;*
> *We are regarded as sheep to be*
> *   slaughtered.' "*

During the years the Lists were in Rochester, the Syferts lived in Illinois with their three boys, where they were even then looking forward to and making plans for Gene's retirement from the air force. Except for the year John and Helen went to Europe, they spent their summer vacations visiting Jean and Gene. Gene, an easygoing man with a routinely bemused air, even found himself tolerating John somewhat better, though he still couldn't put the term "mama's boy" out of his head when he saw John do something like pull on a sweater and a hat and look worried whenever the sun disappeared behind a cloud.

"The Lists seemed to enjoy our family," Jean recalled of those visits. "We'd go sightseeing and take the kids to the beach. The List kids, Patty and John and Freddy, just loved having our kids to play with." The Syferts were Patty's godparents.

Jean also liked having the opportunity to spend time alone with her sister. But she was beginning to notice just how seriously Helen was taking her newfound financial status. Helen seemed to see money as a validation, not just a way to buy something.

It was quite apparent one afternoon when they went shopping together, leaving John to watch the kids. Helen had just bought a number of pricy accessories when she tapped her younger sister on the shoulder.

"Did you notice the way the saleslady was looking at my shoes?" she asked brightly.

Jean shook her head. She hadn't noticed any such thing.

"Well," pouted Helen, bustling along, "you know, you can tell a lot about a person by how much they spend on their shoes."

Years later, Jean laughed at the memory of the differences between herself and her sister, who often drove her to distraction. "We were very close, at least after we grew up, but we were totally opposite," Jean said. "We were both Capricorns, but as to likes and dislikes, we were worlds apart. Helen liked to read. She would rather read than do housework anytime. Oh, did she read a lot! Myself, I would rather do something that when I got through, you could say, 'Well, I did something, I made a dress or something.' Helen wasn't that way at all.

"She was an excellent cook, a gourmet cook really. When she died, she had 350 cookbooks in her house. I counted them.

"I remember as a child," Jean said, recalling a childhood in North Carolina when Helen often announced she was in charge of dinner. It had not been an easy childhood for any of them. Helen was a child who kept to herself as much as possible; only in the kitchen, really, did she seem to blossom. "She *loved* to cook—and I always had to help afterward in the kitchen. Guess who did all the clean-up work. What she cooked was really wonderful. But when she got through you thought, 'My gosh, it'll take an hour to clean all that up.' "

But Jean also admired Helen for her brains. "My sister was a very intelligent woman," she said. "She really had a lot on the ball. In a lot of ways, she was smarter than John was."

Helen was a reader, not a television watcher, but one television show she did enjoy was the quiz program *Jeopardy*, on which contestants had to have knowledge of a wide range of subjects. "Once, in 1963, she wrote a letter applying to be a contestant, and they wrote back accepting her," Jean said. "She kept the letter on her dresser."

As they had anticipated, the Syferts saw with growing concern over the years that John was having difficulties coping with such a strong partner.

Helen's first husband "was probably the type of person she needed as a husband," said Jean, who believed that Helen never really stopped mourning for Marvin. "She seemed to be a different person with him. I think she needed someone who was—I won't say domineering, but more than held his own with her. She never really made this point about defying Marvin. But with John, it was starting to look like a different story."

For his part, John did what he always did when involved in anything having a potential for confrontation. He sought advice from a trusted third party, invariably a woman. On their vacations with the Syferts, he began confiding in Jean, whose marriage he saw as a model for the one he wished he and Helen had.

"John would talk over things to me about the family, things that I could see and that he could see were going wrong, even when the kids were little. Where he wouldn't talk with Helen about it," Jean said.

John envied the equality of their partnership. "I've been married since I was sixteen, and I think Gene and I have kind of grown up together and had a fairly easy life," Jean said. "There have been times when we didn't have as much as we would liked to have. But when I was twenty-one years old, we knew where we were going. We planned it right then. We said, well, when the twenty years in the air force is up, this is what we're going to go. Gene is going to go to school to get his teacher's certificate, and he is going to be a schoolteacher. Then he is going to retire again, and we will enjoy each other's company for the rest of our lives. We walked it together every step of the way."

Nevertheless, Jean wouldn't let John feel sorry for himself when they discussed their respective marriages, "The Lists can have that kind of marriage," she told him bluntly. "It takes two people working together."

"But she doesn't seem to want to work together," he replied.

Jean realized Helen wasn't pulling her share of the load. But she had seen a different Helen with Marvin. She suspected part of the problem was that John was just as content to retreat into himself and sulk—exactly the sort of behavior that brought out the very worst in Helen.

One thing was clear. The Syferts could certainly see Helen's point that John was decidedly odd.

There was that funny way he always stood with his shoulders squared, and walked as if he were in a parade, for one thing. And the way he read the newspaper sitting at stiff attention.

"For a real kick, you'd watch him reading the paper," Jean said. "He read every page, front to back. He'd get to the funny pages and he'd laugh out loud, such an odd, funny little laugh that you'd come in from the other room to see what was the matter with him."

The part of this routine that intrigued her, however, was his fastidiousness. He would start with the Sunday paper in a neat stack on one side of the chair. Then he would carefully pick a section up by the margin of the pages, to avoid getting ink on his fingers, and read it. Every page, top to bottom, right to left, like an automatic scanner. Then he'd put each section down, one by one, right side up, on the other side of the chair. "When it got done, it would be lying there on the other side, perfectly rearranged as if nobody had ever touched it, like it was new," Jean said.

She also noticed something else on those visits from her sister and brother-in-law. For a man who was supposedly doing so well at Xerox, he seemed to be having certain cash-flow problems, and a fairly cavalier attitude about how to cover them up.

Jean was going to her bank one afternoon when John took her aside and asked if he could go along to cash a personal check because he was short of cash. Jean said that would be fine. But at the bank, the teller wouldn't cash an out-of-state personal check unless Jean guaranteed it with her own bank balance. She agreed readily.

The check bounced before the Lists' vacation was over. "It was only for forty dollars, but forty dollars was a fair amount of money then," Jean said. When she told John about the returned check, she could tell that he was lying when he replied in an uncharacteristically haughty manner: "Oh, that money is in my account. Your bank has obviously made a terrible mistake. I'll straighten them out when we get home." He never mentioned it again. More than the loss of forty dollars, the incident stayed with Jean because it had shown her a side of John—a man capable of casual deceit—that she hadn't seen before.

At Xerox, John prospered as the company's fortunes swelled. In 1964, he earned $25,000, including $7,900 in bonuses. He and Helen raised their standard of living in turn, going into debt to buy appliances and other things for the house. The same year, Xerox sent him to a convention in Mexico, and he paid for Helen to come along. On their way back, they stopped in Kalamazoo to see Brenda; John took the occasion to visit Sutherland, where he told Slesdet and several other colleagues that Xerox had rewarded him for helping to solve one of its most nagging problems in the early days of its workhorse 914 copier: exactly how to bill customers.

During his scant leisure time, John added to his military-strategy-game collection. He even brought simple versions of some games in to play with coworkers in the Xerox cafeteria at lunchtime.

"He was a superb strategist," his boss, Clayton Hutto, noted. "He won every battle."

In the lunchroom, that is. But Hutto knew better than anyone that John was beginning to lose points where it counted, in the office.

By the end of 1964, John was telling associates that he had his eye on a vice presidency at Xerox, and sooner, rather than later. His superiors, when they heard of this, were amazed and uneasy. No one else seemed to foresee such a future. After the extraordinary five-year rocketship ride in the early sixties, Xerox executives were managing to catch their breath and assess what they had, before going on the next growth spree. And a closer look at John over those years was not sufficiently impressive to warrant his expectations of a big title.

The company had barely known what it was doing four years earlier when John was among thousands of good-looking candidates swept up in the hiring net it flung overboard. Now, with the need to take a second look, some of those people were adjudged less flexible, less promising than had been hoped. Xerox was undergoing constant shifts in emphasis, in executive duties, as it found its footing. Some people inevitably would be locked in place on the wrong path.

This finally became clear to John, who was, however, not the sort of man who looked in the mirror first when things went wrong. Instead, his gaze fixed on the next closest image. Helen.

True to form, she was certainly giving him cause for discomfort.

His job required attending business parties in the company of his wife, who hated being dragged along and expected to perform like a trained seal. To overcome nervousness, she would have a few quick drinks before they went out, and more than a few after they arrived. Early on in an evening, Helen always made a fine impression. An attractive, shapely woman with a sharp wit and the ability to disarm the most uptight of stuffed shirts, she was delighted to be out of the house and away from the kids; what's more, she scorned the other timid, frightened wives and didn't hesitate to become the life of the party. She liked flirting, and she didn't care who knew it.

As John sulked, other men clustered around his wife, lighting her cigarette, looking into her eyes, offering her the last thing she needed, which was another drink. And Helen, seeing his long face with that basset-hound look on it, and fully aware that she would have to suffer through an hour of his whining on the way home in the car, "would say the hell with it and have a few more drinks, obviously just for spite," a woman who knew her said.

With John seeming to invite her wrath with every drink she took, the inevitable moment would arrive when Helen would attack. "Helen would get drunk, and then she would start talking about Marvin, her first husband," recalled Hutto. "John's face would get blotchy; he would grit his teeth, steer her away, and take her home."

En route, he would complain about her making "advances" to other men.

From time to time, even as long as twenty-five years later, long after Helen's death, John would manage to convey to friends his impression that Helen had been the cause

of the trouble that always seemed to leap out from hiding
to nip his career in the bud.

But corroborating evidence was not easy to unearth.
Most men who knew Helen at least liked her as a genuine
human presence who knew how to talk about something
other than office politics. If she drank too much at social
events, one man said, so did others. "It was the middle of
the sixties," he said. "It wasn't real unusual to get shitfaced
at a party." At the end of the night, few people even seemed
to have noticed, he said.

There was another recurring theme, moreover. After a
few years, in job after job, John invariably would manage,
evidently quite on his own, to wear out his initially enthusiastic welcome.

In August 1965, John's title at Xerox was director of
accounting services, and that was as high as he would go.
It wasn't just a deficiency in management skills that held
him back, though this was a factor. The truth was, he
didn't have the necessary presence.

"At conferences, when he had to talk under stress, his
face would suddenly break out into big red welts," said
Hutto, his boss. "I imagined they were hives. His face was
always blotchy, and when he did talk, his face would
twitch, his head would fall forward, and he would shift
his body from side to side, like a kid volunteering an answer
at a spelling bee on television."

In an aspiring vice president, this was not a valuable
trait. John had hit the end of the road in Rochester.

"What he really wanted was a big title," Hutto said.
"And when he kept asking for advancement, we had to tell
him to look for another job."

Chapter Five

IN MANY WAYS, JOHN LIST EMBLEMIZED THE FIFTIES: MAterially acquisitive; rigidly controlled; timid in the face of authority; proud for no reason that would be readily apparent in hindsight. With pursed lips and eyes that were quick to judge, John's countenance projected the attitude that while the world was a somewhat offensive, morally inferior place, it nevertheless owed him a living.

But it was no longer the fifties, which should have been his time. In 1965, John was forty years old, right at the brink of middle age, and unlike many of his contemporaries, utterly unable to adapt. He was a man whose doors were slowly being squeezed shut by forces, inside his family and out, that he was increasingly unable to control.

Exacerbating tensions, Helen's health had deteriorated again. Though it would be years before her illness was diagnosed, Helen was suffering from the early stages of cerebral atrophy, a degenerative shrinkage of the brain tissues that can be symptomatic of a variety of ills, including the viral infection that had caused her to be rushed home from Korea. Alcohol and depressants such as tranquilizers only aggravate symptoms, which can include sporadic mental disorientation and paranoia.

For several weeks in the early summer of 1965, Helen was confined to bed. "John did everything," one neighbor said. "He'd cook dinner, take them out to social things."

Patty, now ten and a half, was expected to fill in the

gaps and look after her brothers, who followed her around like anxious puppies. In fact, Patty had begun to act more in the role of parent as her mother, sometimes heavily medicated, drifted in and out of the household's daily routine.

"The kids would say, 'Mom doesn't feel good. She's in bed,' " said the neighbor, who noticed that the List children had a "very protective attitude" toward their mother, a woman whom she had never seen much of, but now saw hardly at all. "Patricia would say, 'I'm going to clean the house today because my Mom doesn't feel good.' "

Her impression of the List children was clear over the years. On several summer nights, when her husband started a barbecue out back after work, the List kids, waiting for their father to come home, would drift over to the fence, looking so forlorn that they usually were invited to come over.

It wasn't that Patty, Johnny, and Fred were deprived. There was food in their house; Patty was perfectly capable of fixing something quick if they were too hungry to wait for their father to get in. No, the children were mostly just lonely.

By the end of the summer, however, Helen was back on her feet again. More important, John had been diligently dispatching his résumés across the country. The résumé, by itself, reflected none of the realities of his career problems. Xerox, like Sutherland before it, was only too happy to send John off with a glowing endorsement to become someone else's problem.

His dogged persistence paid off. And it looked like the best job offer yet. Not only was the money, $25,000 a year, comparable to his Xerox salary, but this time the title had the right resonance: *vice president and comptroller*, First National Bank of Jersey City, New Jersey.

Ecstatic, John left for New Jersey, renting an apartment in Jersey City that he used as a base to look for a new

house while Helen prepared the household for the move
from Rochester. Confident about the future again, John
quickly located the ideal new town to match the impressive
new title.

Westfield, New Jersey, was settled in the seventeenth
century by Dutch and English burghers from nearby Elizabeth who built their country homes there, at the foot of
the Watchung Mountain range and alongside the well-
traveled Minisink Trail, which Lenni Lenape Indians used
on their annual warm-weather trek from the Delaware
River across central New Jersey to the seashore fishing
grounds.

For most of its early history, Westfield was a placid and
sleepy place where a wide brook flowed through the center
of the town, crossing Broad Street near Elm. As the town
grew, the brook was bridged and finally covered completely;
today, few people even know that it is underfoot.

Westfield's biggest growth didn't begin until after the
Civil War, when the Jersey Central Railroad bridged its
tracks over the swampy North Jersey meadowlands, offering direct service by the 1870s to Jersey City. From there,
the burgeoning financial world of Wall Street was only a
short ferry ride away.

The railroad eventually enabled Wall Street to find
Westfield as land agents touted the country life to ty-
coons who were weary of the choking smoke and insuf-
ferable congestion that even the privileged had to suffer in
late-nineteenth-century Manhattan. Printed bills plas-
tered all over the financial district touted the advantages
of pastoral Westfield, which "indeed hath charms. Where
in the wide, wide world is the grass greener, the sky bluer
or the air purer? Why, the very exhilaration of such an
atmosphere sets every nerve a-tingle and the whole world
aglow."

The enticement appealed to John Samuel Augustus

Wittke, a rich manufacturer of business forms, who fled the city for the country and began a daily commute from Westfield that he would continue until his death almost a half-century later. By the 1920s, the town would be known for its lively contingent of such Wall Street worthies, rushing back by train after their offices closed at noon on Saturdays to get a starting time at the exclusive Echo Lake Country Club, where the subsequent Saturday night parties were legendary.

At first, Wittke lived in a cottage on Broad Street, near the brook. But the town was growing rapidly, and Wittke disliked congestion. In 1895, he bought twenty-two acres of land a few miles northwest, and built a grand Victorian house atop a gentle knoll on the highest point between the Watchung Mountains and the Port of Elizabeth, ten miles to the east. Wittke, who had an eye for landscaping, set his estate amid tall trees and left a portion of the grounds wild, with paths carved through thick clusters of wisteria and honeysuckle, whose blossoms scented the summer air. As time passed and his fortunes grew, Wittke also amassed a fine art collection and built a ballroom extension on the house to display it. He called the ballroom his "art room." The parties held there in the twenties were major events on the local social calendar.

Wittke called his estate Breeze Knoll.

In 1965, long after the estate had been subdivided and the big house itself had been sold by Wittke's grandchildren, long after Wittke's art collection had been disposed of and his flower gardens and reflecting pools consigned to old photo albums, John List arrived in Westfield and decided that he and Helen must have Breeze Knoll.

The house, which still had more than an acre of rolling ground fronting on Hillside Avenue, had been on the market for some time before John brought Helen to see it. It was a sprawling white edifice with green shutters that badly needed painting. Its nineteen rooms, with oak floors throughout, had among them a total of ten fireplaces, some marble, some with hand-carved teak mantels, and five baths. Wittke's ballroom was thirty-three feet long and twenty-three feet wide, softly lit by a stained-glass skylight that filled almost the entire ceiling. Underneath the ballroom was a billiard room. There were two living rooms, a dining room, a big kitchen with butler's pantry, and a laundry room. The long hall on the second floor had five bedrooms off it. Upstairs, on the third floor, were servants' quarters with two bedrooms, a living room, and a kitchen. Outside, great arching trees, among them a magnolia and an old silver maple, reminded Helen of summertime in her beloved North Carolina hills.

But, like most old mansions that had been sensibly sold off in the 1950s by heirs, Breeze Knoll had seen far better days by 1965.

An indication of just how badly in need of repair it was is that the house was carried on the local tax rolls with an assessed valuation of $100,000—but was on the market, and had been for some time, for only $57,000.

Yet what might have been one person's white elephant became John and Helen's dream house; a monstrance for their new status. Nervously they offered $50,000.

The offer was promptly accepted. A twenty percent down payment was required.

John took out the monthly budget book he had kept faithfully since college to do some figuring. Taxes were $1,040 a year. The oil for heating looked to be about $1,000. The mortgage would come in around $300 a month—assuming twenty percent down. But he and Helen had never managed to save. Even in flush times, they lived right at the limit of their income, if not slightly beyond. Where was the $10,000 down payment going to come from? John only knew one person what that kind of cash who would be willing to part with it for him. That was Alma, his mother.

She agreed to supply the money, but there was a catch, Jean Syfert recalled. "Mother List's condition for the $10,000 down payment was that she have a place to live—there."

Luckily for John, Helen's reluctance to share any domicile with her mother-in-law paled by comparison with her longing to own Breeze Knoll. So it was that Alma, who had never lived more than ten miles from her birthplace in all of her seventy-nine years, came to spend the last five years of her life on the third floor of a ramshackle old mansion in Westfield, New Jersey, where she knew not a soul beyond her son and his family, and where even as simple an act as going to the grocery store required a ride in an automobile. In letters to friends before her death, Alma would confide that these were the unhappiest years of her life.

The town that the Lists moved to in the autumn of 1965 was an affluent, well-tended municipality with a population of thirty-three thousand. It had fifty-one police officers, thirteen public schools, fourteen churches—the Lists' church, Redeemer Lutheran, was founded in 1930; at the other chronological pole, the Presbyterian church was founded in 1728. Its affluence was solid middle-class Republican.

In 1970, only three out of ten Westfield households had a woman who worked full time. The town was known for its regard for its young people. Westfield High School sports teams were often state champions; it was not unusual for ten thousand people to turn out for a high school football game. Besides an excellent school system, Westfield maintained a municipal recreation department whose budget was nearly half that of the police department's. Its staff of 125 ran a year-round program of sports, cultural, and craft activities that was often cited by newcomers as one of the reasons they chose to move to Westfield. It was a town that prided itself on the quality of life available within its borders, and on its lack of strife.

Besides its position on the railroad line twelve miles southwest of New York City, Westfield's history contains little of much note to anyone who doesn't live there: The official history of the Echo Lake Country Club boasts that "the 17th tee appears to be the remnants of Indian mounds." In 1910 and 1911, before the movie industry moved to California, the Biograph Film Company made seven Mary Pickford movies in town. Charles Addams, the famous cartoonist of the macabre, grew up in Westfield, where he studied the architecture for the Victorian perspective that would come to characterize his drawings.

Aside from the artist, Westfield's most famous citizen, albeit a most transient one in a town where many students in the high school had the teachers who had taught their parents, would be John List himself.

The scion of the Wittke family, Jack Wittke, lived with his wife, Dot, in the converted carriage house on a street about a hundred yards behind the main house. Soon after the Lists moved in, John sought Wittke out with a slew of detailed questions about the history of the house he had just bought.

"He asked me if I would supply him with a lot of the historical pictures of the house that we had kept in the family," Wittke said. "What he and his wife wanted to do, he said, was put the whole estate, or what he owned of it, back to its former glory. Well, I didn't think he had the chance of a snowball in hell of ever doing such a thing, but I was happy to lend him the pictures." John and Helen would spend their best moments together in Westfield making plans with that photo album on their laps.

When John showed Helen the fat photo album with interior and exterior scenes of Breeze Knoll in its days as a grand estate, she was enthralled. In fact, the two of them began acting like newlyweds again, bubbling with enthusiasm as they planned a restoration they believed would be substantially complete within five years.

Jean Syfert remembered talking with her sister and John for hours as they described their dreams. "When they started out, they had such intentions," she said, raising her eyes at what became her last happy memory of John and Helen's marriage. "You just couldn't shut them up about it. The first thing they did was, in the center-hall stairway that went all the way up, at the very top of it they put in an absolutely gorgeous chandelier, very expensive and massive. It was their project together. They saw such possibilities together in that house."

John was especially diligent about tending the grounds, raking the leaves almost nightly in the fall, mowing the grass every week in the warm months. This activity, in fact, led to the first rumblings of what would later become a roar of gossip about the Lists. Neighbors, curious about the new family living in the biggest house on the block (and anxiously waiting for the new owners to *paint* the place) began noticing odd things about the man at 431 Hillside. Not only did he usually pretend not to see them when they were outside and waved or nodded a greeting, but the man always seemed to be wearing a coat and tie, winter and summer, night and day. On Hillside Avenue, where most people in fact hired workers to tend the grass, no one had ever seen such a curious sight as John List in a suit and tie, earnestly marching up and down his lawn behind his mower.

"They would laugh at him. He was becoming a joke up there," said George Van Hecke, a longtime Westfield resident who heard about John List's lawn-mowing sartorial habits from seven blocks away. "I guess he was the antithesis of a slob," Van Hecke said, scratching his chin.

Even friends of the List children thought there was something unusual about John. Brad West, a former friend of Johnny's, recalled: "Every once in a while, we would be tossing around a football with John and Fred in this huge front yard they had, and maybe we'd get too loud or something, and Mr. List would come out in his suit and tie, 'Don't do that, don't do this.' He was always dressed like that. Always! It was always white shirt, dark suit, dark tie—come hell or high water, summer or winter."

As the children started growing up, another dimension opened on John's life. No longer toddlers who could easily be supervised and directed in their activities, the children were increasingly exposed, in John's view, to outside influences beyond his control. As they got older, he became stricter, more like the disapproving Teutonic presence that his father had been than the man who would take a step-daughter ice fishing.

Indeed, there were grumblings even in the Sunday school class he taught at Redeemer, where John was becoming known as what one parishoner called a "pious grouch who treated those kids like they were in reform school."

Van Hecke, a local teacher at the time, occasionally got to see John close up, and he bristled at what he encountered. Westfield's various churches were active in sponsoring Cub Scout and Boy Scout troops, and not long after moving to town, John became co-leader of the Cub Scout pack that his sons Johnny and Fred belonged to at Redeemer Lutheran Church.

The various scouting organizations in Westfield often gathered, each with their own adult leaders, for parades or other civic events. Van Hecke recalled the first time that he and the other Scout fathers laid eyes on John List: "He had his kids marching in like little Prussian soldiers, while our kids would sort of saunter in," he said. Alongside these spit-shined boys in their little blue uniforms was their tall, gawky, and mirthless leader practically goose-stepping in his own adult Cub Scout uniform.

"Jesus," Van Hecke said. "We'd never seen anything like that."

Once a year, the Westfield Cub Scout troops participated in what was known as the Pinewood Derby, in which individual dens would compete with tiny racing cars they made from wood. There were small prizes for the fastest, the fanciest, the most unusual. "It was just a fun event for the boys," Van Hecke said. But John won the lasting enmity of other fathers with an attitude that was regarded as unseemly. "Here's this martinet, this tinhorn tyrant, barking orders to a bunch of little kids! As if this event was an exercise in discipline," sputtered Van Hecke. "He was a methodical son of a bitch with an arrogance that most people don't possess. A right-wing nut, in my opinion, who stood out in a cosmopolitan town like Westfield."

But, like anyone else who had known John, he was quick to add this counterbalance: "Now, don't get me wrong. He was otherwise a complete gentleman. The Old World kind."

On Sundays, John was proud to be seen with his mother, his wife, and his three well-groomed children at services at Redeemer. After services, while he taught his Sunday school class and the boys stayed with him, Helen and Patty usually got a ride home.

Predictably, Helen was the first to peel away from the little squadron. Though she liked Westfield very much, liked its cultural quality and its proximity to New York City, she was quickly put off by Redeemer.

"Helen told me she went to a church picnic when they were fairly new in town, and she got the cold shoulder from those people," her sister Jean said, adding with a laugh: "With Helen, you only got one chance."

Never one for the subtle approach, Helen finally insisted to her husband that he go to the church office and formally have her name removed from the roster of the congregation. A mortified John meekly told her he had complied, but never actually did withdraw her name. Anyway, as if to further muddy the waters and let them know she could do as she pleased, a defiant Helen would impulsively decide on occasional Sunday mornings to go to church with her family again. But never two Sundays in a row.

When the children died in 1971, with their father proclaiming his belief that he was saving them from drifting away from religion, Patty still sang most weeks in the church choir. Johnny drew almost all of his friends from the congregation. And Fred was a member of the confirmation class.

John's new job as a bank vice president and comptroller lasted one year.

The title had been somewhat misleading. What the job actually demanded was a person with the innovative ability to seek out new business in the rapidly expanding suburbs around the old industrial cities of northern New Jersey. Social skills and the ability to follow through, to close the deal, were of paramount importance. John was fine with structures and procedures. But as a salesman, he plunged hopelessly in over his head. This time there would be no grace period to find a suitable new job. This time there wouldn't be the salve of a warm endorsement on his résumé. This time, he was unceremoniously fired.

Overcome with humiliation, he was unable to confront his wife with a truth that threatened to demolish whatever happiness they had managed to find in Westfield. Instead, he continued leaving the house each morning with his briefcase and his *Wall Street Journal* tucked under his arm. He got into his car and edged it around the house and down the long circular drive onto Hillside Avenue. He drove to downtown Westfield, parked the car, and walked into the train station. And he sat there all day, on cold days inside the building, on warm days in the little park outside, reading a book. For six months of 1967, this was how John spent every work day.

Occasionally, his face burning with shame, he would make a stop at the bank where both he and his mother kept their accounts. Using the power of attorney she had given him when they moved to Westfield, he began to make regular withdrawals from his mother's account, loans that he believed he would pay back once he got on his feet again.

At night, he began confiding more in his mother. John would come home and excuse himself after dinner to go to Alma's quarters on the third floor, where they read and discussed the Bible. To her he could confide his fears, his failures, and his troubles with Helen, who had become more demanding and contemptuous.

But he didn't tell his mother about the money. And he didn't tell his wife about losing his job until he found a new one.

This job, which came later in 1967, had the requisite cachet in its title: vice president and comptroller, with a firm called American Photographic Company in New York City. But the salary was $12,000, less than half of what he had made in his previous two jobs. And he was out of work again within a year, when the company decided to relocate. John said he was reluctant to part with the house in Westfield. "Nobody was sorry to see him go," one official of the company said.

While John was still working at American Photographic, Helen was hospitalized, at Columbia-Presbyterian Medical Center in New York, where her condition of cerebral atrophy was diagnosed as a symptom of general paresis, a fatal disease.

The Syferts came to visit during Helen's long recuperation and were shocked by the deterioration they found

not only in Helen but in John, who looked puffy and un-
healthy himself. There was nothing to do for John. But,
after consulting with a local doctor who knew Helen, Jean
recommended that he consider having his wife institu-
tionalized. John wouldn't hear of it, she said.

During this visit, while touring the house with John,
Gene noticed for the first time the extensive collection of
strategy games that his brother-in-law had acquired over
the years. Gene also saw that John also had stacks of books
on crime, criminals, and weapons in the room he called
his billiard room. For a man who Gene "didn't think knew
which end of a gun the trigger was on," this was surprising.

John also took his brother-in-law into the damp cellar
beneath the main part of the house, pointing out the dark
nooks and blind passageways. "Gene, a man could hide for
six months down here if he had food and water," John told
him. Gene thought that was such an odd remark to make
that he mentioned it later to his wife.

In September 1968, feeling a real financial squeeze after
Helen's illness, John took out a loan for $4,000 at Suburban
Trust Company, securing it with a lien on the house. Two
months later, he got a $7,000 second mortgage on the
house, and repaid the earlier $4,000 note.

After he left American Photographic, John found a new
job, this time in an entirely new field, selling mutual funds.
He worked out of his house. For a time, though it did not
improve markedly, his financial condition seemed to
stabilize.

Helen, at least by Brenda's account, did not, however.
"Mom just couldn't stop drinking, and she kept making
Daddy buy her all these clothes," said Brenda, who came
to visit with her husband and children. Brenda also noticed
that Helen was now voicing aloud what had been private
complaints about John's sexual abilities. "I don't think John
really satisfied her sexually," Brenda said.

John's instinctive reaction to buy his wife's happiness

now seemed to extend to the children as well, Jean Syfert noticed. "There weren't many fights in that house," she said. "But there were very unpleasant times when money was very tight. If Helen said the kids needed something, John went right out and got it, whatever it was she said they needed. Even in the bad times, he would always buy the best. I remember one particular time when we were there, one of the children needed eyeglasses. They cost like $250, and I'm sure he could have probably got glasses that would have been just as good for less money. But that just wasn't John's way."

But now there was no money to purchase anyone's happiness and love. The walls were closing in. An overwhelming sense of persecution filled his soul. In his despair, he prayed to a God who had forsaken him, pleading for a way out.

Chapter Six

JOHN HATED EVERYTHING THE SIXTIES REPRESENTED: license, irreverence, disobedience. As a Cub Scout leader, he liked to call the boys to attention and strut up and down the ranks like a drill sergeant on inspection. But a scout pack in the New York suburbs wasn't the Marine Corps, and few parents in Westfield were prepared to allow their boys to be publicly rebuked by a man in a Cub Scout uniform, so John kept his disapproval to the level of a sneer when he found a boy with hair creeping down past his collar.

At home, he was terrified of Helen. But the children were a different story. He insisted on his right to approve their playmates. He drilled them in religious and school lessons. He was the final arbiter of their daily schedules. The children, at least, were under control. They obeyed. Until Patty became a teenager right at the height of the counterculture movement and the Vietnam War. For John, deeply alarmed by the moral decay that he believed had begun to pervade the nation, the sixties came home every time Patty walked in from school with her leather jacket and her waist-length blonde hair.

Worse, as far as he was concerned, the girl had obviously inherited certain personality traits from her headstrong mother.

"Pat at sixteen was the most independent young woman that I have ever known," said a Westfield friend of the girl's, Barry Cohen. "She had an attitude and an outlook that people her age admired, and even envied. She had outward qualities of brazenness, haughtiness, and non-chalance, but inward qualities of warmth and kindness. She had tremendous allure for a girl of sixteen."

Like her mother, she also had a mouth that she some-times used to great effect. Once, after being lectured snidely by an imperious male high school teacher for some minor inattentiveness, Pat was heard to mutter "Oh, go fuck yourself" as she buried her head in a book. While the suggestion caused merriment and even prompted mur-murings of "I'll second that!" in the classroom, the re-sulting phone call to her father was no laughing matter. John was horrified that any daughter of his would be heard using such language. She was grounded for what her friends believed was an inordinately long time.

The boys were still too young to sense the trouble that was gathering. John was just turning fifteen, with Fred two years behind him. Their father still accompanied them on scout functions, including camping trips in the summer. On occasion, John would even play catch on the lawn with his sons. One neighbor noticed that John threw a baseball from the wrist, with his elbow bent, "like a girl, before girls began playing baseball that is." Whatever, John was proud of his sons. Young Johnny was a budding athlete, a strong boy with a quick temper who played on his junior high school soccer team. Freddy was a cherub-faced charmer who covered games for his school paper and had dreams of being a sportswriter. Both boys were avid fans of the New York Mets.

As to Helen, the children's classmates have differing recollections. Some say they never saw her. "She was al-ways sick in bed," said one. To others, she was a gracious presence who welcomed her children's friends into the home and often served them snacks after asking them not to make noise that would disturb John at work in his ground-floor office.

The boys clearly believed that their mother was ill. But they told friends that she was gradually getting better. All she needed, they said, was rest.

Pat—the only people who called her Patty anymore were relatives—sensed that this was not the case. Pat didn't say much at home, but she took it all in. She knew her mother was seriously ill, and she knew there were severe problems between her parents.

Pat had noticed that her father did not spend every night with her mother. Sometimes John slept in one of the boys' rooms. Sometimes he spent the night in a spare room down the hall. She had heard him crying in there more than once. Sometimes, she knew, he even spent the night on a cot in the room where he kept his games and books, under the ballroom.

And she knew something else. She knew they were poor. It was clear her father was struggling miserably all day in his office, sitting there in his suit and tie with his two dozen file cabinets and his envelopes. Oh, he was on the phone; he had stacks of mail. But the man did not have a job. You could see it in the haunted look on his face.

Without making a major issue out of it, at the end of her sophomore year in high school, the girl went to her guidance counselor and switched her curriculum from college prep to vocational. That way, she could take advantage of the work-study program in the fall, attending classes in the morning and working in an office, for credit and pay, in the afternoon. That way, she at least would have a job and a few dollars of her own. Pat got an after-school job as a file clerk at KMV Associates, an insurance agency in downtown Westfield. Shortly afterward, she got her kid brother Fred a job at the same office. For ninety minutes each afternoon, the thirteen-year-old boy came in to do

basic janitorial chores such as sweeping floors, emptying
trash cans, and cleaning ashtrays.

Pat kept her worries to herself as a matter of course.
As the sixties swept over Westfield, the girl bought a
second-hand guitar and even wrote her own songs. As a
child of the Midwest transplanted into a new culture at
adolescence, she overcompensated a little, affecting a cool-
ness that one classmate said "struck some people as hoody."
But her friends, and she had a lot of them, boys and girls,
mostly remember her as an earnest, friendly, and amusing
girl who had come to Westfield from upstate New York
and wanted nothing more than to be liked and accepted.

And while she mainly achieved that with her teenaged
peers, it had become disturbingly apparent to Pat that she
had failed abjectly with her father, that, whoever she was
and whatever she was all about, he now did not trust her
and, ultimately, did not even much like her.

Even in high school, Pat needed to obtain permission
from her father for routine forays beyond Hillside Avenue.
It always seemed to present some sort of a problem.

"Daddy, we're going down to get an ice cream cone. And
then we might stop at the Dungeon," a Westfield friend,
John Rochat, recalled Pat saying to her father after supper
one evening.

Her father knew what the Dungeon was—a teen club
operated by a local church, where kids came to dance to
records on Saturday nights. They drank soft drinks. Even
the bolder ones knew better than to try to sneak anything
else in, or even to disappear into the parking lot for a nip.
The place was always chaperoned. It was about as tolerant
of teenaged rowdiness as the public library.

But John, who was so unassertive when dealing with
adults, liked to twist the screws when dealing with children. "There's not going to be any *liquor* down there, is

there?" he growled in disgust, needlessly embarrassing the girl in front of her friends.

Sometimes, the friends noticed, he even got in his car and followed her into town, to be sure they were going where she had said.

"John List was quiet, well-spoken," Rochat said. "But he never seemed to have very much to say. He was the sort of guy I then classified as a bookworm. He had this air about him. He always seemed to be thinking."

Rochat liked Pat very much. They did not date—dating by then was something of an outmoded activity. Kids showed up at places, usually in a group. People would pair off eventually, but it would have been laughable for a boy to arrive at a girl's front door with a bunch of flowers, stammering his greetings to the girl's father. John always seemed to blame his daughter for not knowing that kind of boy.

"Pat wasn't a straight-laced conservative," Rochat said, "but she was by no means what you would have called a hippie. We had some hippies, and Pat was not one of them. In no way was Pat out of line. She wasn't a bad kid. She wasn't promiscuous. Now, I cannot say that she didn't drink an occasional beer. I never saw her, but I'm sure she did. New York was a short drive away, and you could buy alcohol at eighteen in New York. Westfield had any number of teenaged bootleggers. There was beer around. Big deal, right?

"I also never saw her do any drugs, never. She might have smoked marijuana, but I never saw it, which is to say that she wasn't making a big point of it," said Rochat, who went on after college to become a small-town police chief in Ashland, Virginia. "Pat was a good kid. That's what I remember. Now, she wasn't any Holy Roller, maybe she wasn't holy enough for her father. She didn't go around

talking about saving people. But she was what I would call
a nice Christian girl."

In the last eight months of her life, Pat discovered the
theater.

Ed Illiano noticed the girl as soon as she strolled in. She
stood there for a long time at the edge of the group, transfixed as she listened to the young people rehearse their
lines. Actually, Ed *thought* she was transfixed, with her
eyes wide and mouth agape. In fact, Pat List was stoned.

A girlfriend had brought her to one of the twice-weekly
workshop sessions of the Westfield Drama Club, which
was sponsored for local teenagers by the Westfield Recreation Commission. Pat had been reluctant. Drama workshop did not sound especially cool. It sounded something
like marching band, which she had left behind with junior
high. But she had shared a joint in the park; there wasn't
anything better do to. She decided to stop in for a look.

It turned out to be the best thing she ever did. Not only
did she discover a love of the theater that she hadn't known
before, she also found in that group of perhaps thirty teenagers, about evenly divided between boys and girls, something that approximated a family. It would sustain her for
the rest of the life she had left.

The drama workshop was begun in 1968 by Ruth Hill,
the director of the recreation commission, who hired Ed
Illiano, a freelance voice and drama teacher who had a
number of private students in Westfield, to run it. In 1969,
a group of students in Westfield High School, dissatisfied
with what they thought was a timid and unimaginative
school drama group, broke away to form their own splinter
group, Theater 69, which affiliated with the recreation
commission workshop and Ed Illiano.

A brochure published by the group at the time said,
"Our young performers soon learn the sometimes harsh

realities of theater . . . our ambition is to channel our graduates into professional theater."

Ed, in his early forties at the time, believed passionately in community repertory theater and in the ability of young people, given hard work, to grasp the essentials.

"Ed was a good, strong coach, very traditional in his approach, with high standards," Ruth Hill said. "He demanded a lot of the kids. They liked it—they put on one excellent production after another under Ed, who was a real taskmaster."

She was amazed at how Pat List plunged right in, and at the positive change that came over her. A girl who had been a lackluster student in school suddenly was transformed into someone who studied scripts, showed up on time for rehearsals, and gave it all she had.

"This was a girl who was obviously having some difficulties, and the drama group was something, the one thing, she was really excited about," Ruth Hill said. "She was really a very outgoing child, and this was an opportunity she had never known existed for her."

Like most of the other teenaged members of the group, she was in awe of Ed Illiano, an unlikely Pied Piper indeed at the end of the sixties. A Korean War veteran with extensive operatic training, a strict conservative in a room full of borderline hippies, Ed seemed to use the sheer force of personality to make his students pay attention.

"The man threw chairs," said Barry Cohen, who belonged to the group. "He pounded his fist on walls. He shouted. But in spite of that, we came back for more. There was a charisma, a strength—we were all bound together tremendously. If anything happened to one of us, we all felt it."

In the drama group, Pat List found a direction for the first time in her life.

One night, after members of the group had worked for

several hours on scenes from Rostand's *Cyrano de Bergerac*, Pat approached Ed with tears in her eyes.

"What beautiful, beautiful language," she said.

Ed snorted impatiently, "It's always been there. All you have to do is reach out and take it."

The drama group met twice a week, on Wednesday nights for three hours and on Fridays for four hours. It was a tremendous investment of time for teenagers, who were also expected to memorize their lines at home and, when their twice-yearly stage productions approached, put in even more time on rehearsals and such mundane chores as building sets.

Ed was touched when Pat came to him one night in the spring and asked if he would take her on as a private drama student for lessons he gave several nights a week in the music room of a Westfield resident and friend, Barbara Sheridan, who served as the assistant drama coach.

He agreed. The fee was six dollars an hour. In Westfield, it went without saying that a parent paid for a child's lessons. Later, Ed would learn that Pat, not wanting to burden her father with a request for money, was paying the fee out of the few dollars she made from her after-school job.

As a young aspiring actress, he said, "Pat wasn't the type who hit you between the eyes. She wasn't one of these sweet-faced sexy kids at all. After a while, you just knew she was there, but it took time. But her staying power was very great, and she got better. Sometimes you see some in the beginning and they're spectacular, then they fade, they drop out after the first week. But there was something about her. She just stayed and stayed with it.

"I have never in my life, before or since, known a girl like Pat," he said. "She wasn't a child. She wasn't giddy, wasn't pretentious. She had the face, the figure, the intelligence, the stick-to-itiveness. She could have made it.

The kid *wanted* to work. She'd show up with her lines memorized, every time, without fail. And we're not talking about easy stuff."

Actually, Pat's stage debut was easy stuff. The spring production in 1971 was *Li'l Abner*, the first musical the group had attempted, and all that was required for the small part she was considered for was the ability to act comically sexy, which she had, and the ability to execute a small bump and grind, which she lacked.

"Mr. Illiano," she asked him during a lesson. "Would you teach me how to bump and grind?"

It must have been an interesting sight to see this fiercesome Italian taskmaster demonstrating the bump and grind to a sixteen-year-old. "It was only a side-grind, very modest, even for Westfield," Ed laughed years later. It seems to have gone over fine.

The role Pat played in *Li'l Abner* was Stupefyin' Jones, the sexpot who appears at various points in the play. Both of Pat's parents were in the audience in Edison Junior High School's auditorium on May 22, 1971, when Pat made her stage debut in *Li'l Abner*, which was presented with a full cast and an orchestra. The happiest moment in her life came during the curtain calls after the last act, when she stood in a spotlight on the stage basking in enthusiastic applause and scattered anonymous wolf whistles.

The only person in the audience of several hundred who did not seem to join in the fun was Pat's father, who sat rigid in his seat, his face and lips taut. While Helen came backstage after the production to congratulate Ed and the cast, John waited in the car in the parking lot with the engine running and the windows up, even though it was a warm spring evening.

"He must have died to see that because she was wheeled on stage in a box with a curtain in front of it, and she stepped out," said Eileen Livesey, a friend of Pat's from the group. "She didn't have any lines. All she had to do was bump and grind, and she certainly did that," she said with a laugh. "She really had the physique for it."

Pat mentioned to only a few people that her father had expressed serious objections to any notion she might have of a career in the theater. That might well have been because no one talked about their parents anyway. "Parental influence was the thing people were trying to get away from, so that's why I didn't know anything about Pat's family life," said Eileen, who added, "Pat was no shrinking violet. She was a very strong-willed individual."

So she stayed in the drama group despite her father's disapproval. Moreover, in Ed Illiano, she had now found a new authority figure.

In the summer of 1971, she told her drama teacher that she was in love with him, a declaration she reiterated in letters to several friends at the time. "She told me that she wanted to marry me," Ed said, though she added that this would, of course, have to occur at some point in the future. "She was very matter of fact about it." Illiano knew that Pat had several boyfriends, none of whom her father approved of. He dismissed her talk as adolescent prattle.

All the same, he was strangely taken with the girl. He found himself paying more attention to Pat than might have been considered appropriate in a teacher-student relationship. They met in innocent social situations, such as when group members would adjourn to a local diner after workshop. Knowing that she now loathed calling her father for a ride home, Ed began driving her, even though he lived in the opposite direction. And sometimes, when Pat wanted to talk things over, they began taking the long way home, and then even pulling over to sit and talk. It was just talk. But he knew well the peril if some people in Westfield, ever mindful of the comings and goings of teenagers and out-of-towners (Ed lived well on the other side of the tracks, in Elizabeth), began gossiping about a relationship.

"I was close to Pat," Ed said. "She confided in me, and I liked being with her." He believed he had helped her channel her energies and deal with some frustrations. But he wasn't a social worker or a psychologist. He was a teacher, employed by the town. And he was uneasy—undoubtedly more in hindsight—about being too close to the girl.

Another proclamation Pat made that summer was that, the sorry and hypocritical state of the godfearing world being what it was—with bombs raining down on Vietnam and students being mowed down by the National Guard at Kent State—she had turned her back on religion. Even though she continued to attend church at Redeemer every Sunday, she was doing it under silent protest. She didn't tell her father about renouncing religion, but she made it very clear to her friends. Just to drive home the point, she announced in the summer of 1971 that she was becoming a witch.

Such a declaration, in context, is not as odd as it might seem. One of the hit television situation comedies of the era featured a pretty witch who could do housework with the twitch of her nose. And teenaged girls, especially those who perceive an inability to control their own fate, often fantasize about being witches, psychologists have found. Usually, they keep it to themselves.

Not Pat, with her newfound sense of the dramatic. Encouraged by several older members of the drama group who happened to dabble in witchcraft and the occult, Pat made such a point of her belief that it came to the attention of her counselors at a YMCA-YWCA summer camp on the Delaware River where she spent two weeks from August 22 to September 4 in a counselor-in-training program.

"Pat List thought she was a witch," recalled Glenn Pontier, who was a supervisor of counselors at the summer camp. "Now, you can take that at a couple of levels. One level is, camp is a fantasy that you go to to get away from your life, from where you live. They had a camp persona that maybe was a little different than their real life, and that would be perfectly normal. So if somebody comes in and is a little into witchcraft or something, it doesn't seem all that unusual to me. It's part of camp."

However, with Pat, he said, "I think she believed it at a more serious level. I think she was involved with people who took witchcraft seriously. Pat was a pretty confused teenaged girl, confused and afraid."

Because the purpose of the training program was to evaluate aspiring counselors as potential employees for the next season, Pat was given extensive counseling herself, he said. The result was disquieting. "This girl feared for her life," he said. It was unclear, given the quasi-professional counseling of a summer camp, what the nature of that threat was, he said.

As to drugs, "Maybe she was using marijuana on occasion. Everybody was using marijuana then. But clearly, she did not have any kind of a drug problem that was noticeable at a level that would suggest intervention," Pontier said. In fact, it was decided that Pat had qualified to be offered a job as a paid counselor the following summer, he said.

"I don't recall her being a smart-ass or anything. Guys had crushes on her. What stands out is, she thought she was a witch. You really only noticed her because she was talking about real fear. That, and the fact that she was murdered shortly afterward, is why I remember her."

In October of 1971, John List referred to his budget book ruefully. Among the frightfully mounting debts were three mortgages on the house, for $41,446.89; $6,513.16; and $1,562.75, all months in arrears. But the entries for monthly income showed the grimmest news of all. So far that year, he had earned less than $5,000, selling insurance from home.

A sixteen-year-old girl and her thirteen-year-old brother with after-school jobs now accounted for the only regular paycheck being brought into the List house.

For John, the hill at last had become too steep to climb, at least with so much baggage.

He prayed and thought it through carefully. One *could* lighten the load. One could start the climb again, alone. Without the baggage.

On October 14, he walked into the Westfield police station to fill out an application for a gun permit. Routinely, his fingerprints were taken. But then, inexplicably, he never returned to pick up the permit.

A week later, Pat approached her father to ask if she could have a Halloween party in the ballroom for friends from the drama group. He looked at her and nodded, but she told a friend he didn't speak.

About thirty teenagers, most of them members of the drama group, showed up in costume for the party on the Saturday night before Halloween. Pat had decorated the ballroom with luminous hobgoblins and other such Halloween festoons.

"Pat was dressed as a witch," Eileen Livesey said. Eileen didn't see Pat's mother at all that night. "I just knew that she didn't come out of the house very much and that she spent a lot of time in bed," she said.

Pat had insisted that her two younger brothers stay upstairs during the party, which they did—to a point. Guests stepping into the center hall off the ballroom could see the boys hiding behind the banister on the second floor. The boys began writing notes on folded squares of paper and dropping them down. And as some of the guests scribbled friendly replies, young Fred would come scurrying down the double-winged staircase to fetch them and run back before his sister saw what was going on.

During what was remembered as a good party, with good music thumping from a record player on the floor, and lots of dancing, John List himself caused the only untoward incident. He had been seen from time to time during the night glaring down on the costumed partygoers from the upstairs landing. At one point late in the evening, John actually stormed down the steps to confront a boy sitting on the lower steps with a girl. It is not clear what incurred his wrath—perhaps the teenagers had a can of beer, or just a cigarette; maybe they were necking. Or perhaps a long suppressed shame from a long-ago Halloween darted angrily from the shadows of memory. Whatever, John took off after the frightened boy, aiming a kick that just missed him. He chased the boy out of the house.

John Rochat noticed one other unusual thing. Rochat's grandparents lived next door, and he had been a regular visitor to the List house since he was in junior high school. "Where did the furniture go?" he wondered during the party.

"At first, I thought, hey, the old man's worried that we all are going to do some damage," Rochat said. But he saw that it wasn't only the ballroom that was bereft of furniture, it was the center hall, where there had been antique high-backed chairs and area rugs, and the other rooms he could see. "Except for a few things like the kitchen table and chairs, and the file cabinets and desk, I didn't see any furniture at all to speak of on the first floor," he said.

The fact was, as John List would have been mortified to have any of the neighbors know, he already had sold some of the furniture downstairs. It hadn't amounted to much. He also sold the second car. Now he drove a nine-year-old Chevy, and it had a bright red sticker on its windshield that indicated it had just failed state motor vehicle inspection.

Helen was no longer drinking. But that was only because she was so ill, drifting in and out of lucidity, that booze no longer occurred to her. To accept the increasingly apparent fact that his wife was mentally ill would have been impossible, even without the other terrible burdens that had piled up. To accept the fact that Helen was in fact dying, on the other hand, would have been inconvenient.

He spent long nights without sleep, and his tortured mind groped for rationalization. He wasn't to blame. John never blamed himself for anything. Helen was to blame. And Patty was growing up just like her. And now he would act to save them for another world, and himself for this one.

For it was written:

> *Fallen, fallen is Babylon the great!*
> *It has become a dwelling place of demons,*
> *A haunt of every foul spirit,*
> *A haunt of every foul and hateful bird;*
> *For all nations have drunk the wine*
> *of her impure passion,*
> *And the kings of the earth have committed*
> *fornication with her,*
> *And the merchants of the earth have grown*
> *rich with the wealth of her wantonness*

And:

> *Render to her as she herself has rendered,*
> *And repay her double for her deeds;*
> *Mix a double draught for her in the*
> *cup she mixed.*
> *As she has glorified herself and played*
> *the wanton,*
> *So give her a like measure*
> *of torment and mourning.*

And this:

Alas! Alas! though great city,
Thou mighty city, Babylon!
In one hour has thy judgment come!

After dinner on Friday, November 5, John List stood in the kitchen at the rear of the house. He told one of the boys to go get his sister and brother.

When Pat, John, and Fred were seated anxiously at the table, John looked reproachfully at them. He told them directly what he had been hinting at for several months. Sternly, with no equivocation whatsoever, he advised these children to be prepared to die, because they would do so soon. Would they prefer to be buried or cremated? he asked. "Buried," the shocked children replied, one by one. Then he walked out of the room and calmly shut his office door behind him.

No one knows what the children might have said to each other that night, but it is evident at least that the two older ones, Pat and Johnny, now believed they were about to die.

Pat attended drama group rehearsal the same night. The production of *A Streetcar Named Desire*, in which she was to understudy the role of Blanche DuBois, was only two weeks away. Pat had memorized the play—not her lines, but the entire play, Blanche and all of the other parts as well: Stanley Kowalski, Stella, Steve, Harold, and even the minor parts. She knew every word of it. But she didn't seem interested now. Her eyes were red from crying. She seemed to cling physically to anyone who came near her.

Worried, Ed offered to drive her home after the workshop ended.

Hearing her sniffing in the dark beside him, he stopped the car in the park right behind the Municipal Building and turned off the lights. Looking straight out at the path, he asked, "Pat, what's the matter?"

She didn't reply. She kept a tissue pressed to her nose.

Ed was uncomfortable, as he usually was when he was alone with her. It was after eleven o'clock at night, and he was in a parked car in the town park with a teenaged girl who was in tears. "Was it something that happened tonight at rehearsal?" he asked.

She shook her head. Then, composing herself, she said calmly, "It's my father." She had stopped crying. "Mr. Illiano, my father is going to kill me. He's going to kill me." She began weeping softly again.

Ed smiled, aware that he had probably conveyed the same sentiments on occasion to his own teenaged daughter.

In an avuncular tone, he assured her, "Nobody's going to kill you, Pat."

She looked at him as if he were an idiot.

Angrily, she repeated: "He said he is going to kill me. My brothers too. He said that, Mr. Illiano." She pushed herself across the seat as far away as she could get. Her eyes glowed with resentment. "He said that!"

Ed looked straight through the windshield across the car's hood, which reflected the street lamp. He drummed his fingers on the dashboard, lost for words. Pat was many things, but hysterical was not one of them.

"What are you talking about?" he said, lamely.

Her eyes were accusing. "He took us into the kitchen. He sat us down and he said, he flat-out told us we should be prepared to die."

"He said he would kill you?"

"That's exactly what he was saying. There was no doubt about it."

Ed made a soundless little whistle with his lips. He wondered what time it was. He didn't want to look at his watch. It was getting cold in the car. He turned on the engine, waiting for the heater to kick in. He could hear the girl beside him sobbing softly.

He tried middle-aged bravado. "Look, Patricia," he said

quite sternly. "I'm not going to let anybody kill you. Let's get that straight."

Her look said, What bullshit! Her look made him feel as if he was the child, and not she.

"Listen," she said, as if explaining something carefully to a six-year-old. "If he tells you he's going to take the family on a trip for a couple of weeks, that's it. That's how he's going to do it."

"Do what?"

"*Do* it. He's going to make it look like we went away."

"He told you that?"

"Yes."

Ed was dumbfounded. "Why would he tell you something like that?"

At this, she laughed. That was a good question, a very good question. The girl laughed at the patently ridiculous knowledge that her father had been so deliberate that he had told them, right down to the details. Maybe the man was simply out of his mind after all.

All she could say in reply to Ed was, "I don't know." She said it with a chuckle and a toss of her long blonde hair. Grinning in the face of the truth. She laughed, her eyes wet with tears. "I don't know."

Ed took out his handkerchief to wipe off the steam that fogged the windshield. He put the car in gear and took Pat home. He waited until she disappeared through the door before driving away.

Two days later, on Sunday, Ed invented an excuse to visit the List house. He returned a book he had borrowed from Helen several weeks earlier. He came early in the afternoon, without calling first.

Young John answered the door and let him in. Like his father, the boy was tall. But where the father was rigid, with squared shoulders that moved as if they had no joints, the boy was loose and relaxed, and usually quite animated.

But this time, the boy couldn't even manage a smile. He took him into the dining room, where Helen, apparently in good health that day, was seated at the table.

Pat didn't seem to be anywhere downstairs. Helen beckoned to him from the table, where she had the big Wittke photo album open in front of her.

Helen was always glad to see Ed, and on this day she seemed particularly vivacious and in good spirits. She moved closer to him when he sat down.

"We're going to start on the rest of the house as soon as John is better," she said, showing him a photo.

Ed was surprised. "Is John not well?"

"Oh, he'll be all right," she said cheerily, expelling a short breath, as if to blow away a feather. "He'll be back to work soon."

Finally, still with no sign of Pat, he disengaged himself from Helen and her dog-eared black-and-white pictures and put his coat on to leave.

At the door, he was surprised to find young John waiting. Physically blocking the exit, the boy grabbed Ed's arm in a tight grip and looked him directly in the eye. "Mr. Illiano, whenever you are in this neighborhood, please come by," John said with a firmness that was unusual for an adolescent addressing an adult. "Please understand," the boy said, choosing words slowly. "You are welcome here any time." Then he let Ed pass.

"There was quiet hysteria," Ed recalled years later. "That young boy was scared." As he backed his car into the driveway, he noticed that a sheer curtain was parted in a window on the ground floor, in the room where John kept his office. "It was John List, looking daggers at me," he said.

The next night, Monday, November 8, Pat phoned Ed at home. She sounded more sad than frantic.

"Mr. Illiano, you'd better get over here pretty quick," she said evenly. It was almost in an "I-told-you-so" tone of voice.

"What do you mean? What's the matter? I can't do it. You come *here* to see me," he replied, aware that he couldn't come up with another plausible excuse to visit the List house. Ed was already on thin ice with his wife, from whom he would shortly be separated.

"I can't," Pat whimpered. "I'm having my period and I've got violent cramps."

This was exactly the sort of thing that complicated the relationship with this girl, he thought peevishly. It was as if she meant to keep him uncomfortable. He was tired and annoyed at this. There was nothing he could do, not at eight o'clock on a Monday night.

"I just can't come over," he said flatly, putting an end to the conversation. "I've got a full schedule."

Chapter Seven

IN BETTER TIMES, JOHN LIKED TO TAKE OUT THE MONTHLY budget book and admire the columns of numbers he entered with his fountain pen. He was proud of the neat, nineteenth-century dress of the figures, the precision with which they marched down the thin blue lines, one after the other, squared off and squared away. He was proud of the fact that by the time the little figures hit the bottom line, every item would be accounted for, with assets sufficiently, even if sometimes just barely, in excess of liabilities. For years now keeping that balance just barely on the black side of the ledger had required the movement of certain future gains into the category of current earnings. This was a somewhat unorthodox accounting practice, but John could live with it. Mother's estate was to be legally his upon her death anyway. He was only borrowing his own money. He had always assumed he would be able to repay what he had taken, in the unlikely event a woman in her eighties should decide she wanted it.

By the end of 1971, Mother's money was all almost gone, too. The old woman didn't know it, but she was now almost flat broke. In an accountant's terms, those gains on John's balance sheet were nonrecurring.

Now, in the pale, cold hour before sunrise, on November 9, 1971, John wasn't dwelling on past accounts. With a pen, he drew an indelible line beneath the final set of figures.

It was only five-forty-five, a full hour before the children would stir upstairs, probably a good three hours before Helen would wander down to have her coffee and Mother would start puttering in her kitchen on the third floor. John adjusted his desk lamp for better light and glanced through the budget book, starting back in January and working his way up to October, where he had finally given up.

It was all quite hopeless. The oil bill was $1,072.76 and counting. He could hear the burner running even as he read. The mortgage, three months in arrears. On and on went the liabilities. The situation was irretrievably, irrevocably hopeless. His fate settled over his shoulders like a shawl. It had come to this. His pleas to God had brought him only to this. Now there would be detachment from all else. So be it. Amen.

He closed his budget book for the last time, putting it aside on the desk, beside his Bible. He twisted his class ring off his finger, Michigan 1950, and lay it there too.

From the red-covered Lutheran hymnal, the 1941 Concordia edition that was in use in the Missouri Synod, he read the words, humming softly as his eyes followed the verse:

> *The world is very evil,*
> *The times are waxing late;*
> *Be sober and keep vigil,*
> *The Judge is at the gate;*
> *The Judge that comes in mercy;*
> *The Judge that comes with might,*
> *To terminate the evil,*
> *To diadem the right.*
>
> *Arise, arise good Christian,*
> *Let right to wrong succeed;*

Let penitential sorrow
To heav'nly gladness lead,
To light that hath no evening,
That knows no moon nor sun,
The light so new and golden,
The light that is but one.

O home of fadeless splendor,
Of flow'rs that bear no thorn,
Where they shall dwell as children
Who here as exiles mourn.
Midst pow'r that knows no limit,
Where knowledge has no bound,
The beatific vision
Shall glad the saints around.

Amen

Now, having suffered to do the will of God, the time had come for a terrible journey of faith.

The door to his office was open, and across the entrance hall one could see the aquamarine glow of the fluorescent lights in Helen's fish tanks, which sat side by side on a table in front of the windows that opened from the dining room onto the side porch. The aerators in the tanks gurgled in the quietest hour of day.

Outside, the sky had begun to lighten. Sunrise, he knew, for he had planned this day to the last detail, would be at 6:36 A.M. Until then, there would be time for quiet reflection in the comforting gloom.

A shaft of white light glanced into the room, destroying reverie. John tensed with the day's first unwelcome intrusion by the outside world. A car slowed at the upper end of the driveway, on the side of the house where his office was. A newspaper thumped onto the ground somewhere in the general vicinity of the front steps.

This was not good. This was a hitch. He had phoned days ago to have the newspaper delivery stopped. But here it was again, and God knew how long it would keep piling up out there, drawing attention to the place. Later in the day, he would phone again to halt delivery.

John always read a morning paper, and in Westfield it was *The New York Times*. He had time to do so this day as well, for the plan was well laid and there was no sense of urgency. Outside, it was freezing. The temperature on the porch thermometer read twenty-eight degrees. A breeze from the northwest shook down some leaves that still clung stubbornly to a tree. John always put on his coat and hat when he went out, even if it was to fetch the paper from the lawn ten feet past the front door.

That day's *Times* contained the usual blend of what would have been both informative and annoying to a man who had come to blame the media for fomenting much of what he found wrong with the country. The front page led with news of a 5.5 percent limit on employee wage increases as part of the federal government's economic stability program. Five years ago, such news would have caused him severe consternation, but it was of little consequence now to a man without a job. The front page also carried a headline offering more disheartening proof of just how out of kilter John believed things had become in such a short time:

School Prayers
Blocked by House
By 28-Vote Margin

Street crime, so bad that the newspaper's own drivers had held a one-day strike the previous day to protest the murder of one of their members near Times Square. Elsewhere, a particular bête noire continued unraveling, the My Lai travesty, which was making criminals of soldiers he strongly believed were only doing their jobs, dragging its way through the courts. On page nine was a headline that would have assuaged his dismay, if it wasn't also a blunt reminder of the apparent interminability of a war the United States wasn't being allowed to win:

U.S. Planes Raid
The North Again

And another outrage lay in the news section: A *full-page* photograph of the satanic, smirking Charles Manson in an advertisement promoting a book on the Manson case. Even the entertainment pages rankled: Ads for the blasphemous new Broadway musicals *Hair* and *Jesus Christ Superstar* overwhelmed the notices for such wholesome shows as *Fiddler on the Roof.* The depraved *Oh! Calcutta* was in its "third big year!" Sex manuals with titles such as *Any Woman Can* and *The Sensuous Man* leered from ads on the book page. One of the biggest best-sellers of the year was called *The Exorcist*, a book that John had only needed to read a few pages of some time ago before denouncing it as a clever-glorification of Satan.

John always perused the television page last before neatly rearranging the paper in the order in which it had come. Once, John had objected to television in his home, insisting that the set be turned off as soon as the evening news was finished. But with children around, it had wormed its way in. By now there were in fact four television sets in the house, two of them color: the one in Mother's room and the one in the parlor. John sometimes let people know that his house had two color television sets in it.

But there wasn't much point in checking the television

listings now. There wouldn't be any television that night in the List house.

Soon after daybreak, a faint rush of water through the pipes indicated that someone had just flushed a toilet on the second floor. It was about seven o'clock. Before long—at last—the children would be down and on their way to school.

As a car edged down a neighbors' driveway, wheezing steam with the first welcome stirrings of the day outside, John had the opportunity to go over his paperwork one more time. There was the passport, issued in the name of John Emil List. He wouldn't have any use for that document, but he wanted it to appear to others that he might. He would take this with him. The credit cards would stay behind. All they were good for lately was a rueful look from a cashier. The driver's license would stay, of course. His billfold now held only a few dollars, but by afternoon it would have enough cash to tide him over for some time, if he watched his pennies.

He had packed a briefcase and a small suitcase. No heavy baggage, for once. Not even the raincoat and galoshes his mother would have insisted on. In every sense, emotionally as well as physically, John was ready to travel light.

Around eight, Patty came downstairs. As usual, she rummaged in the cupboard and shut the refrigerator with a whump after she looked inside for milk. There wasn't any. The milkman was due later in the morning, John knew. Besides, the kids usually left the cereal soggy and half-eaten anyway.

John waited quietly until he heard her go to the hall closet for her black leather coat. She left by the back door and presently came around the side of the house. Impassively, he stood by the slightly parted curtain at his window and watched her make her way down the long driveway.

She kept her head down against the cold, and hugged her schoolbooks to her chest. Long, whispy blonde hair trailed behind her in the breeze.

Her hair had been so curly when she was a tot. "Shirley Temple!" the ladies in Inkster would coo when he took the baby out in the carriage. This was the baby that liked to laugh, just loved it. A mildly funny face would do it. She would giggle, and if you scrunched your face a little more, she would laugh herself silly, with those pudgy little hands raised in delight.

Now she was almost an adult. In a minute, a late-model car stopped and she got in. Pat never had a problem getting a ride to school. In Westfield, where money was easy, there was always a boy with a car.

Soon the two boys were down.

Once, there would have been lively voices, laughing, teasing, a wail of injured protest, a clatter of bowls and spoons, the hiss of a faucet, the scrape of chairs on the floor. What a long time ago that was. But now mornings were subdued. There wasn't any chatter. At twenty minutes past eight, the boys gathered up their school things and stomped down the back steps.

They trudged along the drive past his office window in their bulky coats with knit ski caps pulled down on their heads. Young John carried a blue and white gym bag with "Westfield" lettered on it. John had really shot up the summer. He was going to be a six-footer or better, Johnny was. Would. Freddy still looked like a little Cub Scout. "Little towhead," his grandma called him when he was a baby, stroking his thick hair. His bangs, darker now, spilled out from the blue cap over a ruddy child-face.

He was proud of the boys. The boys, true to the Boy Scout oath that John had insisted they memorize, still believed that they must do their best to do their duty to God and country, to help other people at all times, to keep themselves physically strong, mentally awake, and morally straight.

Morally straight? Where tranquil tree-lined streets led to moral deviation? Where the danger zone began at the curb?

There was insolence in John already, at fifteen, in the flash of those dark, defiant eyes. In Freddy, at thirteen, a close observer could detect the faint hint of slackness, of lack of resolve. Temptation would have no contest here. Evil was only a phone call away, a short drive in a car, a whistle in the night. There was would be nothing he could do, once it came, as it would.

Yes, there was a fortress. And this fortress was impregnable. But, oh God! it was humble. That is what John had finally come to realize. The fortress was just too small. It only had room for one.

> *I love thee, O Lord, my strength.*
> *The lord is my rock and my deliverer,*
> *My God, my rock, in whom I take refuge,*
> *My shield, and the horn of my salvation.*

The boys waited for a few minutes down by Hillside Avenue. Their breath made little vapor trails in the cold. It would not do for them to be late for school. The last thing John felt like dealing with was a phone call from the school. Finally, their regular car-pool ride, Barbara Baeder, a neighbor with a son Fred's age, pulled up. The boys got in. As the car drove off, brittle brown leaves skittered behind in the street.

Once the house was silent again, John went to a file cabinet where the label "Guns and Ammo" was affixed to a drawer, which he slid open. Inside were the two pistols, one a little 22-caliber automatic, so small it could almost hide in the palm of a hand. That gun, a Colt, had been

his father's. And the other was a beauty, the Steyr 1912
automatic he had brought back from World War II, a classic model that had been carried by officers of the Austro-
Hungarian Army during World War I and was refitted by
the Nazis in World War II to take a certain cartridge
known as the 9-millimeter parabellum. The cartridge's
name was derived, John knew, from the Latin motto *si vis
pacem, para bellum*. "If you want peace, prepare for war."
Both pistols accepted magazines that held eight rounds
each. The weapons lay on the desk gleaming with oil.

A few minutes after eight-thirty, Herbert Arbast, a milkman, drove his truck up the drive at 431 Hillside, and
parked behind the house. As was his custom twice each
week, he entered the house through the unlocked back
door and walked across the kitchen to the adjacent butler's
pantry to check the note which Helen usually left taped
to the refrigerator. Most times, the List order was for six
quarts of milk and some butter and eggs. Arbast set his
carrier on the floor by the refrigerator. Oddly, the note
was from John, not Helen. It said to stop deliveries "until
further notice" because the family was going on vacation.
John would call to resume delivery when they returned.
The milkman shrugged. He didn't see anyone else around.
With bottles rattling in his carrier, he left by the back
door and returned to his truck, where he made the appropriate note on his clipboard to halt deliveries to 431
Hillside Avenue until further notice.

At the window of his office, John watched quietly until
the truck turned onto the street.

Within ten minutes, Helen came down, filled the kettle,
and banged it on the stove. John's office had once been the
library at Breeze Knoll. It was the front room on the left
side of the house. Behind it were a parlor and then the
ballroom. One door of the office opened onto the center
hall, where the twin staircases swept up on each side.
Beyond the hall, through an open door toward the rear of

the right side of the house, lay the kitchen. It was a commodious room with knotty-pine cabinets and countertops that held a toaster, an electric frying pan, a juice squeezer, and a blender.

Since they barely acknowledged each other's presence anymore, Helen would have made no attempt to ascertain her husband's whereabouts when she came down wearing her bathrobe. He had always disapproved of appearing downstairs in nightclothes. There was so much John disapproved of. Helen had tried to be accommodating. But perhaps because she had spent so much time sick in bed, she had always had a much less formal attitude about attire.

In the kitchen, the kettle made a shrill whistle, then pitched down as Helen turned off the flame and took it from the burner.

John stood, the Steyr in his right hand. He was calm and alert as he stole out of his office and across the center hall. Helen sat with her coffee at the table on the far side of the kitchen, beside a window where the morning sun streamed in through canary yellow curtains. Silently, John approached from behind, just a bit to the left.

As he raised the barrel of the Steyr about eighteen inches from his wife's head, she sensed movement just over her shoulder and turned her head slightly, with her chin tilted up just a bit, the way a woman would to be kissed on the cheek at a party. John fired. The bullet hit her in the jaw and knocked her to the floor with its force. The amount of blood pooling at her head told him it had been quick, final. Without taking aim, John fired several more quick shots that slammed into the wall beyond the table. One bullet ricocheted off a radiator into the next room.

The kitchen stank of gunpowder. Helen lay motionless, face down in the blood that spilled across the broad striped pattern of the lineoleum floor.

Now he scrambled up the gold-carpeted back stairs to the third floor. For the first time in his life, he didn't knock before entering his mother's quarters. Barging in, he found her in the small kitchen holding a plate that had a pat of butter on it, waiting beside the toaster, her silver-gray hair untidy from sleep. Alma looked startled as he moved toward her. "What was that noise downstairs?" she asked. In reply, he raised the gun and shot her once above the left eye at point-blank range. The plate smashed to the floor as the gunshot blew the old woman off her feet. Involuntarily, John squeezed off two more shots that smacked into the wall. Alma was sprawled on the checkerboard tile in the kitchen, quite still. On the counter beside the sink, her toast popped up.

He had planned to drag her downstairs, but quickly realized that the task was impossible. She was a large woman, not fat but big-boned and tall. He couldn't move her that far. But he couldn't just leave her lying there in the middle of the kitchen. He looked around desperately, then remembered the long plastic carpet runner she kept by the door in the sitting room. That would do it. He brought it beside her and, sweating, unmindful of the blood that drenched her housedress, pushed his mother's body onto the runner and dragged her to the narrow hallway just off the kitchen. Still struggling, he forced the body into the hall near a cistern that provided an auxiliary water supply for the house, and crammed the bloody runner in behind her.

As best he could, he cleaned the floor, wiping up the blood with dampened sections of the Sunday newspaper she had placed in a trim pile on a table. He found an old towel and used that, too. It wasn't perfect housework. He wasn't trying to hide anything. It was more of a gesture toward propriety, a respectful nod at the neatness his mother insisted on.

He hurried back down to the kitchen to ponder the problem of how to move Helen. Finally, he simply grabbed her feet and dragged her, struggling at first and then moving more smoothly as momentum eased the way, across the center hall into the other side of the house, through the entrance of the ballroom. The path from the kitchen to the ballroom was marked now with a forty-foot-long trail of blood.

John left Helen on the ballroom floor and took the steps down to the billiard room. He came back with three rolled-up sleeping bags in his arms. He knelt on the oak parquet floor to unfasten the square knots on the cords that held the fat round bundles in place. He unzipped two of the sleeping bags all the way around, opening them side-by-side like beach blankets. The other he did not open fully. This one he lay perpendicular to the two.

He rolled Helen's body onto that one, face down, with her feet to the wall where a small pool table was piled with clutter, including some stacks of Styrofoam cups from the Halloween party, some artificial flowers, and a game called Where's Willie? that Freddy had long since grown out of. The forest green sleeping bags were official Boy Scouts of America equipment, with the Boy Scout insignia and the motto "Be Prepared" repeated on their inner lining. As usual, John had bought quality, even when he couldn't afford it.

The light pouring down from the skylight showed the walls of the ballroom cracked and badly in need of attention. A good plasterer could have fixed the whole room in a couple of days. Had John and Helen managed to continue their renovations, they would have hired one. On the wall just above the children's pool table was the bare spot where a painting of Hessian soldiers had hung during the halcyon days when the room housed the Wittke art collection.

John arranged Helen's bathrobe to cover her legs. She was wearing only a red satin teddy underneath the robe. He found a bath towel and covered her body with it, and placed a kitchen towel over her face.

He used a roll of paper towels, and when he had gone through that, newspaper to wipe up the blood around the spot where Helen lay atop the sleeping bag. Sunlight streamed through the multicolored skylight down onto her.

He knew he was badly soiled. On his way to the bathroom on the second floor, John stopped first in Helen's bedroom—he hadn't really considered it his and Helen's bedroom for months—and did something that had not been part of his plan. He wiped his bloody hands on the sheets on her unmade bed. Again and again, he streaked the bedsheets with his grisly message, until he was convulsed with rage and nausea. He ran to the bathroom and vomited into the toilet, leaving a bloody palm print where he had leaned on the porcelain lid. Then he showered and scrubbed his hands and nails, and put on clean clothes. It didn't matter that he left his dirty clothes and blood-spattered shoes in the open in the bedroom. He wasn't trying to hide anything. He combed his hair neatly and went back down in a business suit with his necktie neatly adjusted.

The first phase had gone well, essentially according to plan, virtually like clockwork. But there wasn't much room for adjustment or deviation in the next phase, the delicate part, which required contact with outsiders. John knew that the rest of his life could depend on remaining dispassionate and orderly throughout the rest of the day.

Outside, there was no sign that any neighbor or passerby had heard a disturbance. Hillside Avenue wasn't the sort of street that strangers had any reason to stroll along. And the neighbors tended to stay on their own grounds when they weren't in their cars. Most of the houses on Hillside were big; not many were as large as the List house, but they all had space and ample ground separating one from the other. The crack of gunfire inside a house with thick masonry walls, a house set back away from the street and the neighbors, wouldn't carry far on a cold November day when people were at work, or at school, or snug inside their homes.

The sun hadn't warmed things up much yet. By nine-thirty the temperature had inched only two degrees above freezing. At other houses storm windows were secured fast in place, keeping the heat in and keeping most intrusive sounds out. On Hillside Avenue, nothing moved except the occasional automobile and the brittle leaves sifting down from bare branches.

At ten o'clock, he was due for one of the monthly meetings he had with Burton Goldstein, the branch manager at State Mutual Life, for whom he sold insurance from his house. Even once a month, getting out to Jericho, a ninety-minute drive that managed to combine the worst commuting headaches of New Jersey, New York City, *and* Long Island, was a chore. He had no intention of making the trip today.

Not wanting to leave open the opportunity for any inconvenient rescheduling of appointments, he waited until that morning to call Goldstein, and phoned the office just before Goldstein's usual arrival time to get the answering service. He left a message canceling his appointment and saying he wouldn't be able to reschedule for some time because his wife's mother was very ill, and he was taking his family to North Carolina to be with her.

The next details to tend to involved the children's absence from their schools, Westfield High for Patty and Roosevelt Junior High for the boys. At his desk, he wrote notes of explanation:

Westfield High School

Our daughter Patricia is a student in the 11th grade at Westfield High.

She will be out a few days since we had to make an emergency trip to North Carolina. We left after the school was closed so I'm sending this to you to explain her absence.

> John E. List
> 431 Hillside Ave.
> Westfield

Roosevelt Junior High

Our sons John and Fred, 9th and 8th grades, attend Roosevelt. They will be out for several days as we had to make an emergency trip to N.C. This happened after the school was closed.

> John E. List
> 431 Hillside Ave.
> Westfield

He also wrote a similar note to KMV Associates, the insurance office where Patty and Fred worked after school. After addressing them, he put them aside on his desk.

This done, he had a little time to relax. With nothing pressing to do for a while, John decided to go out and rake the leaves one last time. A neighbor happened to be outside when he did. She would recall the exact date a month later because she remembered that the temperature had broken the record low for November 9. She recalled that John pretended not to see her as he strode up and down his lawn with his rake, in his overcoat and dark tie, dressed as if he was going to church. When he came back in, he fixed himself a sandwich for lunch.

The first unwelcome deviation in his agenda of murder occurred just after noon when the phone rang. It was Patty, who wasn't due back till after five o'clock. She said she wasn't feeling well and wanted to come home right after school rather than going to work. There wasn't a ride available. Would he mind picking her up?

John was annoyed at this hitch. But he got in the car

and drove to Westfield High. Patty, looking pale and unhappy, thanked him for coming. They rode in silence on
the short drive home.

John parked the car in the usual spot out back, and
hurried to get inside the house first. Patty collected her
books from the back seat and followed a minute or so later,
coming in through the laundry room to the kitchen. She
never even saw the hulking figure waiting in the corner
behind the door. John leveled the pistol and shot her once,
at close range, in the back of the head.

Like her mother and grandmother, Patty died facedown
on the floor. When she lay still, he dragged her by the feet
through the kitchen, across the hall and into the ballroom,
where he tugged her onto one of the sleeping bags open
on the floor beside her mother's body. There were now
parallel paths of blood that looked like railroad tracks from
the kitchen to the ballroom.

Around one o'clock, he washed and changed his clothes
again to begin the day's errands. He drove downtown,
stopping first at a drive-in branch of Suburban Trust Company, where he cashed a personal check for $85 drawn on
his joint checking account with Helen. Neatly he entered
the balance, $24.14, in the front of the checkbook.

Then he went to the post office and made two trans-
actions at separate windows. At the first, he mailed a
special delivery letter, addressed to himself, inside which
was a blank sheet of paper folded over a small flat key. At
the other window, which he chose as if he had forgotten
something during his initial transaction, he filled out a
standard form asking that the List household mail be held
at the post office for a full thirty days, effective immediately. On his way out, he mailed the letters to the children's
schools.

After this, he drove back to another window at the drive-
in bank branch and cashed a second personal check, this

one for $200, the balance in a joint account he shared with his mother. Next he drove three blocks away and parked outside the main office of Suburban Trust. Besides the checking accounts, Suburban Trust held two of the three mortgages currently in force on the house, the last of which, for a paltry $1,800, he had taken in June in a pathetic attempt to stay afloat until something came up. The bank also held what remained of his mother's savings, which John had access to because she had granted him power of attorney when they moved to Westfield.

After he first began using it, John had actually repaid the small sums he borrowed, a few hundred here and there to pay bills or buy things for Helen or the children. Then he tapped in more frequently, to hold off insulting calls from bill collectors and several times to pay the overdue mortgage. He wasn't returning the money by then. He kept meticulous records, however. Over the years, and without her knowledge or consent, he had borrowed—*embezzled* was the word some would use, but he told himself that it was to be his money anyway at some point—a total of more than $50,000 from the money his father had left his mother. All the old woman had left on the day she died, in fact, was a stack of mature U.S. Savings Bonds that John stored in a safe-deposit box. Having just murdered the woman and crammed her body into a hallway, he now was going to steal the last of her money.

There were only a few people waiting at the windows in the lobby. A teller, Gay Jacobs, led him back to the vault where the safe-deposit boxes lined the wall. The time on the access slip he signed was stamped 1:37 P.M. Besides Alma's bonds, the box held a few decent pieces of jewelry he had given Helen in Rochester, but there wasn't much John could do with that. He was interested only in easy liquidity. He was uncomfortable but calm as he cashed each bond—all told, they yielded just over $2,000—under the watchful eye of the teller. She thought it odd when he was through that he made a point of asking her to make a list of the bonds and their value "for his mother's records, so his mother would know what the value was." She complied, however, and initialed and sealed an envelope with the cash, all but $200 of which was in hundred-dollar bills. The teller had also noticed how blotchy the customer's face had looked as he stood there shifting his weight from one foot to the other and signing his name. He signed out of the vault at 1:57 and headed back to Hillside Avenue, where three people lay dead.

Young Fred showed up for work as usual at KMV Associates at three o'clock, and employees there, who were genuinely fond of the diligent little boy with the blond hair, noticed that he seemed dismayed when he learned Patty had called in sick. Immediately, Fred phoned home. A secretary, Margaret Koleszar, never forgot what she heard the boy say to his father on the phone.

"What happened to Patty?" he demanded.

Shortly afterward, John made another unplanned trip, this time to pick up Fred, who told his employers he needed to go home early. As he had with his daughter, John hurried into the house first and grabbed the gun he had left in the corner just behind the kitchen door as he heard his son enter the laundry room just inside the back entrance. Like his sister, the boy never even had time to take his coat off. He died with a single bullet wound to the head.

Again the grisly trek was made to the ballroom. The father pulled his son's body onto the sleeping bag beside Patty. Fred's head was positioned so it just barely touched his mother.

Then there was yet another unexpected change in schedule. It was such a cold day that young John's soccer team couldn't practice outside. So the boy also was done for the day earlier than expected. When he happened to see John sauntering up the drive around four o'clock, swinging his gym bag as he walked, his father had to scramble to get into position behind the door.

Indeed, young John may have heard this scurrying because he didn't come into the kitchen as unwarily as the others. He saw his murderer coldly level the gun at him. For the boy managed to dodge; the first bullet caught him not in the head, where it was aimed, but in the back. The next shot didn't kill him either. The boy wouldn't die! With a pistol in each hand, his father began firing wildly. The brawny teenager tried to crawl across the floor to safety, but it was hopeless. He was on his knees, with his back to his murderer. But the gunman was in control of the situation, firing now with the .22. The room thundered with gunfire. The boy refused to die quickly. Again and again his father fired the .22 until it clicked empty.

Finally the boy stopped moving. He lay still on the floor, still wearing his winter gloves.

John had not wanted any of them to suffer, and anyone could see that this one had died in agony. But it was done now. He dragged his fifteen-year-old son along the bloody trail to the ballroom, where he positioned him on the far end of the grim tableau atop the unfurled sleeping bags that John List and his two boys had once shared happily in the woods, on camping trips where they lay to sleep, father and sons, listening to crickets chirp in the summer darkness beyond the fading embers of a campfire.

Ever meticulous, John put the finishing touches on his terrible display. Still clad in their winter coats, his children's bodies now reposed side by side, face up. John tugged at the sleeping bags until their edges all met neatly. He bent down to move Helen's stiffening arm carefully so that it rested on Freddy's shoulder, in what appeared to be a futile gesture of protection. From ten feet away, the bodies appeared to be arranged in the form of a cross. In the waning light of day, their murderer knelt on the ballroom floor beside them to pray in the name of Alma, Helen, Patricia, John and Frederick:

Almighty, everlasting and most merciful God, Thou who dost summon and take us out of this sinful and corrupt world to Thyself through death that we may not perish by continual sinning, but pass through death to life eternal, help us, we beseech Thee, to know and believe this with our whole heart, to the end that we may rejoice in our departure and at Thy call cheerfully enter into Thine everlasting kingdom; through Jesus Christ, thy Son, our Lord. Amen.

To which John added, on his own authority as worldly protector of their departed souls:

Depart in peace, thou ransomed souls, in the name of God the Father Almighty, who created thee; in the name of Jesus Christ, the son of the living God, who redeemed thee; in the name of the Holy Ghost, who sanctified thee. Enter now into Mount Zion, the city of the living God, the heavenly Jerusalem, to the innumerable company of angels, and to the general assembly and Church of the first-born which are written in heaven. The Lord preserve thy going out and thy coming in from this time forth and forevermore. Amen.

In the dusk just before five o'clock, the doorbell rang, shattering the deathly stillness in the house. The intrusion caused John the only real panic he had felt all day. Except for the single light at his desk, the house was dark. He made his way carefully into the parlor and peered through a part in the curtain.

It was the mailman with, obviously, the special delivery letter John had posted to himself that morning. Who would have thought the post office would take this particular day to be so efficient? He stood frozen as special delivery notice slid under the front door and only took a breath when the postman sauntered back to his truck. John left the notice on the floor where it lay.

Calm gradually returned. Around seven o'clock, John stirred to make a telephone call to his pastor, the Reverend Eugene A. Rehwinkle, at Redeemer Evangelical Lutheran Church. The chat was brief but friendly; the minister thought John sounded tired and worried, but he attributed this to the concern over the consuming troubles in his life. John lied to Rehwinkle, saying his family was already on a plane for North Carolina and that he would join them soon. He said he wouldn't be available to teach his Sunday School class for at least the next week. Rehwinkle, who considered John a personal friend and was very fond of the two boys—Fred was a member of the church's current confirmation class, in fact—said he understood. The pastor advised him not to worry, and promised to remember the family in his prayers.

Now only a few details remained. One of them was to head off Patty's friends at the drama club. He didn't want any of that crowd nosing around. At about seven-thirty, he dialed the number Patty had given him for Ed Illiano. Barbara Sheridan, Ed's assistant, answered.

Barbara thought the man sounded agitated on the phone, but she had never known John well—he had only attended one or two productions—so she didn't make much of it. He was calling to say that Patty would miss workshops and rehearsals for "a while," though he didn't estimate how long. It could mean that she wouldn't be able to continue understudying in *Streetcar*, which was scheduled to open November 20.

"I just put my wife and family on the plane for North

Carolina," John said. "My mother-in-law is very sick, and they're going to visit her."

In her room, Patty kept a copy of the script for *A Streetcar Named Desire* on her nightstand. It was there when she died. She had been studying it every night for over a month, whispering the lines to herself over and over long into the nights when the rest of the household was asleep.

In the evening, John wrote letters. At his desk, he took out a memo pad, each page of which had a logo printed at the top in green letters: "A Few Words From John E. List, Career Builder" He had ordered the stationery for the consulting business he was trying, with little success, to get going. The first letter was to his mother-in-law, the woman whose illness was providing him with the excuse for his family's sudden disappearance. This was a touchy one. Eva Morris was in fact quite ill in North Carolina. A kidney infection had caused her to postpone a visit that would have brought her back to the List house for the entire month of November. John didn't mention what would leap out as being terrifyingly obvious to the woman when she later read his letter:

Mrs. Morris

By now you no doubt know what has happened to Helen and the children. I'm very sorry that it had to happen. But because of a number of reasons, I couldn't see any other solution.

I just couldn't support them anymore and I didn't want them to go into poverty. Also, at this time I know that they were all Christians. I couldn't be sure of that in the future as the children grow up.

Pastor Rehwinkle may add a few more thoughts.

                With my sincere sympathy,
                John E. List

To Helen's sister Jean Syfert he wrote:

Mrs Jean Syfert

By now you have heard of what happened to Helen and the children. I'm sorry that it had to go that way but when I couldn't support them I couldn't let them go on welfare etc.

Please accept my sincere sympathy.

John

To Alma's sister, Lydia, in Frankenmuth, he wrote:

Mrs. Lydia Meyer

By now you know what has happened to Mother and the rest of the family. For a number of reasons this was the only solution that I could see for the family. And to save Mother untold anguish over that result I felt it best that she be relieved from this vale of tears.

Please accept my sincere condolences.

John

Despite what he had done during the day, John still managed to devote attention to pending business. His next letter was for Burton Goldstein at State Mutual. In it, he made suggestions to follow up on sales prospects:

Hello Burt

I'm sorry that it all had to end this way but with so little income I just couldn't go on keeping the family together. And I didn't want them to experience poverty.

I want to thank you for everything that you did for me. You treated me better than any associate I've ever dealt with and I am sorry that I have to repay you in this way.

The files are marked so that they can be turned over to you.

Maybe Paul Greenberg can follow up on some.
The best prospects for a quick sale are:
Douglas Moe
Edward Varga
Odendahl
Also be sure to contact Charles Jacobson CPA. I
worked with him on the Swokenden thing and that
worked real good.
Also don't fail to follow up with Harvey. He may
be just about ready.

Best wishes,
John

John then composed a separate message to Goldstein
concerning a $500 loan his boss had advanced. "This is a
lawful debt which the administrator is to pay to you," John
wrote. "Included should be a payment of interest at 6
percent per year. John E. List."

Each of the notes were placed in unsealed envelopes on
which he had written the addressee's name and placed a
postage stamp. John tucked the envelopes into a big manila
folder, on the outside of which he scrawled: "For Pastor
E. A. Rehwinkle of Redeemer Lutheran Church."

There was but one more letter to write, the most difficult
of all. He wrote a confession to his minister on the thin
lines of a yellow pad, dating it "11-9-71." It was slow going
at first, as if it required great effort to drag the pen across
the page. But then the writing became easier, as wretched
thoughts found their way into precise syntax in well-
defined paragraphs of excuses for murder:

Dear Pastor Rehwinkle:
    I am very sorry to add this additional burden to
your work. I know that what I have done is wrong
from all that I have been taught, and that any reasons
that I might give will not make it right. But you are

the one person that I know that, while not condoning this, will at least partially understand why I felt that I had to do this.

1. I wasn't earning anywhere near enough to support us. Everything I tried seemed to fall to pieces. True: we could have gone bankrupt and maybe gone on welfare.

2. But that brings me to my next point. Knowing the type of location that one would have to live in, plus the environment for the children, plus the effect on them knowing they were on welfare, was just more than I thought they could and should endure. I know that they were willing to cut back, but this involved a lot more than that.

3. With Pat being so determined to get into acting, I was also fearful as to what this might do to her continuing to be a Christian. I'm sure it wouldn't have helped.

4. Also, with Helen not going to church I knew that this would harm the children eventually in their attendance. I had continued to hope that she would begin to come to church soon. But when I mentioned to her that Mr. Jutzi wanted to pay her an elder's call, she just blew up and stated that she wanted her name taken off the church rolls. Again this could only have given an adverse result for the children's continued attendance.

So that is the sum of it. If any one of these had been the condition we might have pulled through, but this was just too much. At least I'm certain that all have gone to heaven now. If things had gone on, who knows if that would be the case.

Of course, Mother got involved because doing what I did to my family would have been a tremendous shock to her at this age. Therefore, knowing that she is also a Christian, I felt it best that she be

relieved of the troubles of this world that would have
hit her.

After it was all over, I said some prayers for them
all—from the hymn book. That was the least that I
could do.

Now for the final arrangements:

Helen and the children have all agreed that they
would prefer to be cremated. Please see to it that the
costs are kept low.

For Mother, she has a plot at the Frankenmuth
Church cemetery. Please contact

Mr. Herman Schellhas

Rt. 4

Vassar, Mich. 41768

He's married to a niece of Mother's and knows
what arrangements are to be made. She always
wanted Rev. Herman Zelinder of Bay City to preach
the sermon. But he's not well.

Also, I'm leaving some letters in your care. Please
send them on and add whatever comments you think
appropriate.

The relationships are as follows:

Mrs. Lydia Meyer—Mother's sister

Mrs. Eva Morris—Helen's mother

Jean Syfert—Helen's sister

Also, I don't know what will happen to the books
and other personal things. But to the extent possible
I'd like for them to be distributed as you see fit. Some
books might go into the school or church library,

Originally I had planned this for Nov. 1—All
Saints Day. But travel arrangements were delayed.
I thought it would be an appropriate day for them to
get to heaven.

As for me, please let me be dropped from the congregation rolls. I leave myself in the hand of God's
justice and *mercy*. I don't doubt that He is able to

help us, but apparently he saw fit not to answer my prayers the way I had hoped that they would be answered. This makes me think that perhaps it was for the best as far as the children's souls are concerned. I know that many will only look at the additional years that they could have lived, but if finally they were no longer Christians what would have been gained?

Also, I'm sure many will say "How could anyone do such a horrible thing?" My only answer is it isn't easy and was only done after much thought.

Pastor, Mrs. Morris may possibly be reached at:

802 Pleasant Hill Dr. Elkin—Home of her sister.

One more thing. It may seem cowardly to have always shot from behind, but I didn't want any of them to know even at the last second that I had to do this to them.

John got hurt more because he seemed to struggle longer. The rest were immediately out of pain. John probably didn't consciously feel anything either. [*The murderer then crossed out the word "probably" and continued.*]

Please remember me in your prayers. I will need them whether or not the government does its duty as it sees it. I'm only concerned with making my peace with God and of this I am assured because of Christ dying even for me.

P.S. Mother is in the hallway in the attic—3rd floor. She was too heavy to move.

John.

(*Even in his confession, John lied. The autopsies of the bodies would subsequently make it clear that of the five, only Patty had been shot in the back of the head. For the others, their last vision in life clearly was that of John aiming a pistol at their heads.*)

When he was through, his writing covered five pages. Without using an envelope, he slid the letter into the manila folder with the other notes. He found his checkbook on the desk and dropped that into the folder too.

Now he prepared his work space for the inevitable discovery of the carnage. He put the two pistols, along with an envelope containing extra bullets, into the bottom right-hand drawer of the file cabinet beside his desk. On the outside of that drawer he taped this note: "Guns & Ammo."

On the drawer above it he taped another note, which said: "To Pastor Rehwinkle, Burton Goldstein and Administrators."

He put the manila envelope containing all of the letters into the drawer, which locked in place after he shut it.

John then wrote another, unsigned, note and taped it to the top of his desk. It said:

To the Finder:
   1) Please contact the proper authorities.
   2) The key to this desk is in an envelope addressed to myself.
   3) The keys to the files are in the desk.

Having done this, he dropped the file cabinet keys into a desk drawer where they would be easily found once the authorities received the special delivery letter now being held at the post office, containing the key to the desk. The desk drawer also locked in place when he shut it.

The death sentence had been carried out righteously. Once more, in exhaustion, he fell to his knees on the cold oak floor and prayed.

He realized he was hungry. It was late, but he went into the kitchen and made dinner, which he ate slowly. Afterward, he washed his dishes and left them on the drainboard. Then he went to the billiard room and slept. He was up before dawn and ready to leave.

He remembered to turn the thermostat down to fifty degrees, high enough to prevent any mishaps such as the pipes bursting in an unexpected cold wave and drawing attention to the house from some helpful neighbor; low enough to make the fuel oil last as long as possible into the winter; cool enough to retard decomposition of a body. He went around the house switching on lights. Except for the ballroom, which was now dark, he left lights burning in every room.

He placed the three supermarket bags he had filled with bloody newspapers, paper towels and other debris in the kitchen near the back door where he had ambushed the children, as if waiting for one of the boys to take them out on trash night.

In a closet off the main hall was a stereo receiver wired to an intercom system with speakers throughout the house. John never let anyone tune it to any radio station except WQXR-FM, the classical music station. And now his last unopposed imposition of authority over his family was to fill its death chamber with quality music played at a moderately high volume.

As usual, he satisfied himself that the house was neat, clean, all hatches battened down.

With almost $2,500 in his wallet and a new lifetime on his hands, which were now scrubbed quite clean of blood, John gathered what little he intended to take from the inventory of the first half of his life—the suitcase with a couple of days' changes of clothes, the briefcase with a few personal documents and a handful of motor club maps.

He left by the back door. The night was a little milder than the previous one; snow flurries were expected by morning. He walked into a chilly drizzle. There was a bit of fog in the glow around the street lights.

Luckily the old Impala started right up. He eased it down the driveway, his foot light on the accelerator to minimize the racket from the broken muffler that had caused it to fail inspection. As he pulled out onto Hillside Avenue, his house, Breeze Knoll, blazed behind like a ghost liner on a moonless sea.

Still exercising care not to draw any attention to the noisy muffler, he turned right onto Broad Street, and headed down into the business district, where the wet sidewalks glistened with the nightlights from closed shops. The marquee of the Rialto movie theater was dark. But the letters could be made out against the white panels. The feature movie was called *Billy Jack*. John wouldn't have seen it as he drove by, but a poster in a frame near the ticket booth described the film as being about "a person who protects children and other living things."

A block away, on Elm Street, he eased the car to the curb in front of the darkened office of KMV Associates where Patty and Fred worked. Casually, he got out and slipped the envelope with his letter excusing their absence under the front door.

With that, Westfield was behind him. He drove east, and soon could see the lights of Manhattan twinkling through the fog. But then these, too, faded as he headed more to the south, finally crossing the Goethals Bridge from New Jersey to Staten Island, and then the Verrazano Narrows Bridge over the bay, to lower Brooklyn. The road signs for Coney Island passed by in a blur through the rhythmic sweeps of the windshield wipers. Brighton Beach, Manhattan Beach; across the inlet, the Rockaways. Once it reached cruise speed, the Impala hummed rather than rumbled on the rain-slicked highway along the cusp of Jamaica Bay.

Soon billboards appeared indicating that the airport wasn't far, billboards depicting stewardesses and the salacious invitation "Fly Me!" But on this night, the airport offered far more than the lure of exotic locales. It offered anonymity to a man who needed it badly.

He followed the signs for long-term parking. The machine at the automatic gate spit out a ticket, which he placed on the seat. He headed for the most crowded section of the lot and edged his car into a spot between two others.

He turned off the engine and the lights, locked the doors and moved the seat back for comfort.

As dawn streaked the skies over Long Island, he removed his keys from the ignition, tucking them away from casual view just under the front seat. He made sure to lock the door behind him.

He didn't have much to carry, though his journey would be one that would last for eighteen years. In his loping gait, shoulders squared against the dawn, he made his way across the vast parking lot toward the lights of the terminals, a figure fading gently into the mist as it crossed the concrete island and blended in with the other faceless stragglers wading silently into the boundless transient sea.

Chapter Eight

ED ILLIANO HAD THE IMPRESSION THAT THE CALL HAD been meant for him. Since had been sitting right there, he was a little put out. He wished she had just handed the phone over instead of taking a message.

"Who was that?" he asked when Barbara Sheridan put the phone down.

"Pat's father."

"Pat List? What did he say?" Ed was nervous whenever the subject of Pat List came up.

"He said he just put his family on a plane for North Carolina," she told him. "They've gone to stay with Patty's grandmother, who is sick." She added that the caller had sounded strange. He wasn't speaking in his usual monotone. He sounded "excited and out of breath."

Ed felt like he had just been punched in the stomach, but he didn't say anything to arouse alarm in Barbara. Yet his mind raced. Maybe the girl had known about the trip last week. Kids project, dramatize their fears. But Pat's tears hadn't been an overwrought teenager's plea for sympathy or affection. What had struck him most about the scene in his car four days earlier, aside from the confusion and nagging guilt over his own motives in being alone with her at all, was that Pat hadn't been looking for consolation from anyone. Hers were tears of anger and frustration. At once, he knew that she girl had felt utterly alone and vulnerable.

"What do you mean, 'kill you'?"

He saw her eyes burning through those angry tears.

He had become too involved, he told himself. He was a drama coach, not a social worker. Ruth Hill saw the thicket that could lay ahead, and had warned him. He knew she meant Pat specifically, though she didn't come right out and say it. And he knew she was right.

On the way home the night of November 9, he found himself driving down Hillside Avenue again. He slowed down as he passed the List house and tried to be inconspicuous while attempting to inspect it from the passing car. At the bottom of the hill, he made a U-turn and cruised by once more. Everything looked normal. Lights were on throughout the house. He had been there often enough at night to know the routine. When she was well, Helen would be in the kitchen, finishing the dishes or even cooking for the next day. If he wasn't down in the billiard room, reading or hunched over one of his war games, John would usually be upstairs with his mother. They still read the Bible together most nights, Pat had told him once, rolling her eyes. The boys would be upstairs, doing homework or watching television in John's room, where a long banner taped on the wall said "Let's go Mets." Down the hall, Pat would be studying. Not schoolwork, but a script.

Ed couldn't see anything amiss. The house at 431 Hillside looked still and quiet through barren trees.

Pat wasn't the most popular girl in the drama group, and she wasn't one of the best known. In any repertory group, there are stars and workers, and there are comers. Pat was a comer, one of those who was watched with interest by group members, who often speculated on who among their number might actually make a stage career some day in New York. Pat worked like a maniac. She seemed to be getting better every week. She had the fire in her belly, as Ed called it. Some of the others believed she was just driven enough, and just screwed-up enough, to make it one day.

So her abrupt absence, during rehearsals in which she was to understudy one of the most attractive female roles in the modern repertoire, was widely noticed, especially as the weeks passed without a word.

"Even when Pat went away for a weekend, she always was in touch with someone," Barry Cohen said. "She wasn't one to just disappear on a trip somewhere." In one of the few traits she inherited from her father, Pat was in fact an inveterate letter-writer. Even on a short trip, she would send a postcard to stay in touch with her friends.

By November 20, when *Streetcar* was presented, no one had heard from Pat since the first week of the month. People were starting to worry.

The old white Pontiac, with Ed behind the wheel with his right arm draped nonchalantly over the seat so he didn't look like a burglar scouting the territory, became a familiar sight coming down Hillside Avenue. Ed, sometimes accompanied by a few members of the group, began cruising past the List house almost every night on his way home from group workshops or from giving private lessons in the Sheridans' music room.

The Lists, like their neighbors, always kept a lot of lights on, so there wasn't anything terribly unusual about the way the house was illuminated, since it was known they were away.

On several occasions, Ed parked his car in the drive and knocked on the front door, stamping his feet loudly, so that any neighbor who noticed him would know he wasn't being furtive. He rang the bell and knocked, but it was obvious that no one was home. The mail had obviously been stopped. So had the paper.

Once he worked up the nerve to try the door. Unobtrusively, he jiggled the handle. He was relieved to find it

locked. He didn't know what he would have done if the
door had opened. He thought he heard music playing somewhere inside the house as he turned to leave.

Without going into detail about the cause of his suspi-
cions, Ed managed to convey his misgivings to some of the
group. People recalled how distraught Pat had seemed just
before she disappeared. This was a girl who had recently
proclaimed herself a witch, so a certain amount of odd
conversation might be expected from her. But now people
recalled that she had spoken vaguely of fear for her safety
in the week after the Halloween party. Of course, talk was
cheap and eminently disposable, especially after a couple
of joints, or even a bottle of Boone's Farm Apple Wine.
But Pat never had seemed frightened before.

Reluctant as they were to turn to any authority, some
members of the group suggested that the school was the
right channel for inquiries into the whereabouts of Pat
and her two brothers. Weren't there truant officers who
could come to the house and check? School authorities
were quick to get on your case for everything else; wasn't
being absent for almost three weeks a good enough reason
to intervene?

In fact, school attendance officials had made inquiries
when the "few days" in John's letters to them turned into
a few weeks. In mid-November, the Westfield school district's attendance officer, Mildred Kreger, looked up the
List children's records and noticed with some misgivings
that these were not children with any history of inordinate
absences from school. Worried, she went to the List house
and rang the bell. When no one answered, she looked in
the narrow windows beside the door. She saw no sign of
activity. There was no mail in the mailbox. For some reason
she decided to stroll around the house. The only thing even
remotely unusual she noticed was that while all of the
other curtains were tightly drawn on the ground floor,
the one in the front-room window on the left side of the

house—she did not know that this was John's office—had been left slightly parted, as if someone had used it to keep watch.

A week later she returned. Nothing had changed.

Meanwhile, Pat's friends began asking themselves, what about that church she had to go to every Sunday? Her father even made her sing in the choir there, something that was so totally uncool that only Pat's closest friends knew about it. Didn't the church want to know what happened to the Lists?

And how about the cops, who seldom had anything better to do than hassle kids hanging out listening to music in the municipal park? The cops stuck their noses into everything else. Couldn't they go up to the List house, just to check on things?

The kids didn't know that Ed had already approached the police, in the first week after the call from John List. He phoned a friend on the department and told him he believed there might be a problem at the List house, where the family was so suddenly reported to have gone away. Could a patrol car swing by and maybe have a look inside?

The officer was sympathetic. But there wasn't much the police could do. "Ed, nothing has happened," the officer said. "What's your evidence? We can't just go into a house. We can't even look in the windows. How can we do that?"

Even though Ed was reluctant to go over his friend's head, a week later he phoned the police again. As he had expected, they weren't interested in a drama teacher's daydreams. Ed said he felt he was being treated like "the village idiot."

The church was another dead end. The pastor, the Reverend Rehwinkle, was a good friend of John's, and John himself had called to explain where the Lists were going so suddenly. John was the head of that household, and if John said something, that was that.

The minister also made it clear that he wanted nothing

to do with Ed Illiano. "Rehwinkle talked to me on the phone like I was a nut, a full-blown nut," Ed complained.

Of course, Ed was getting increasingly agitated, and Rehwinkle had no reason to guess that he was being anything other than overly dramatic. "I was rather shrill," Ed conceded.

Without confessing embarrassing detail about how he *knew* something was wrong—to do so would have been to reveal those long, intimate conversations with a teenage girl in a parked car late at night—he felt unable to proceed along routine channels.

On Sunday afternoon, December 5, he drove to the List house. Someone had hung a yellow advertising book on the door knob. He also noticed that the Lutheran minister had left his calling card in the mailbox. There was no sign of activity. He left.

But that night, after brooding through dinner, Ed decided he had to go in.

Ed had never broken into a house before. He was so rattled as he drove through Westfield to that he inadvertently ran two red lights on his way to Hillside Avenue.

Ed and the members of the drama group weren't the only ones concerned by now about the Lists. Neighbors on Hillside Avenue, who had already made note of the fact that the lights hadn't gone out, had become suspicious now that the lights *were* blinking off, one by one, as they finally burned out.

Aware that the neighbors had begun to cast at least the occasional curious glance at the big rambling house at 431 Hillside, Ed parked his car on the street behind. Casually, he strode past the old outbuildings of the former estate and onto the List property to the place where, on occasion, he had stopped the car to talk with Pat before she slipped into her house through the back door.

Breeze Knoll loomed in front of him. He almost turned back when he saw how bright it was out back with those lights that still were on in the windows. The last thing he needed now was to attract the attention of a nosy neighbor and get collared crawling through a window—he could just see the headline in that week's Westfield *Leader*: Local Teacher Nabbed as Cat Burglar. Yet he was determined at least to have a look inside, to assure himself that everything was fine. What he hoped and indeed expected to find, and as quickly as humanly possible, was a cold, empty house. Then he would sleep better.

He couldn't explain the dread that weighed on him. He dismissed it as mere fright at the prospect of entering someone else's house uninvited.

With a bright moon low in the sky, he was glad for the cover of long shadows cast by the tall hedges bordering the rear drive. He knew the house well, and headed for the ground-level windows in the back wing just beside the rear chimney. The screen came off easily because the wood frame was rotted on one side. The window wasn't locked. Grunting, Ed got down on the ground and pushed it open, clambering down backward until his feet found the basement floor inside the house. He dragged in the small flashlight he left on the ground.

He dropped down clumsily and stood motionless in the dark. His heart pounded. Then he heard the music upstairs. It took him a few seconds of cold sweating before he figured it out. Jesus, he thought, they left the stereo on!

Stepping carefully, he moved toward the light showing in the stairwell. The room through which he passed was the one John insisted on still referring to as the billiard room. Everyone else called it the basement. Ed noticed John's stacks of strategy games on the shelves.

Like the ballroom just above, this room was dominated by a marble-fronted fireplace big enough to roast an ox in. Above the teakwood mantel hung pairs of antique gas-globe light fixtures that had been wired for electricity. Everything seemed quiet in the room. At least he hadn't stumbled across John List asleep on his mattress.

Ed edged carefully up on the wide, softly lighted staircase that led to landing at the entrance to the ballroom. Each step seemed to creak more loudly than the last. All of his senses of smell and hearing were alerted before his brain could evaluate the information. The house had an off, dank odor. And the classical music that he had heard faintly downstairs seemed to fill the ground floor.

At the top of the stairs, to the right, a heavy drapery was stretched across the entrance to the ballroom. Cautiously, Ed parted it and peered in. The moon hadn't yet risen high, so not much illumination came through the skylight above the spacious chamber. An unmistakable haze hung in the air, like mist off a swamp. Otherwise, he noticed nothing amiss. He backed out to look into the library, which was deserted. To save on heating costs, John had installed a vinyl folding door at the entrance from the ballroom landing to the center hall. Ed opened it and gazed into the main section of the house. Except for the music and the chill in the air, nothing was unusual. There was no sign of recent activity.

He went back to the ballroom entrance and poked the flashlight beam into the gloom. Pat's folk guitar lay in its case on a table just to the left of the entrance. A few stray decorations left from the Halloween party still were taped to a wall on the left. Dime-store hobgoblins, gap-toothed pumpkins, and good-natured witches leered in the light beam. He thought he saw some bundles of clothes dumped on the floor to the right, near the fireplace.

Then the flashlight fixed on a child's face in the dark clutter on the floor fifteen feet away.

Ed snapped the switch off, as if that would erase the image he had just seen appear in the yellow beam.

Sick with fear, he came closer. He kept the flashlight turned off. At his feet, he could make out the body of

Helen List, grotesquely bloated. The children were beside their mother, whose arm lay across one child's shoulder.

Ed shouted "Pat!" into the unyielding gloom. Then he turned and ran—not the way he had come in, but across the hall and into the kitchen, and out the back door, which he shut securely behind. He fled to his car. He does not remember driving home the ten miles to Elizabeth. Nor does he remember what he told his wife when she asked him what was wrong.

Incapacitated by grief and guilt, he kept his discovery to himself. For two nights and days he lived in a panic, the cold depths of which he will carry to his grave.

On Tuesday night, December 7, he returned. This time, he made sure the neighbors would notice and do something about it.

Early that evening, some of the regulars got together at the municipal building where the drama group had its workshops on Wednesday and Friday nights. There was a lot of talk of Pat. Too much time had gone by. A couple of boys even suggested going up there themselves to see just what the hell was going on. Ed did nothing to discourage this. "The kids used to go up there and walk around the place," Ed said many years later. "But now there was talk of going in. By this time, every kid in my group was expecting me to go in the window any day anyway. They were going to go in if I didn't. So what I did was—I made a loud report—'Well, I'm the leader. I'm going to go!' " Barbara Sheridan, who also had been concerned about Pat's disappearance, volunteered to come along.

With Ed behind the wheel, the two of them drove up to Hillside Avenue. Ed made a point of pulling right up the driveway with his bright lights on. Leaving the headlights on, he slammed the car door when he got out. It was about nine forty-five as Ed and Barbara stood in front of the house, wondering what to do next. For the benefit of the neighbors, Ed talked as loudly as he could.

"Well," he announced to his frightened companion, who stayed back on the lawn beside the car, "I'm going to go up and take a look."

Next door to the List house, a very suspicious neighbor, Shirley Cunnick, heard this activity from her front porch. Shirley had lately begun paying particularly close attention to what was going on at 431 Hillside. It wasn't just the lights burning out. It was also that battered white Pontiac cruising by and sometimes pulling into the drive. And here it was again.

Shirley had relayed her concerns to her husband, William, a physician. When he arrived home nights, he too had begun looking over at the List house. People might go away for one or maybe two weeks, he thought, but this long was very unusual. Still, his concerns had to do mostly with the potential for vandalism or robbery presented by such an evidently unoccupied house.

But there had been something else. His wife was one of the few friends Alma List had in Westfield. She liked the lonely old woman, who occasionally visited to chat, sometimes bringing with her a sheet of fresh-baked cookies. Late in October, on one of those infrequent visits, Alma had told Shirley that John was going to send her back to Bay City in November to visit relatives. Alma, excited to be going home, had even asked Shirley if she would drive her to the cobbler shop in town so she could have her shoes repaired. It bothered the neighbor that Alma, who had been so intent on having those shoes in their best condition, had disappeared without ever following up her request for a ride. That was not like Alma List at all.

So with the commotion on the front lawn on the night of December 7, William Cunnick decided to walk over to investigate. While he did, his wife went to the phone and called the Westfield police to report an intrusion at 431 Hillside.

On the front porch, Ed banged on the door and tried the handle. Then he lumbered up onto the veranda on the right side of the house, where he knew the tall ground-floor window offered easy access to the dining room. But as he was raising the unlocked window, he heard the siren of the Westfield patrol car boring in on the neighborhood. He hurried back to the car where Barbara Sheridan waited apprehensively.

Within minutes, the Westfield patrol car screeched into the driveway, blocking the Pontiac. Two patrolmen got out with their weapons at their sides. The ground was soggy from a recent rain and their shoes made a squishing noise as they approached. The officers, Patrolmen Charles Haller and George Zhelesnik, relaxed when the woman identified herself. "I'm Mrs. Sheridan," she said.

Once the officers ascertained the identities of the intruders, and learned that they, too, were expressing concerns about the property, Zhelesnik began checking around the outside of the house, working clockwise from the front porch. Ed waited on the side porch for the officer to complete his inspection of the exterior, where the only thing that appeared unusual to Zhelesnik was a basement window he noticed ajar in the back, under the ballroom wing. Zhelesnik came around the house and found Ed on the porch by the open window. After a brief discussion the two men decided to go in.

As they eased over the sill into the dining room, Zhelesnik noticed a musty, slightly offensive smell. There were aquariums near the window. In one of them, dead fish floated belly-up on the surface of the water. In the other tank, which had an automatic feeder, the fish were alive.

Music was playing loudly in the house. With Zhelesnik following him, Ed crossed the center hall past the staircase and through the vinyl folding door that opened onto the landing beside the ballroom. Shaking, Ed led the officer to the ballroom. Zhelesnik shone his light in and gasped when it settled on the bodies.

Ed, meanwhile, ran to the front door and threw it open from inside. Barbara, Patrolman Haller and Dr. Cunnick hurried in from the porch.

"Something terrible has happened," Ed said in a resonant voice. He led the three into the foyer and through the center hall, pointing to the ballroom where Zhelesnik stood rigidly beside the bodies.

The twenty-six-year-old Haller rushed up. Getting down on his knees, he took the woman's arm. To his horror, he found it felt like a piece of wood. "Hey," he said inanely. "Hey! Wake up!"

Someone snapped on the lights.

None of them would ever forget the sight. The children lay in their school clothes and coats. A towel covered Helen; when it was lifted, her stomach was horribly distended. The bodies were badly decomposed. Horrified, Cunnick, a specialist in internal medicine who was barely acquainted with the List family, knelt to examine the victims. It was apparent that the bodies had lain there for some time. He saw disintegration of the fingertips and toes. Small maggots swarmed on the bodies, all of which were bloated. As the doctor identified the dead as Helen, Patricia, John, and Frederick List, Haller rushed back out to the patrol car and grabbed the radio. The dispatcher logged the alarm in at ten minutes after ten.

Ed and Barbara retreated into the dining room as the officers, themselves stricken with shock and disbelief, searched the rest of the ballroom. The music swelled on the radio. Ed, who had studied at Juilliard and later at La Scala on a Fulbright scholarship, recognized the music readily as orchestral excerpts from *Götterdämmerung*.

With their weapons still drawn, the two cops quickly

went through the adjacent rooms, although the deteriorated condition of the bodies was an obvious indication that
the murderer was long gone. Haller found the phone and
called Chief Moran, who was working late that night at
headquarters to supervise departmental promotion tests.
Moran could tell there was major trouble. Haller's voice
was a full octave higher than normal.

"Chief, you got to get over to 431 Hillside Avenue,"
Haller gasped.

"What's going on, Charlie?"

"Chief, there's been a mass murder. There's bodies all
over the place."

The statement sounded almost like a joke. Westfield
hadn't even had a regular murder in eight years. A *mass
murder?* Moran sped from police headquarters on Broad
Street. He found the scene easily. Two other patrol cars
were already in the driveway, their red lights pulsing across
the long, dark lawn. More sirens wailed in the distance.

Haller met him at the door and showed him inside,
where the ground floor of the house had already taken on
the grim routine of a crime scene. A Westfield detective
had arrived and was talking calmly on the phone. Outside,
flashlight beams pried into bushes and dark corners.

Moran went to the bodies and was sickened to see that
three of them were children. But it was the blaring music
that made the next strong impression on the police chief.
Moran, who didn't know a concerto from a waltz, thought
it was liturgical music filling the house where four bodies
had just been discovered.

"Somebody turn off that goddamned music!" the police
chief shouted.

He was annoyed to see two civilians in the center hall,
and further annoyed when he saw that one of them was
the drama coach. One of the cops had brought in blankets
for them to put over their shoulders. The temperature

outside was forty-five degrees, but the house seemed colder inside.

Suddenly, Illiano realized he hadn't had the presence of mind to make a full inventory when he looked at the bodies on the floor. There were only four.

"Something's missing!" Illiano cried. "The old lady! She lives upstairs!"

Moran turned to the officers. "Did you search up there?"

One of them shrugged and looked at his shoes.

"Well, go look upstairs!"

Someone had located the stereo in the front hall closet and turned it off. The officers made enough noise to frighten ghosts as they bounded upstairs with their guns drawn. They rummaged through bedrooms on the second floor, banging doors and drawers. When the second floor seemed secure, one of the cops dashed up the steps to the third floor.

A sudden shriek froze everybody in their tracks.

Then the man came running down, his face drained of all color.

"Was she up there?" someone demanded.

He had literally stumbled over Alma's grossly swollen body when he turned into a hallway in her apartment. All the cop could do was nod in response to the question.

With the gruesome 1969 murders committed by the Charles Manson cult still fresh in people's minds—the trial had ended only that year and its appeals were still in the news—the first chilling thought at the murder scene was that someone had come into this house and done this. But after a thorough search that included an inspection of the cistern, it was apparent that one member of the List household was not on the premises.

Down in John List's office, the police chief thought he knew why. Moran was reading the notes John had taped to the file cabinet beside his desk. With his appreciation of strategy, John had apparently expected that the police would read the notes left in the open and then follow the rules of the game.

A cop with five bodies on his hands and no murderer in sight is not usually so inclined, however. While John evidently expected that the police would wait for their explanation until after they retrieved the keys from the special delivery letter which was now among 162 pieces of mail being held, by the murderer's order, at the Westfield Post Office, Moran had no time for games. And he wasn't about to wait for business hours to begin at the post office.

"Open it," he said.

An officer forced open the cabinet with a crowbar.

Years later, Moran explained his actions at the scene: "I had called the prosecutor's office and the county medical examiner's office to come up, done all the stuff you had to do," he said. "There was a desk, and I started to search. I went through it. I pulled out a drawer and found an envelope, a sealed envelope addressed to the pastor of the Lutheran church, plus two guns that had been fired . . . in the drawer. They were left there to be found. I don't know why he just didn't heave them out in the back yard or something like that. He put them right in the drawer with the envelope. So I opened the envelope and I read it."

After he'd read the confession letter, he phoned Rehwinkle at Redeemer. Around midnight, the shocked minister arrived and identified the victims.

"Who could have done this?" Rehwinkle moaned.

"The husband did it," Moran told him matter-of-factly. "It's here in the letter."

Moran let the minister read it, but he didn't intend to let the letter out of his sight for a second. With the police chief hovering over his shoulder, Rehwinkle slumped at the dining room table and began reading: "Dear Pastor Rehwinkle. I am very sorry . . ." When he reached the end—"P.S. Mother is in the hallway in the attic—3rd floor. She was too heavy to move. John"—he was too stunned to get up.

"You finished with the letter?" Moran demanded.

"Why?" asked the minister.

"It's evidence," the chief grunted, holding out his hand.

"I'll be finished in a few minutes," the pastor said. He read the letter through twice more. Then, without dissent, he handed it to Moran. He told the police chief that he believed the letter should be kept "confidential" and asked him to use discretion in divulging its contents. This was advice Moran neither needed nor welcomed. The chief knew what to do with evidence: seize it and secure it. In fact, Moran hadn't even shown the minister the other letters in the folder.

Rehwinkle returned to his church office that night without the letter.

As he did, the crime scene was bustling with police activity. A crime of this magnitude had never occurred before in Westfield, or even in Union County. Detectives arrived. So did the FBI, which would share jurisdiction if there were indications the murderer had fled across state lines. A police photographer knelt by the bodies taking picture after picture.

Finally the ambulances arrived and took the dead away. The green sleeping bags lay on the ballroom floor blotted with dark stiff bloodstains. In the kitchen, someone noticed that a large skillet and some breakfast dishes had been washed and left to dry in a drainer next to the sink. Bananas had turned black in a bowl on the counter. Upstairs, in Alma's own little kitchen, her toast was still waiting in the toaster.

Neighbors had gathered on the lawn, some of them with coats tossed over their nightclothes. Reporters, alerted by night city desks that monitored police frequencies, were pulling up with their notebooks and measuring eyes. Photographers scurried around, buzzing as close to the windows as they could get. Inside the house, the phone jangled again as soon as someone put it down.

There was nothing more he could do. Early in the morning, Ed Illiano went to the Westfield police station and gave his statement.

Chapter Nine

LIFE IN THE MINISTRY HAD PREPARED HIM FOR MANY things, but it hadn't prepared him for this. As John List's confessor, as the man whom he had chosen to burden with the tortured reasons for murdering five human beings, the pastor of Redeemer Lutheran Church was suddenly and quite publicly on the defensive.

Matters were very confused. Procedure was most unclear. And the press was pounding on the door. A well-ordered world at the helm of a quiet, conservative congregation was suddenly under siege in the middle of the night.

The five-page confession letter would be nothing but trouble to everyone who came in contact with it except its author. From the beginning, there were serious questions about a minister's role in protecting the confidentiality of a communication from a congregant. There were also questions about the police procedure in opening a sealed communication and reading it on the crime scene, though these questions wouldn't surface publicly with any force until eighteen years later.

Rehwinkle, an energetic man with a shock of thick brown hair who had an unsigned contract with the New York Yankees farm system in his pocket when he chose the ministry instead, resolved to take charge of the situation before it took charge of him and destroyed his close-knit congregation in the process. But the confession letter was like a crazed dog with its teeth sunk into his ankle.

At one A.M., when he arrived back at the church office, shaken and confounded by what he had just seen at the List house, Rehwinkle spoke openly of having read List's "confessional letter addressed to me," according to one of the people who happened to have come to the office after a tag-line of phone calls alerted key members of the congregation. But then it appears that the initial problems with the letter as possible evidence had occurred to someone in authority. Two hours later, after meeting with police and an FBI investigator, Rehwinkle spoke to reporters clamoring outside the Municipal Building in Westfield, but he made no mention of the letter or the stunning revelations it contained. The police, however, made it clear to the news media that John List, whereabouts unknown, was the only suspect in the murders.

By this time, the bodies had been removed to Sullivan Funeral Home, a county-designated morgue-keeper, in nearby Roselle, where an autopsy was scheduled for the next day.

There would be no sleep that night at Redeemer Lutheran Church. Parish records produced the name of a next-of-kin, and Rehwinkle made the call as soon as he got back from the Municipal Building.

It was two-thirty in the morning when the phone broke the stillness in the Syferts' comfortable ranch home in Midwest City, in the suburbs of Oklahoma City. After Gene's twenty years in the air force, from which he had recently retired as a lieutenant colonel, the Syferts were no strangers to urgent phone calls in the middle of the night. But this time, as Jean listened to her husband's flat, emotionless tone as he spoke, she knew there was something terribly wrong. Her first panicked thought was that something had happened to one of their three grown sons. But her husband shook his head and motioned for her to wait.

Gene had taken the call in the dark. His wife got up to turn on the light and listen.

"Yes," she could hear him repeat. "Oh, good God," he said. "And you're sure?" he said. "Oh, my God."

Jean couldn't bear listening to the monotone on her husband's end of the conversation. She only knew that someone was dead. She went into the kitchen, where she couldn't hear, and paced until she couldn't stand it any longer. She went back into the bedroom, where Gene put his palm over the mouthpiece and told her briefly that Helen and the children were dead. He went back to his conversation with Rehwinkle without saying how they had died.

Jean lay on the bed in disbelief. When her husband put down the phone after a half hour of talking to the minister, "our lives had changed forever," she said.

The morning after she found out what had happened, Jean was able to give words to certain misgivings she had felt for weeks about her sister's family.

"Right before that, on Thanksgiving Day, we were watching television and there was a fellow named List playing in the Nebraska-Oklahoma game, and when we got through dinner, I said, 'Gene, let's call Helen and John.' Because I had written three or four letters and had no answer whatsoever. I said to him, 'Of course, you know they could be lying there dead and nobody would ever know it.' And of course, it turned out, they were."

A couple from next door who had been dinner guests even volunteered to call a close relative who happened to live in Westfield and ask him to stop by the house to check on the Lists. Jean demurred with thanks. "I said no, if it was me and someone did that, came by like that, it would kind of irritate me. Same thing with calling the police. We just kind of let it slide. But I had a strong feeling something might be wrong."

*   *   *

After midnight, the property at 431 Hillside Avenue was starting to look like a small carnival that was just setting up. Floodlights cast a cold glow across neighboring lawns. Spectators milled around, behind police barricades that were starting to go up. Frustrated reporters had to hustle for what little information seemed to be coming from the police, who hurried to and from the house and their cars parked in clusters on the circular drive. Moran had ordered the lights turned off in the ballroom to prevent any enterprising reporter from getting a picture inside, which would have been a major accomplishment anyway, since the only windows into the big chamber were an opaque stained glass panel at the far wall and the skylight high on the roof.

The morning newspapers were past their deadlines anyway by the time the news broke. Among the reporters was Joe Buscaino, a veteran photographer for the only paper that still had a deadline ahead, the afternoon Elizabeth *Daily Journal.* With that deadline fast approaching, Buscaino was determined to get into the house in time to take pictures for that day's paper. But first, he decided to get rid of the others.

He began complaining loudly, to no one in particular. "These sons of bitches won't tell us a goddamn thing," Buscaino grumbled as the reporters milled behind the barricade the police had set up to keep them away from the immediate house. "We'll be out here freezing our asses off all night for no reason. I know these Westfield bastards."

Some of the others began squinting at their watches in the glow of the emergency lights and thinking of hot coffee.

"My boss is keeping me here, for Christ's sakes," Buscaino continued, really carrying on now in an effort to get rid of the others. "What an idiot. There's nothing to do. We're not going to get anything. It's all over."

This reasoning made sense to the others. As long as they all decided to leave, there wouldn't be a problem. No one would be beat in the remote chance the cops might toss out a crumb of information. The others began drifting back to their cars, leaving Buscaino alone.

When they were gone, he rushed next door to call his desk.

"I alerted my night editor, who wanted me to come back in and put through some crap that I had shot of something else earlier in the day," Buscaino recalled. "I said, 'You're crazy! I'm not going to leave here!' I told him to try to hold the presses, and he did. I was taking a chance."

Now he began working on Moran, whom he had known for some time. He confronted the police chief when he stepped outside around three o'clock.

"I had a hunch I would be able to talk Moran into it," Buscaino said. "Knuckles Moran, they called him, because he used to be a boxer. I pulled every trick in the book. Crying, 'My boss is a lousy bastard; he'll fire me,' and all of that stuff. Moran had known me for a while. I had always been square with him. I was very persistent that night. 'Moran, jeez, come on, will you? Look at all the favors I've done for you,' I told him. Every chance I had, I kept hitting on Moran."

In the process, Buscaino was gleaning information that no one knew except the police. He heard about the confession letter, for example, and alerted his night editor to send a reporter to the church, where the reporter was when Rehwinkle returned to his office and casually discussed the letter, the existence of which the police and prosecutors subsequently wished had remained secret, and might have, had Buscaino not learned of it.

"Around three o'clock, I got the biggest shock of my life," said the photographer. "Moran came down and he says, 'Stick around.' So I knew to stick around."

Buscaino called his desk to have a reporter come back to the scene. A short time later, Moran allowed them into the house under strict orders not to touch anything.

They complied. "I was really surprised that he gave me

the okay. I promised Moran I would be very careful. I
didn't want to overstep my bounds; they were very touchy
about the whole thing. I knew we weren't really supposed
to be in there," said Buscaino, who used a floodlight to
take pictures of the bloody sleeping bags on the ballroom
floor and of the disheveled mess in Alma's kitchen. "I got
in there before the prosecutor's men even arrived on the
scene.

"We had everything. It was a big, gloomy house. To me
it looked like a big mausoleum. It had the smell of death.
Besides the death scenes, all I remember is this guy seemed
to have a lot of paraphernalia for a house that was sparsely
furnished."

Buscaino's paper proudly printed his crime-scene photographs the next day. Then, after the county prosecutor
raised a ruckus, the same paper promptly threatened to
fire him for the enterprising venture, a threat that Buscaino's labor union ultimately thwarted.

"The next day, the prosecutor was really pissed off—
pissed off at me, and pissed off at Moran," Buscaino said.
"Moran says to me the next day, 'Jesus Christ, you got me
in a lot of trouble.' "

Eighteen years later, the confusion and commotion at
the crime scene in Westfield hadn't been forgotten at the
Union County prosecutor's office.

"A lot of people were on the scene . . . so many lay
people," Eleanor Clark, a deputy prosecutor who had inherited the List case, said pointedly. "It was very bad police
procedure, I will tell you that."

Given a full day to look for new angles before their stories
would come out, the newspapers came up with the obvious
one. How could a well-regarded family, active in its
church, with three children in school, one of them fully
involved in a theater workshop, have been missing for a
month without generating some sort of an inquiry? If the
Lists had essentially disappeared from the face of the earth

on November 10, where were the authorities in the month that had passed? Didn't school authorities want to know why the children hadn't returned? Wouldn't police in a small town have some inkling that something seemed amiss? And if the family was as intimately involved with its church as it appeared from the descriptions of the murderer's religious bent, why hadn't the minister sensed something was wrong?

It was becoming clear that the perpetrator of this mass murder had had the benefit of a month to get away.

Chief Moran irritably took several questions along those lines. There just wasn't sufficient reason for anyone to suspect something was wrong, he said. In fact, the police chief said, school authorities and an employee of the office where Patricia had worked had made "routine" requests to police to look into the absence of the children, Moran said, and on two occasions in mid-November, patrolmen were sent to the house, "but left when no one answered the bell because everything appeared to be in good order from the outside." There was no logical reason to investigate further, the police chief said, "especially in view of the arrangements made by List on November 9."

Finding himself also uncomfortably on the defensive, and anticipating a church funeral that he knew would form the center ring of a media circus, the pastor felt compelled to hold a press conference.

"The matter of 'no one knew where they were' or 'why didn't someone check up on this' because 'something was not right,' is not the case," Rehwinkle said in a statement he spent a long time writing. "We were informed by Mr. List that he had put his wife and children on a plane to North Carolina to visit the ailing and perhaps dying grandmother . . . I had personally stopped by the home a number of times, called by telephone at various times with no answer, and finally on December 3, at 5 p.m., I left my calling card asking Mr. List to contact me.

"My assistant, Vicar Zerbst, had also stopped by the List home. I had the son Fred in my confirmation class and wanted to touch base with Mr. List on his absence from class. I also checked with Mrs. Bilden at Westfield Senior High School about the children's absence. She informed me that they had not been in school since November 10th. Members of the parish did have close relationships with the family, and the fact that they were a noncommunicative family is not altogether true. Certainly not at church."

Then, in a move that deftly diverted attention from the month-long disappearance, the minister made what he called a "pastoral appeal" addressed to the confessed murderer: "John, as your pastor, I am still very much your friend who will always support you, stand by you, and help you. The Lord God whom you know and believe in will not forsake you in these most agonizing times. Please contact me. If you are prevented by other circumstances at this time, wait, pray and contact me when you can, any time, day or night."

Rehwinkle then added a fillip guaranteed to catch a tabloid editor's attention. He read a what he called a "personal plea" from Brenda, John List's stepdaughter, now twenty-five years old and living near Kalamazoo as a divorced mother of five children. "Daddy, you are all I have left," said the statement the pastor read from Brenda. "Please call me."

Actually, the last thing Brenda wanted, a close friend explained later, was to hear from her stepfather. The FBI had asked to use her name in the statement in an attempt to flush the murderer out. After hearing of the slayings of her mother, Patty, John, Fred, and Alma, "she was absolutely petrified of anything and anybody," said the friend from Kalamazoo, Portia Hageman. "She knew she was the only living one left from the family, and she was afraid he was going to come and kill her and her children. For a long time, the FBI was watching her, checking the place."

John List about 1970
(AP/Wideworld).

Helen List in the mid 1960's.

(From left) Freddy, Johnny, and Patty List in Rochester, NY. The Lists used this photo as their family Christmas card in 1962.

The house in Bay City, Michigan, where John List grew up, sleeping in the front parlor, which he would have to vacate during the day. The top floor was rented to tenants. (Nancy Sharkey)

John Frederick List's old store in the Salzburg section of Bay City had seen better times by 1990. The name "List" can still be seen in the cornice. (Nancy Sharkey)

(From left), Helen Taylor, Jean Syfert, and John List on October 13, 1951, the night they met outside a bowling alley in Fort Eustice, Va. Helen and John were married less than 2 months later.

The beaming new father, John List, with Patty, January, 1955.

Proud new grandmother, Alma List, shows off toddler Patty.

Helen List and her children, shortly after they moved to Westfield,
New Jersey, in 1965.

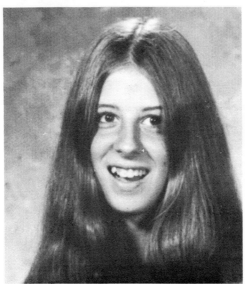

Patty List's last high school photo, 1970.

When John List attended this presentation of "L'il Abner" in Westfield, in May 1971, he decided his daughter, shown here playing Stupefyin' Jones, was bound for damnation. Police believe he began planning the murders around this time.

Ed Illiano, 18 years after he discovered the grisly tableau at the List house. (Carolyn D. Albaugh)

The Westfield drama group receiving an award for a benefit peformance for disabled veterans. Pat is fourth from left, with her hand on a friend's shoulder. Ed Illiano is at right center, receiving the award.

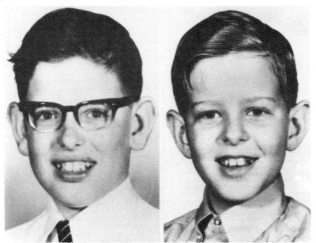

John and Frederick List in Westfield, New Jersey, 1971.
(AP/Wideworld)

The house on Hillside Avenue where John List murdered his
family in 1971. This photo was taken the night the bodies were
discovered. (Joseph Buscaino, © *The Daily Journal*)

Bucolic Westfield, New Jersey, its downtown little changed since the day 18 years earlier when the List murders rocked the town. (Carolyn D. Albaugh)

The Westfield train station where John spent six months reading books and newspapers during the daytime when he was too embarrassed to tell his wife he had lost another job, in 1968. (Carolyn D. Albaugh)

The ballroom at Breeze Knoll as it appeared in the 1920's. (Courtesy John Mittke)

After he killed Helen, Patricia, John, and Frederick, List dragged them to the once elegant ballroom where he laid them on Boy Scout sleeping bags, and arranged them with Helen's arm reaching across the children's bodies in a protective gesture. (Joseph Buscaino, © *The Daily Journal*)

Reverend Eugene Rehwinkle, to whom the murderer wrote a confession letter, conducts graveside services for Helen, Patricia, John, and Frederick on Dec. 1, 1971. (Ed Hausner, New York Times Pictures)

Redeemer Lutheran Church in Westfield, where the Lists worshiped and Patty sang in the choir. (Carolyn D. Albaugh)

Bob Wetmore: a fugitive's good friend in his new life in Denver, August 1989.

Wanda Flannery, who identified her neighbor, Bob Clark, as wanted murderer John List.

The trailer park at the foothills of the Rockies in the Denver suburbs where John List began to shape his new life as Bob Clark.

St Paul's Evangelical Lutheran Church near the state capitol in downtown Denver, where John List, as Bob Clark, made a new start in his religion.

Retired Westfield Police Chief James Moran, after the arrest, holding a copy of the FBI flyer he carried with him for 18 years. (Mario Ruiz, *People Weekly,* © Time Inc.)

Philadelphia artist Frank Bender with the bust of John List he created for *America's Most Wanted.* (Mario Ruiz, *People Weekly,* © Time Inc.)

Delores Clark with lawyer David Baugh at press conference in Richmond, Va., after her husband's arrest. (AP Wideworld)

John List, age 63, being led into federal court in Richmond, Va., after his arrest in June 1989. List was still maintaining that he was Robert P. Clark. (AP/Wideworld)

Back in New Jersey, 18 years after the crime, List confers with court appointed attorney Elijah Miller, during a court hearing. (Kathleen Freidrich © *The Daily Journal*)

Jean Syfert at her home in Midwest City, Oklahoma, August, 1989.

At her murderer's instructions, Alma List was buried in
Frankenmuth, Michigan, in her family's plot. (Nancy Sharkey)

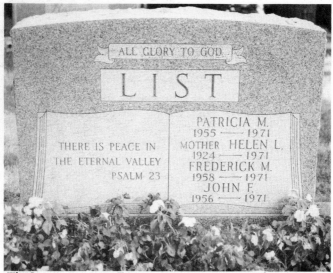

The List gravestone at Fairview cemetery. For years after the
murders, Westfield detectives staked out the cemetery on certain
anniversaries hoping John would pay a visit. (Carolyn D. Albaugh)

That kind of terror, the terror that stalks the sleep, was John List's legacy to the few people who would call themselves his friends, and to what was left of his wife's family.

Though they kept their concerns among themselves, members of John's congregation at Redeemer also worried that a man who could massacre his loved ones in such a manner might also have some twisted reason to come to the church with a gun. For weeks, eyes darted warily to the back whenever the church door burst open during services.

Rehwinkle wasn't without his own fears, said C. Frederick Poppy, the undertaker who handled the funeral. "He was really upset; even after the funeral we would talk about it, and he would say, 'Gee, I hope he doesn't come around with a gun on us, Fred.' He was really into it. And his wife, like my wife, they were concerned. You'd hear a knock on the door, and you would worry: Who's at the door?"

The Syferts, when they got the phone call from the minister in the middle of the night, had been too stunned to consider the question of John's whereabouts, and they don't recall Rehwinkle's having brought it up. In an era when Charles Manson still filled the television screens on many nights, they had assumed initially that the murders had been committed by an intruder. It didn't even occur to Jean that John wasn't among the victims until well after daybreak, when she received a call from one of their sons, who had begun making inquiries on his own after his father had called him with the news.

"Mother," he said when it became clear to him that she didn't, "you know Uncle John is still alive, don't you?"

She was stunned. Then she felt a fear that didn't go away with the passing of time. "I always was terrified I'd open the door and there would be John List with a gun," Jean said quietly in the summer of 1989. "I never really got over that."

Nor, Jean added bitterly, did her mother. Before she got sick, Eva Morris had already made arrangements to arrive around Halloween of 1971 and stay with the Lists, where there was ample room and where her daughter's illness seemed to require assistance, until after Thanksgiving.

No one needed to spell out for Eva the fact that, had she not been sidelined with illness, she would have been the sixth body lying in the house on Hillside Avenue. This knowledge, combined with the grief from the murder of her daughter and grandchildren, preyed on the old woman's mind for the rest of her life.

Jean, who had barely turned forty when the murders occurred, knew that she could not spend the rest of her life hateful and embittered. But she knew she would never, ever forget the pain of seeing how her mother finally died, on August 8, 1988, crying and trembling in her last desperate minutes with visions of John List.

In all, investigators counted and labeled about 150 separate pieces of evidence from the crime scene, ranging from the confession letter and blood-caked sleeping bags and spent bullets to the photo album of Breeze Knoll that John had left in the dining room to be returned to Jack Wittke.

The last physical evidence that would be discovered turned up at Kennedy Airport on Thursday, December 9, when a Port Authority policeman making a routine check for stolen vehicles at the long-term parking area, Field 8, came across a 1963 blue four-door Chevrolet Impala with New Jersey tags. The car had caught the officer's eye because it had an expired red inspection sticker on its windshield. He checked the license number, KBN-813, against his list, and found it there. It hadn't been reported stolen, but the police were looking for this car anyway. It was John List's.

When Westfield cops came to pick it up, they found on the front seat the parking ticket indicating that the car had been there since early on November 10. Back in West-field, the police tore the old car apart, but found no further evidence in the car. The glove compartment contained only what one of the cops referred to as the "usual junk." In a neat pile on the front seat, John had also left some cards, among them his membership in the University of Michigan alumni association and his annual registration as a certified public accountant.

Karl Asch, the county prosecutor and now the central figure in the investigation, didn't have much information to give the increasingly restive press. The day after the car was found, Asch speculated that, since List had left the car at the airport after apparently fleeing Westfield with his passport (police had found Helen's passport in the house, but not John's), indications were that the suspect had left the country.

Asch added that a grand jury was about to receive the case. "We probably have enough evidence to indict," he said.

An indictment was easy. The real dilemma confronting the authorities was that it had become abundantly clear that not one of them had the slightest clue as to where John List might be. And the trail, if there ever was one, was now a month cold.

John had left behind instructions for the funeral and asked the pastor to supervise those.

Sleepless since they had received the phone call, the Syferts made their plans on Wednesday to fly from Okla-homa to New Jersey.

Tragedy seldom maintains decent calling hours, and it brings no dispensation from the quotidian demands of one's life. It barged into an otherwise peaceful existence for the Syferts. When John murdered his family, the Syferts were crossing a well-made bridge from one stage of their lives to another. Gene was completing his master's degree and was in the middle of final exams. And while the Syferts had already put three sons through college and were living comfortably, money and time happened to be tight in 1971.

For living victims such as close relatives, unanticipated death brings more than profound shock and grief. In its most mundane manifestation, it also brings profound inconvenience. Even while still reeling from loss and anguish, the survivor is suddenly confronted with the necessity of making certain arrangements: house-sitters to engage, vacation days to be borrowed from, dogs to be boarded, airline tickets to be purchased at full fare. Clothes to press, accommodations to secure, food to buy, coffins and hymns to select. Even in households on well-managed budgets, there is a painful jump in expenses: The telephone bill soars; the undertaker and the gravedigger expect payment.

"Besides the unexpected expense, it was a time when Gene really couldn't afford to be off from school," Jean recalled. "He had to take off during finals time. John just doesn't realize the situation that he left us in."

Jean, who had always been fond of John despite the fact that her husband had not, was devastated by the murders. But she was also deeply injured by the cavalier manner the murderer—*Mrs. Jean Syfert   I'm sorry it had to go that way*—had dumped the wreckage he had made of their lives and his right into her lap. The fact that he had left *detailed instructions* for the funeral flabbergasted her. For a man with all of $24.14 in his bank account, the practical Jean thought, that took a staggering amount of nerve.

On Friday, the day before the funeral, Jean went to the house to sort through Helen's and the children's belongings in an attempt to restore some order. Jean was instructed only to concern herself with her sister's and the children's things. Rehwinkle was in charge of John's and Alma's property.

Detectives were still combing through the mansion,

dusting, sifting, looking into every dark corner. Jean was packing some of the boys' things into boxes when she heard a bloodcurdling scream from the butler's pantry adjacent to the kitchen.

She dashed into the big pantry to investigate, only to find a policeman with a sheepish look on his face and a deep round box in his hands. He explained that he had seen the box on a shelf and decided to open it. Inside was a head with long hair—Helen's wig dummy.

"It scared the daylights out of him—he didn't set it down, he threw it down," Jean said. "You knew what he thought. It was just this wig that Helen had; when she didn't want to go out and get her hair fixed, she would use a wig."

That eased the tensions somewhat. But in general, Jean was appalled by the conditions she found in the house that day. From the comings and goings still in progress, it was obvious that dozens of people, not only law enforcement officials but also town officials and others who had connections, had been allowed in for a look at the horror house. In the time since the crime scene had been secured, dozens of outsiders seemed to have been through the house.

Souvenir-taking began. "Helen always had lots of family pictures around," Jean said. "But I found picture frames with no pictures in them, which somebody had to take from that house. They took pictures right from the mantel! I like to have cried when I saw that. There were ten fireplaces in that house, and pictures over several of them, and you would find the frame empty on the floor.

"Then you would pick up the newspapers and there would be Helen's pictures just splashed all over," said Jean, who had always exchanged family photos with her sister and had her own copies of most of the pictures missing from the mantels. "There was no one there to protect her things. I think they even went through the drawers."

She said she was surprised that no one had taken the

stale cookies and black bananas she found in serving bowls where either Helen or John had left them a month before.

For Jean Syfert, it was the beginning of a long process of disillusionment with the police handling of the investigation. "The whole thing was botched right from the beginning," she asserted flatly.

The funeral was scheduled for Saturday, December 10. Rehwinkle had chosen Gray Funeral Home in Westfield, across from the municipal park and not far from Redeemer. Fred Poppy, the general manager at Gray's, was a good friend.

The Syferts liked Poppy immediately. A plain-talking man who understood that people most closely involved in the arrangement of a funeral have unexpressed concerns that extend beyond the closing of the grave, Poppy took the job only because he liked Rehwinkle, and because Rehwinkle's congregation were regular patrons of Gray's.

The funeral undertaking business is a unique blend of personal service of the most grim sort and show business of the most glib, conducted in an atmosphere that usually combines strong doses of commerce, grief, guilt, resentment, and, quite often, abiding recrimination.

From the onset, Poppy, who was also a wary businessman in a field where, even under ordinary circumstances, emotion could run high enough to spin off into orbit, spotted the extraordinary number of pitfalls presented by the List funeral. Not only were there *five* deceased, three of them were children. Furthermore, each of the deceased had been shot to death by the next of kin, and left hidden, under the most tragic (and, for an undertaker, least appealing) sort of circumstances, for nearly a month. Not to mention the fact that there didn't appear to be any money to pay the funeral bill.

From the beginning of the process, which was the physical handling of the bodies themselves, to the end, which

was commiting them to the grave—not to mention in between, which was to do it all in the blazing glare of publicity
surrounding the biggest mass murder in New Jersey history—Poppy realized that this particular job would be a
thankless one.

The Gray Funeral Home undertook the List proceedings
in good faith that was nurtured by the knowledge that
Rehwinkle's congregation, good solid Lutherans who paid
their bills, already accounted for about fifteen funerals a
year at Gray. Besides, Poppy pointed out to his boss, the
publicity value was substantial, and the church was already
planning to cover a number of costs, such as purchase of
the burial plot. The undertaker was instructed to keep
costs to the absolute minimum.

The first matter of business, then, was the expenses.
The next-of-kin himself being expansive in his directions
but conspicuous in his absence, who was going to pay to
carry out his instructions? Under the circumstances, it
was a particularly touchy question. For a man who sold
insurance for a living, John List had left behind what Poppy
regarded as a sorry mess of a personal insurance portfolio.
Although the murderer himself had a decent policy, with
a $225,000 death benefit, with State Mutual Life Assur-
ance, there was only one policy in effect for any of the
deceased, a paltry one on one of the boys worth $2,000.

And there wasn't any estate value worth mentioning.
The bank accounts were drained. Poppy made a visit to
the house and his sharp eye told him there wasn't much
there. The furniture wasn't junk, but it wasn't the sort
of stuff people buy second-hand. The family car, the 1963
Impala that now sat in the township lot, was just an old
junker. It hadn't been worth the cost of towing it back
from the airport. But even if it had been a Rolls-Royce, it
wouldn't have mattered, given the reality that its owner
was apparently still alive and, so far as the New Jersey
motor vehicles department was concerned, unfettered by

any court judgment whatsoever. To a dispassionate businessman, the assets were not an impressive collection.

"There was some furniture in this place, but it was very sparsely furnished," Poppy recalled. "The man was struggling. I called in two different used-furniture people, to give me a bid on all the furniture. The highest bidder offered $550. That's all I got."

Inside the house, there was nothing of value left except a fancy kitchen stove John List had bought for Helen in 1969. Poppy figured the stove, in excellent condition, was worth over $1,000, but he never expected to see that. "It was a chef's stove, the kind of thing a pro would use," Poppy said. But he found there wasn't much demand for a used oversized stove, particularly if the buyer has to pick it up at the scene of a mass murder. And legally, even that was still John List's property.

"The only thing I had legal custody of was the deceased," said Poppy, who would always regard the List business as the worst ordeal of his professional life. "To me, John List was nothing but heartache."

Successfully putting together a cut-rate funeral that didn't look cheap was one of the few positive aspects about the ordeal for Poppy, who, like most people in Westfield, had never met any of the Lists.

"It wasn't a big bill all told. I had cut it right to the bone," he boasted. "Each and every one of the deceased was placed in a metal casket with an eggshell crepe interior. These caskets were presentable. They weren't lavish. They were inexpensive. But they were presentable." The bill, less than $2,500, was paid in full, covered by the one insurance policy in effect and the money from selling the furniture.

Rehwinkle and Poppy agreed to proceed with as much dignity and as little outside disruption as possible. On Friday afternoon, Poppy and several employees used a nondescript station wagon, not a hearse, to transport the five bodies from the funeral home on Broad Street to the church, about a half-mile away.

"We had made a decision that around four-thirty in the afternoon, when everybody is busy coming home from work, going to the store, the kids coming home from school, here's the best time for us to move," Poppy said. "We made five trips back and forth in the station wagon." The bodies were taken in the back door of the church, wheeled in one at a time on dollies, four of which Rehwinkle had borrowed from other churches in town. The pastor also had to borrow four extra palls, long white funeral cloths with green crosses on them, to drape over the coffins.

On Friday night, for the second time, the bodies of Helen, Patricia, John, and Frederick List were arranged in symbolic repose, with Alma beside them now.

Given the intense media attention, maintaining order at the funeral was a challenge made difficult by the fact that the survivor's instructions had the effect of placing his pastor and his sister-in-law in conflict. As the closest member of Helen's family, which obviously included the three children, Jean considered herself the interlocutor for the deceased, the *victims*, as she saw them. But because of the civil and spiritual burden he had been handed, Rehwinkle was unfortunately cast in some eyes as the agent of the closest surviving relative, the absent next-of-kin, the presumed (but not yet officially charged) murderer himself. Like his comrade Poppy, the minister was well aware that John List had handed him a very thankless task.

With an air of resignation, the minister took charge. With inevitability, Jean resented it.

"John had told the preacher what he wanted done," she said, recalling the unpleasant memories of making the funeral arrangements in Westfield. "Gene and I basically said, well, John has no rights at this point. But the preacher

took over and did whatever it was that John had told him
to do, where Mother List was to go, this and that."

After the autopsies, which determined such things as
the number of times young John had been shot in the back
of the neck and the back and from what angle, the five
bodies were delivered to Gray's, where they were prepared
for the funeral. Despite the serious deterioration of the
corpses, "they had to be embalmed, otherwise we couldn't
have taken them into the church for any period of time
because the odor would have been something terrible,"
Poppy said. "Not only did we embalm them, but we had
other agents that we use, drying agents that we put around
the body, and then we encompass the whole body in a
plastic pouch that you zip up, and put the powder in there
to absorb moisture that's still being lost out of the body."

"There were so many shots and so many wounds," he
said sadly.

Already, a vigil of reporters and townsfolk had been
established outside the funeral home. Rehwinkle decided
against having calling hours. "Nothing happened at the
funeral home. The only thing we did was prep the bodies
and casket them," Poppy said.

A half block down Broad Street, the drama group was
gathered for its biweekly session in the Municipal Building.
Ed Illiano tried to keep them busy, but all anyone could
manage was a lackluster stab at a familiar scene or two.
It was clear that more than the usual number of kids had
come stoned, and some of them were more stoned than
usual. The talk was thick with death and betrayal. Ed was
glad to get out.

It was after ten o'clock when Eileen Livesey, Pat's
friend, walked with some friends past the park on their
way home from the workshop. She was surprised to see a
former boyfriend of Pat's, whose name was Chris, slouched
against a telephone pole, just beyond the glow of a street

lamp. The tip of his cigarette glowed in the shadows as he dragged on it in the cold.

Eileen tried to engage him in conversation. He steadfastly ignored her. Someone suggested a cup of coffee at the diner. He didn't acknowledge the invitation. "All he did was stand there and stare at the building," she said. "He didn't even seem to be aware that anyone was speaking to him. Later, someone said they drove by well after midnight, and he was still standing there. He wouldn't budge."

Meanwhile, Poppy thought it ironic that John would have wholeheartedly approved of the military precision with which the funeral was arranged. The church accommodated about two hundred people, and hundreds more were expected outside, where the television trucks had already staked out their positions on Clark Street. There wasn't going to be a lot of opportunity for improvisation if order was to prevail.

Poppy wanted Helen buried in the center grave, with the children at her side. Alma, as John had instructed, was to be taken to Michigan after the funeral and buried in the cemetery of St. Lorenz. So Poppy had arranged the caskets in the appropriate order: Patricia's was on the far left, with her mother's to the right, followed by the two boys. Alma's, on the far right, would be the last to be wheeled out of the church. Alma's would be placed in the rear hearse, which would peel off from the procession when it passed the funeral home. There, a vehicle would be waiting to transport the casket to Newark Airport and the afternoon flight with connections to Bay City.

Pallbearers were a major headache. Even under normal circumstances, pallbearers personify an undertaker's worst nightmare, which is having the coffin come crashing to the ground with the deceased tumbling down the church steps. At most funerals, one only needs to come up with a handful of able-bodied persons to carry the casket, and even when the pallbearers are borderline infirm, employees from the funeral home can be found to shoulder some of the burden. But this funeral required the services of more than three dozen pallbearers. Eight boys from the drama group carried Patricia's coffin; her brothers' caskets were borne by taller friends from school aided by a couple of adults from the congregation. Men who didn't even know the family were pressed into service as pallbearers for Helen and Alma.

The members of the drama group not actively involved as pallbearers or ushers took up the first three pews on the left side of the church, which Rehwinkle had set aside from them. Ed Illiano sat in the first, next to the aisle and beside Pat's casket. Across the aisle from him, in the first pew, sat Helen's mother, Eva, and next to her the Syferts and Helen's three brothers and their wives. No members of John's family were present. None had been invited.

Far more than the two hundred expected showed up for the service; Rehwinkle hadn't realized until then that his church could accommodate so many people, more than three hundred in all by someone's count. The estimated five hundred spectators massed outside the church were able to hear the service on loudspeakers that Poppy had set up on poles.

As the funeral proceeded, Pastor Rehwinkle's invocation boomed from the pulpit and the outside speakers.

"We have been leveled, but God lifts us up," the minister said in a firm voice. "We are not concerned here this morning about the unexplainable, illogical, irrational or bizarre behavior that led to this tragedy. We have all been leveled. Where are we at this very moment?

"All mankind is grass," the pastor intoned.

At this unwitting allusion to a subject close to their consciousness, a few teenagers in the drama club pews snickered quietly and nudged each other. Ed stared them back into silence.

"They last no longer than the flowers in the fields."
Rehwinkle had taken his theme from Isaiah:

> A *voice says, "Cry!"*
>   *And I said, "What shall I cry?"*
>   *All flesh is grass.*
>   *and all its beauty is like the flower*
>   *of the field.*
> *The grass withers, the flower fades.*
>   *when the breath of the Lord*
>   *blows upon it;*
>   *surely the people is grass.*
> *The grass withers, the flower fades,*
>   *but the word of our God will stand forever.*

To some who were not members of the Redeemer fold,
the pastor's choice of scripture seemed to skirt the overwhelming issues of the day, violent criminality, blame, and
grief, and they would just have seen the notion of the
blameless perishability of life left unexplored by the murderer's confessor and proclaimed good friend.

Among the members of the drama club, who were well
aware already of Patricia's contemptuous attitude toward
the very church in which they now were gathered, the
sermon was especially rankling. Even Ed Illiano, a staunch
Roman Catholic who would brook no show of disrespect
toward any clergyman, was barely out of the church before
he began referring to the Rehwinkle invocation derisively
as the "We Are Leveled, O Westfield soliloquy." Said Ed:
"I just thought, my God, what is this guy doing? Doesn't
he know how much injury John List has caused these
people and how pissed off they are?"

The day was cold and sunny, with a brisk wind that
whipped over the low hills and stung the faces of the

mourners gathered by the plot, where fresh red earth was piled beside four newly dug graves. The funeral procession had stretched the length of Westfield itself; when the last car was pulling into the line from the parking lot at Redeemer, the first had already made its turn off Broad Street and under the gray stone arch at the entrance to Fairview Cemetery. The graves were dug beside a large fir tree, on a hill where the western edge of Westfield begins a gentle ascent toward the Watchung range.

Standing among the mourners, Eileen Livesey, noticing the large number of automobiles parked helter-skelter on the winding drives near the grave, thought of Pat, being laid in her grave a month short of her seventeenth birthday. *We're all so sophisticated and mature*, Eileen thought. *She never even got to drive a car.*

Hundreds of people were clustered near the white graveside tents that flapped in the wind. Muffled sobs mingled with the pattering snaps of the photographers' shutters. Glassy eyes of television cameras searched uplifted faces for emotion. Some of the photographers and television camera people perched atop nearby tombstones for better angles into the faces of the crowd.

Gene Syfert looked around from his place under one of the tents. He had never seen so many people with cameras. He was also surprised to see the glint of gun barrels from the crests of some of the hills. He counted a dozen police riflemen on the hills, waiting for John List to show his face. Gene thought how bizarre they looked in such a setting.

Both the undertaker and the minister were glad, though, for the presence of police sharpshooters. Given the enormity of the violence both men had encountered, neither was entirely assured that the murderer's business was finished. During the graveside service, Poppy recalled, Rehwinkle nudged him, and muttered out of the side of his mouth, "Hey, Fred, you look around to see if this guy is somewhere in this crowd up here. He's liable to take a potshot at us."

"Don't worry," the undertaker whispered. "I'm already looking. So if I see him and suddenly push you into that grave, you'll know why. And I'll be right behind you."

Much to the relief of some county investigators, who were becoming increasingly testy over questions about the lack of progress in the case, the Federal Bureau of Investigation entered the investigation on Thursday, December 9, when a federal warrant was obtained in Newark charging John with the crime of unlawful interstate flight. The FBI published a standard wanted flier, which described the suspect as being 46 years old, six feet tall (he was actually an inch taller), and weighing 180 pounds, with "black, graying" hair, a fair complexion, brown eyes, and two distinguishing scars, a "mastoidectomy scar behind right ear" and "herniotomy scars both sides of abdomen." The flier included this warning: "List, who is charged in New Jersey with multiple murders involving members of his family, may be armed and should be considered very dangerous." Incongruously, it added this remark: "Reportedly a neat dresser."

FBI agents on the case thought the flier was a dead cinch to locate their man. With his picture, full face and in three-quarters profile, he was an odd-looking fellow indeed in the pantheon of career murderers, cop killers and bomb-throwing revolutionaries then crowding the post office walls.

After looking into John List's personality and recent history, the FBI was able to focus on two other approaches as well. Investigation turned up the fact that John suffered from severe hemorrhoids and was, one agent on the case said, a "heavy-duty consumer of Preparation H." It was also learned that John was so badly nearsighted that his eyeglasses prescription had to be adjusted frequently.

Fliers were dispatched to every pharmacy and eye doctor in the country.

More important, though, was John's well-established religious devotion. Every cop who looked into the murderer's personality was convinced of this: If he was in the country, John List would ultimately turn up in a Lutheran church somewhere.

But the fliers never went out to the churches. It was the 1970s, and FBI headquarters was wary. Overtly asking the church in effect to become an agent of law enforcement was politically unwise, even though the Lutheran church itself had indicated to the FBI that it would have no objection to the effort.

Ironically, five years later, when a more relaxed FBI headquarters in Washington finally agreed to allow the Newark office to blanket the U.S. Lutheran churches with John List fliers, the Lutheran church threw up a roadblock. A Senate committee had recently turned up allegations that U.S. intelligence agencies had used missionaries abroad as informants, and the Lutheran church wanted no parts of a public association with the FBI. "They told us thanks but no thanks," said a former FBI official connected with the List case who remained convinced that if the fliers had gone out to the churches, they would have caught John List.

For months, intrigued with the conundrum of John List, the FBI exhaustively combed through what was then known of the man's background. John List's life never quite added up. The patterns eventually seemed clear enough: dashed expectations in a career leading to the edge of bankruptcy, and superimposed over these failures were tensions worsened by a hectoring wife and a zealous religious reaction against the mores of the 1960s. But it never quite pointed all the way to John List picking up two pistols and spending a well-planned day shooting his family to death.

Some minor details previously unknown about John

List's character did turn up, to the merriment of the cops. Like the private post office box the FBI found that John List had rented to receive girlie magazines. Also intriguing was the report of a married couple from the Westfield church who attended a weekend religious conference with John and Helen in the late 1960s. To save money, the couples shared a motel room. At night, with the lights out and each couple modestly tucked in their beds on either side of the room, John List began making sounds, obvious noises, the apparent purpose of which, it seemed to the embarrassed other couple, was to impress on them the fact that he was engaged in sexual activity with his wife.

One bizarre theory that did keep police speculating for many years stemmed from a famous event that occurred on the night before Thanksgiving in 1971, two weeks after the List family was murdered but two weeks before the bodies were found in the ballroom. That was when a polite, soft-spoken man, described as dark-haired, middle-aged, six feet tall, and bespectacled, hijacked a Northwest Orient 727, forcing it to land and pick up $200,000 in ransom money and then, airborne again, parachuting out into the howling wind at ten thousand feet over the Cascade Mountains of Washington. While it was ultimately the firm belief of investigators that the famous hijacker, known as D. B. Cooper, could never have survived the forbidding terrain even if he had hit the ground alive, and although it was furthermore known that John List was utterly without athletic prowess, the strange coincidence of timing—and the fact that there was some slight resemblance to List in a police artist's sketch of the mysterious D. B. Cooper—would be the subject of many a beery late-night bull session among cops whose experience had taught them that strange things can happen.

Wild theories aside, however, whatever chase there was quickly reached the point of obvious futility among the

police in Westfield and Union County. There was *nothing*
fresh to go on. Painstakingly, the FBI had run down the
name of every passenger on every flight that had departed
anywhere near New York on November 10 and immediately afterward, in the hope that a murderer who had so
boldly killed his family, and left such a detailed account
of it, would have had the concurrent audacity to travel
under his own name. Every variation of John Emil List
was looked at, to no avail. Photographs of List were shown
to stewardesses, ticket agents, baggage handlers, and coffee
counter clerks. But the task was impossible. If he had
boarded a flight, he had been one of thousands of people,
and tens of thousands more had passed by in the inter-
vening month. Who would recall such an ordinary man
over that span of time? With a month to cover his tracks,
List had simply vanished.

Even the newspapers tired of the story, given the lack
of any fresh angles to highlight, as evidenced by several
editions of the afternoon Elizabeth *Daily Journal* the Tuesday after the funeral. "List's Trail Cold; Hunt Left to FBI,"
the newspaper's main front page headline blared in an early
edition over a story that began: "Police said Monday they
have exhausted their leads to the whereabouts of murder
suspect John E. List and are now relying on the FBI to
locate him." By the late edition, the "List Trail Cold"
headline had been downsized and pushed near the bottom
of the front page, which now lead with the headline: "U.S.,
France Agree on Devalued Dollar."

Disillusionment was palpable. The same day, Michael
Mitzner, the assistant prosecutor of Union County, ex-
plained the situation this way, to the annoyance of the
FBI: "We have not heard anything significant from the
FBI to date, and if they have any clues, they are not telling
us at this point."

In Westfield, Chief Moran began telling people he was
carrying the FBI flier with John List's picture with him

at all times. He would carry a copy of that flier with him for the next eighteen years. At regular intervals, Moran also dispatched officers to the cemetery, where they lurked behind trees and tombstones, waiting for John List to visit his family's grave.

Despairing of finding the elusive murderer himself, some police decided to go after a more easily identifiable villain, the devil. Word of Pat's fascination with witchcraft had spread quickly as some townsfolk groped for a plausible explanation for the murders. Hadn't a Black Sabbath record album been found in the child's room? For a time, from the tone of their questions, it seemed that some police were toying with the idea that a satanic cult, perhaps operating within the drama group itself, had somehow made its influence on his daughter known to John List, and that the deeply religious man had then snapped under the pressure.

Armed with this preposterous theory, investigators soon focused on a coven of satanists in a nearby town, Mountainside who appeared to have some connections to a motorcycle gang that was believed to be dealing drugs. While it seemed clear that members of this group had never heard of the sixteen-year-old Pat List until after the girl was murdered, the connection—murder and Satan—continued to appeal both to satanists savoring the ironies and to some stymied investigators who didn't have anywhere else to look. Evil being much easier to accept when it has a leering, demonic face, and not the benign countenance of the man mowing his lawn, the devil became a prime suspect in some minds as an accomplice to murder.

One Westfield detective pursued this angle so energetically that he prompted an angry letter to the police chief and the mayor from a banker's wife associated with the drama group. It seems the detective asked the woman, who volunteered to assist drama club productions, point-blank if she herself was a witch. Her letter protested "undue badgering of a private citizen."

Chastized, the Westfield police then began pursuing the devil less aggressively. Nevertheless, some of them never abandoned the theory that the satanism was somehow involved in what they considered to be an otherwise inexplicable crime.

Aroused by the sensation surrounding the crime, however, the satanists did begin causing problems for Fred Poppy who, at the behest of both Rehwinkle and Jean Syfert, had accepted appointment as administrator of the List estate.

One night in January, dozens of motorcycles roared down Hillside Avenue into the driveway of the List place to make a pass around the mansion, as if staking a macabre claim. Later, on some dark nights, neighbors began noticing candlelight flickering through the cracks of boarded-up windows. There were odd comings and goings, stirrings in the bushes, cackles of laughter. Some people heard muffled chants. Gawkers in slow-moving sedans cruising by the crime scene were one thing. Bikers and devil worshippers using the house was quite another.

Poppy, who had the only key to the property, was furious, not only at the late-night trespassers, but at other local teenagers. It had become something of a dare locally to drive up to the murder house and break in. Poppy, by now extremely sorry that he had ever become involved, soon discovered that the intruders were getting in by climbing an arbor at the rear of the house and edging over a roof to the skylight atop the ballroom, then dropping down to the floor. Once inside, they couldn't exit the same way, of course. Instead, a distressed neighbor told the undertaker, they crawled out through a cellar window in the back. The neighbor called him regularly, day and night, "as if I were the chief of police," he said.

One Saturday the neighbor phoned him to report more intruders. Poppy, disgusted that the Westfield police department seemed to assign a low priority to protecting the List property, drove up there himself. He parked his station wagon out back with the bumper completely blocking the escape window. Then he called the police and asked "if they would see fit to stop by." When they did, they nabbed four teenagers, a girl and three boys—all of them, it turned out, children of prominent Westfield residents. Against Poppy's wishes, charges were not pressed.

He wasn't worried much about theft. Souvenir hunters had already taken the mailbox, the house numbers from the door, the brass knocker—anything that could be removed, even the sideview mirror and other removable bits of John List's old car parked near the municipal building.

The real threat posed by intruders, Poppy knew, was fire, especially from what he called the "devil crowd," which favored Pat's old bedroom on the second floor for their nocturnal gatherings. Poppy, who saw the witchcraft fad merely as a pretext for getting high, asked around about the empty aerosol cans of shaving cream that always seemed to litter the scene after one of the sessions, and was astonished when he was told the kids spread it over their naked bodies "so they could slide around on each other— the girls and the boys." Poppy chuckled to think of how the good burghers of Westfield would react if they knew just how many of their well-educated, upwardly bound sons and daughters were "getting naked and dancing around a chicken," vowing their buck-ass-naked loyalty to Lucifer himself, right there on fancy Hillside Avenue.

Poppy also found disturbing signs, candles and other paraphernalia, that the devil worshippers were gathering on moonlit nights at the grave in Fairview Cemetery. "The superintendent of the cemetery, when I would be coming up for other funerals, would say, 'Look, the kids were here laying on the grave last night again.' Kids would come up and lay on the grave!"

On August 30, 1972, nine months after the murders, Breeze Knoll burned down.

With flames leaping through the roof, the first alarm went in at three-seventeen A.M., and again Hillside Avenue was shaken from sleep with the wail of sirens. The house burned steadily until after seven P.M., and by the time it was over, only the front columns and a small section of the dining room area were left above the smoldering rubble. The blaze had started in the open center hall, which acted like a flue to spread the flames.

Poppy got a call early in the morning from the Lutheran pastor, who himself had been notified by a neighbor.

"Hey, Fred, guess what?" Rehwinkle said.

"I know, let me guess, it's on fire," Poppy replied with resignation. "All right, I'll be right over."

The first thing Poppy looked for when he went in, just out of curiosity, was Helen's stove. It had crashed through the back kitchen floor and lay smashed under a pile of charred wood on the cellar floor.

The cause of the fire was apparently not what Poppy had expected, which was kids being careless with candles. Jack Wittke, then living in the converted carriage house a few hundred yards in the back of the old mansion, slept through the commotion. But when he woke early the next morning, he was struck by the sharp smell of kerosene that pervaded the neighborhood. The once beloved mansion was a smoking, stinking ruin. But the devil hadn't done it, and neither had John List. For whatever reason, a skilled arsonist had burned Breeze Knoll down.

Almost as soon as they had come, the satanists lost interest. The gravesite where the Lists were buried began aging into its surroundings on the hill. Friends of the children, when they came home from college, sometimes visited and left flowers. Flowers, in fact, always bloomed at the grave. They were tended anonymously for over a generation.

In the summer of the second year, a handwritten note appeared among the red and white impatiens that blossomed at the base of the gravestone. In tribute to Pat, the message quoted a poem of François Villon, the fifteenth-century French vagabond and adventurer whose jaunty spirit had captivated so many children who grew up in the sixties. It was a single sad refrain from the most famous of Villon's ballads, "The Ladies of Bygone Days," which laments the death of lovely women:

Mais ou sont les neiges d'antan?
But where are the snows of yesteryear?

PART TWO

Resurrection

Chapter Ten

THE DECEMBER WIND HAD A BITE TO IT IN THE HOUR before the sun rose over the high plains that sweep up to the foot of the Rockies. Five inches of powdery snow lay on the ground from the night before. The man's black rubber boots made a crunching sound on the path beside the road.

There wasn't much traffic on the local street, but the whoosh of cars and eighteen-wheelers could be heard from Interstate 70 just up the embankment, where the highway began boring its way into the foothills. It was quite cold, not much above zero, but at this altitude, at six thousand feet, numbing early mornings often gave way to mild afternoons with the bright winter sun defining the jagged mountain peaks. By late afternoon, the snow would be gone.

Early each morning in the two weeks since he had found a place to live on the western edge of the city, the man walked the four blocks to a convenience store. There, among deliverymen warming their hands on cardboard cups of steaming coffee, he would select the two local papers, the *Denver Post* and the *Rocky Mountain News*, from the rack where they were wedged in with the want-ad digests advertising used cars and cheap apartments. It was a morning ritual to walk back home and read the papers carefully in the little trailer he had rented in a mobile home park just off the interstate. He spent a good part of his time reading, historical novels chiefly, and of course the Bible.

The rent was seventy-five dollars a month for the little house-trailer, which had one room with a bed, a table, two chairs, a nightstand on which sat a cassette tape player, a swag lamp, and a small kitchen area with a sink, a counter, and a refrigerator that would do for one person. The tiny bathroom was just beyond, behind a door the size of those on airplane lavatories.

In time, he would buy a television set. Not far away, the Wal-Mart had thirteen-inch black-and-white models for $69. Also some decent cookware. Slowly, the accoutrements of an ordinary life would arrive in place.

He would need a job, of course. But the money would hold out for a while. Then he could find something, probably something menial, to cement him in a little more firmly to the landscape. But not for a while. It would be a mistake to rush into anything. So far, he hadn't made any mistakes.

To augment the Bible, he had begun drawing comfort from the words of Miguel deMolinos, a seventeenth-century mystic who was condemned for heresy, and who had written:

Your center is the Kingdom of God. Within you is a divine fortress, and that divine fortress defends, protects and fights for you . . . When you see your peace assaulted, retreat to that region of peace, retreat to the fortress . . . Do not leave that place while the storm is on. Remain tranquil, secure and serene within.

Serenity, faith, anonymity. Those were his imperatives.

The trailer park had about twenty small units arrayed about a circular drive. It was neat, cheap, convenient, and impersonal. The neighbors were apparent mostly through sounds—a hasty footstep on the gravel, a muffled cough, a car door slamming, an engine being coaxed to life. Faces displayed themselves only fleetingly. Judging by the license plates on the older-model cars parked beside the driveway or fit onto the scrubby slices of land between the trailers, everyone was from somewhere else. Many of the cars were from the Midwest, where the automobile industry was just feeling the first shivers of failure and had begun jettisoning ballast. Day-Glo swaths on one car identified a hippie couple from Massachusetts, evidently holed up for the winter before the last big push to the Pacific. The only eye contact readily available on the premises came from the occasional defeated child standing outside a trailer, hoping for a diversion.

The monthly lease bore the name Robert P. Clark. No identification had been required, only the ability to produce one months' security deposit and one month's rent. The accommodations were fine for his purposes. Years ago, in another life, he had passed through Denver once and noticed the inordinate number of trailer parks clustered just off the exits of the interstate, with signs offering instant move-in and cheap rent.

Now, with little more than an alias that had its only firm footing in a new Social Security number, Bob Clark was prepared to drift passively for a while in the vagabond stream, unremarkable among the dispossessed, the displaced, and the desperate, the fugitives from child support, the hapless adverturers, the immigrants with questionable documentation, the laid-off and hopeful, the ambulant deinstitutionalized, the merely transient and determined, all bobbing just under the surface of American society by the beginning of the 1970s.

For he understood something very basic that had allowed John List to plan his escape with the assurance that, if it was initiated with cunning, a new life was possible. By the 1970s, most middle-class Americans actually believed that, more than any time in their history, they were a

nation of citizens readily identifiable and accountable—as
employees, taxpayers, credit-card users, voters, licensed
drivers, candidates for jury duty—to an essentially benign
but nevertheless monolithic record-keeping bureaucracy
with the ability to spit out any person's whereabouts and
bona fides instantaneously, with the efficient tap of a computer key. They were not aware of the fact that the America they had known in their youths no longer existed for
many people. Then, a man on the run from authorities
was at routine risk. Even the most mundane daily undertaking, such as buying breakfast, required some form of
social intercourse. But the society had changed. Now any
person, especially a neatly dressed adult male with a few
dollars in his pocket and no desperation on his face, a man
with a penchant for keeping his mouth shut and lingering
in the crowd, could get off any bus, come into any new
area, with virtually no questions asked, with little fear of
ever encountering the unexpected. Succor would be found
without challenge in impersonal fast-food joints, K-marts,
7-Elevens, and chain motels arrayed across the land in
utterly predictable pattern.

If only because he had stood against them so defiantly
for so long, John List understood the raging social currents
that had burst through at the end of the 1960s. Now, in
this hour of his need, he was determined to tap into it.
Like much of the rootless society that had evolved around
him, he was resolved to keep his head down and, quietly,
look out for Number One.

He always read the papers carefully. Lately, however,
he had more than a detached interest in the news. On a
snowy day, December 10, he would have finally found what
he was looking for, buried on page 15 of the *Rocky Mountain
News*, where a headline read:

Police Seeking
Accountant in
Slaying of Five

The story was only ten paragraphs long, frustrating in the paucity of the information conveyed. There was Moran, the police chief, saying the two unloaded pistols had been found in a desk drawer. The story didn't say much more of interest; more important, it didn't signal any cause for alarm. The bodies had been found Tuesday night—it was Friday by the time the story made its way to the one Denver paper that had been interested enough to run it. Interestingly, it had taken twenty-eight days to find the bodies. And it was apparent that the police didn't have a clue as to where the murderer might have gone. How could they? He hadn't left one.

In the serenity of that first dark winter, John List receded from mind and Bob Clark bundled himself in a renewed sense of order. He began to establish a routine. Simple meals cooked on the gas stove in trailer kitchen, or eaten quietly out of a paper bag on a table in McDonald's with the other hungry strangers. He had no car yet, of course. A car was expensive. More to the point, a car was dangerous. A car required documents that would be scrutinized. Worse, a car was the easiest place for a law-abiding person to come into direct, inadvertent contact with that most capricious of interlopers, the police officer. A car could wait.

The bus was simple, anonymous, and convenient. There would be no problem learning the schedules and connections. So life wasn't bad. Besides order, there was a new-found sense of self-esteem starting to emerge. Even a middle-aged man set in his ways could adapt to a new life once he put his mind to it, once the reference points started to fall into place.

By the second half of 1972, a man of more distinct dimensions could be seen making his way in the first light of day across the parking lot of a Holiday Inn. He walked around the big tractor-trailers that idled in the rear of the parking lot, under the big green-and-white sign that blazed toward the interstate. He would look both ways before crossing the street to the trailer park, where he would read the newspapers, and then the Bible, before retiring.

Bob Clark liked the night shift for its quietude. He also had come to realize with some irony that all of those unhappy evenings coming home from work and having to rustle up dinner for three hungry children hadn't been wasted. For he had found work as the night-shift cook at the Holiday Inn West, along Interstate 70 where the suburbs of Denver had stretched all the way out to Golden by the 1970s. Among the lively bunch on the night shift—waitresses and waiters, the bellhop, the helpers and cleaning people—Bob Clark was regarded as friendly but taciturn, a man more likely to bury his nose in a book than chat during lulls in the routine. But one could see a bounce to his step again, a sense of diligence and purpose as he worked at the big stove or rummaged in the refrigerator with a hamburger hissing on the grill.

Night work in a kitchen not being an endeavor given to long tenure, it was not long before steady Bob Clark was one of the senior employees on the shift.

The Holiday Inn West was strategically situated. With the popular ski resorts of Vail and Aspen less than two hours away, westbound travelers could stop for the night to take advantage of the reasonable rates and still be on the slopes before lunch, or beyond the Rockies by dark. For the eastbound traveler coming in from the mountains, it offered a haven before the urban glut of Denver and the long, dreary drive across the plains. As a result, people were coming in at all hours, and the kitchen was busy day and night. By mere dint of his diligence and ability to keep things organized, Bob Clark was quickly promoted from the sink to the stove, where he developed a reputation as a deft short-order cook who never ruined a meal and won the respect of coworkers, some of them transients who wandered in for a month or two of work.

As he added shading to his new form, Bob Clark made his first genuine friend in the unlikely personage of a cowboy who had grown weary of working the ranches and ridges of the high country and drifted down to Denver to find comfort and steady work.

At fifty-five, Robert Lavner Wetmore had spent his last winter in the high elevations of the North Park of the Rockies, where he had a small fence-mending business that supplemented the money he earned as a cowboy. It was a decent business. The federal Bureau of Land Management and the Colorado Forest Services department often had work for him. But it was feast or famine, and it was work better suited for a younger man. Sometime before the winter of 1972–1973 managed to get a frigid lock on the high country, Bob Wetmore piled his things into his pickup truck and came down.

"I figured I would wash dishes or something, and study," said Wetmore, who had begun devouring books on Eastern philosophy during the long winters in the mountains. "So I came in and got me a room downtown, in the old Skid Row, which was a wonderful part of town then. Then I drove out to the Holiday West, where I knew the old chef."

As they spoke, he told Bob Clark's boss: "I'm sure glad I no longer have to work four head of horses and take a saddle horse along for salvation in a blizzard, seven days a week."

"Hey, but what you going to do with yourself now?" the chef asked.

"Well, I come in to study. But I got to get me a little spending money, of course," Bob said, and waited.

The chef dried his hands on a towel. He looked around the place. "Well, this kitchen's a bitch to keep clean. You want to work cleaning it up? Night shift, of course."

"Well, I don't care about working nights," Wetmore replied.

The cowboy became a kitchen helper on the night shift.

At first Wetmore didn't take much notice of the night cook, a tall, gangling man who seemed to keep pretty much to himself. But Wetmore liked a man who always seemed to have a book going. He and Bob Clark soon discovered their mutual interests in history. Wetmore noticed that Bob was a good listener, if not much of a talker.

"We just got acquainted and seemed to hit it off," Wetmore recalled many years later. "How it grew, I don't know. He would keep coming up to me with questions. He seemed to be real interested in my life. I told him it wasn't much: 'I spent time in hobo jungles, skid rows, cow camps, cheap jail houses and a few pretty decent houses of ill repute,' I says, and he's all ears at this. He wanted to know all about my life up in the North Park. Life was rugged, but it suited me all right for a while, I told him. 'I only got in two fights, and I was lucky enough to win both of them, right there in a bar.' Well, Bob was extremely interested in that. It was like he never met someone who ever got into a tangle."

Soon, true to tradition, Wetmore was gleefully embellishing mountain stories for his wide-eyed new friend on the night shift.

"He was the sort, if you'd piss down his neck and tell him it was raining, he'd believe it," Wetmore said.

"He had this funny way of laughing. It wasn't really a laugh, it was sort of a little 'heh, heh, heh.' But I did enjoy talking to him." That is, about anything except religion. "You'd get him on religion, and sometimes he would start," said Wetmore. "You get this bullshit from them people about a loving God. 'Well,' I'd say, 'where the fuck is this loving God when he lets a little child die some godawful death?' I'd ask him these questions and he'd get this real sad look on his face. Pretty soon we didn't talk much about that subject."

Another subject Wetmore learned to avoid was Bob's past.

Late one night, they were sitting together at a booth in the dining room while on a break. Except for a waitress smoking a cigarette by the cash register, they were the only people in the room.

"Where did you say you was from before?" Wetmore asked in the midst of idle chat over coffee before they went back to work.

"Michigan."

"You went to college is my guess. You're too intelligent not to have."

"Yes, Michigan."

"What about your relatives back there?" Wetmore enquired casually.

Bob stiffened. "There aren't any!" he snapped. Wetmore was surprised enough to remember it clearly eighteen years later. Bob had never seemed agitated before about anything, let alone a simple everyday question. Wetmore never forgot how oddly Bob had reacted: "That was the only time I remember him showing emotion," he recalled. "We were sitting there in the booth, but he snapped back. He pulled his hands off from the table real fast, like he'd been hit by something."

Like many others who knew Bob Clark in the early years of his new life in Denver, Wetmore recalled a man of no apparent extremes, save for his penchant for detail. Bob didn't curse, but he didn't make a point out of it, Wetmore noticed. He didn't seem to drink much, but again, he didn't make a point of it. Wetmore could recall a few occasions when Bob quaffed a beer or two, but never more. He did seem to be something of a hypochondriac, always complaining of one ache or another. He popped a lot of pills, it seemed to Wetmore, who once asked him: "Why do you, a man with no overt illness, have to take about eighteen different kinds of pills?"

"They're vitamins," Bob replied simply.

And he had chronic problems with his feet, but he wouldn't consider going to a physician. "His feet was bruised, sore, it was the only thing he really bitched about much," Wetmore said. "It was always 'I got to go to the foot doctor. I got to go to the foot doctor.' A chiropractor, he told me."

And when he puts his mind to it, Wetmore remembers unsolicited kindnesses on several occasions when Bob seemed to sense that things were tight.

"How's the money?" Bob would ask.

"Oh, I'm getting by."

"Really?"

"Well, truth to tell, I'm a little short this week."

And Bob would discreetly palm over a ten-dollar bill.

"I always paid him back," Wetmore recalled. "In all, it was probably a total of less than a hundred dollars over a couple of years. But he wasn't making all that much, and I was always grateful for how thoughtful he had been toward me."

In the early 1970s, as more Americans took to the roads, and more often with skis strapped to their rooftops, business was thriving at the Holiday Inn West, which drew not only from the interstate but also from the growth that had pushed Denver's suburbs out beyond Wheatridge all the way to the foothills at Golden.

In late 1973, the hotel brought in a new general manager to manage the growth. The new boss brought with him a new chef, Gary Morrison, a man in his early thirties with a good reputation in the local food-service industry not only as a cook but, more important, as a manager. An axiom in the food business is that the best cook in the world isn't worth much if he or she cannot efficiently keep the kitchen running. Gary knew that one of the first things he had to do was to identify those people he could depend on.

The tall, bespectacled, middle-aged night cook weighed in at the top of Gary's list.

"I took over as chef," Gary explained, "and generally you find going into a situation like that, people kind of like the guy they used to work for, the old chef, who in this case happened to be a very nice guy. Someone new comes in, it's a new regime, a new set of rules. People start to buck the system.

"Bob wasn't that way. He was extremely cooperative from the first time I met him, and it didn't take long for us to develop a bond without laying ground rules.

"I accepted him as a professional who knew his job and didn't hesitate to do it, so immediately there was the ca- maraderie that comes from withstanding the daily pres- sures and being able to smile and talk as friends at the end of the day. He was night cook. That meant not only the dining room, but the coffee shop and room service.

"Bob showed a remarkable amount of skill in that busi- ness, plus he lived in that little trailer park just across the street, which gave him a great deal of flexibility."

In short, the new boss had found himself an assistant. And when, as is inevitable in the restaurant business, the chef ultimately moved on to another establishment, he took Bob Clark with him.

The move occurred in late 1974, when Gary was offered the job as head chef at the sprawling Pinery Golf and Country Club in the suburbs southeast of the city. Gary invited Bob along as his deputy, with the title sous chef. At Bob's request, Wetmore was invited to come along as a kitchen steward.

Sometime before Christmas, Wetmore drove his pickup truck to the trailer park where Bob lived to help his friend move to a new place on Columbine Street, near the University of Denver, not far from where Gary was living. This way, Bob, who had no car, could commute to work with Gary. The apartment was a furnished place in a three-story complex that looked like a motel and was called Columbine Plaza. Across the street was a fraternity house, Zeta Beta Tau. The front door of Bob's new apartment opened onto a small courtyard with a swimming pool in the center. The rent was $150 a month. On average, tenants stayed about six months. Bob would stay there for three years.

Wetmore had never been inside Bob's old trailer, a nine-by-eighteen-footer with windows that looked like portholes on a ferry boat. Wetmore was surprised that all of Bob's things fit into the flatbed of the pickup in one trip, with room to spare. Besides some lamps, a small television, and things like kitchen utensils, Bob's possessions were all neatly stacked in cardboard boxes. For a man with so few other worldly possessions, Wetmore thought, Bob seemed to have an inordinate amount of clothes.

Soon, as Bob and Gary began riding to work together, a drive that took about thirty minutes, Gary discovered that Bob shared his interest in classical music and news. The music station of choice was KVOD-FM, which called itself "The Fine Arts Voice of Denver." Gary found they even liked the same composers—the nineteenth-century Hungarian composer and piano virtuoso Franz Liszt was a mutual favorite. And at the top of the hour, the radio would be switched to the all-news station for a few minutes.

"He *had* to know what was going on in the news," Gary said. "If it came up in the news, we would discuss it. He wouldn't compromise and I wouldn't either, but we could discuss things in such a way—'Well, this is the way I feel about this, and I think I'm absolutely right . . .' and 'Well, I feel this way, and I believe I am absolutely right . . .' "

Years later, Gary was angry to read some newspaper accounts that depicted his friend as arrogant and dogmatic. Bob was nothing of the sort, he said. Unlike Bob Wetmore, Gary never baited Bob Clark on matters of religion, but he did discuss it with him often over the years they were friends in Denver. "There was an ease about him with regard to religion," he said. "He never spoke out or in any way indicated that he was an extremely devout religious person, but you knew that he drew a lot of strength from his religious beliefs."

He added, "Bob in some ways is very difficult to describe, because the relationship that we had very trusting, in ways very close, but at the same time it was not intrusive.

"If I had something that I wanted to tell Bob, I would tell him, and he would me, but neither one of us would pry. As a result, there's a lot about Bob that I wish I had asked about.

"When you have a friendship, it doesn't come with rules. When you put rules on a friendship, you've lost it. We had a lot of times sitting talking, driving to and from work, or when things would quiet down at work, and we discussed a lot of things. There were things that we both had an interest in—history, music, the news. We always had something to talk about. It was a friendship that didn't require a lot of personal questions."

Bob had known that he would need a new Social Security number to find secure work in Denver, and obtaining one had been no problem. But so far, he hadn't had any need for a job résumé in the restaurant business. Gary hadn't even asked Bob about his work experience when he invited him to be his assistant at the Pinery. The restaurant business is famously fickle, with tremendous turnover in every job from head chef to dishwasher. Gary knew all about Bob's work habits that he needed to know.

"I never required references from my people," Gary said. "You go by skill. I already knew Bob had skill because I had worked beside the man. You go by what a man can do, not what he might have done somewhere else. You could work at McDonald's for six years and put down on a résumé that you'd had six years experience cooking. I had already seen for myself what Bob could do.

"I had offered him the position of sous chef, the equivalent of assistant manager, because he had shown the ability to keep things under control.

"As a cook, the guy was a natural. It was amazing for me to learn over the course of our relationship that he was actually an accountant by training and had never really had much experience in a kitchen."

Also, it was useful having an accountant on the payroll, even one who worked behind the stove, because the ability to keep numbers straight is crucial to running a profitable kitchen. And Bob seemed to be as adept with numbers as he was with dishing up a ham-and-cheese omelet while making sure the steak didn't burn. "Bob had this natural aptitude for numbers," Gary recalled. "As a chef, of course, you are also responsible for food costs, labor costs, figuring your overhead, profit margins, and so on. There were a lot of times, once I knew he had this aptitude, that I just dumped figures on him."

Even in the car on their way to work, "he'd run percentages for me in his head. He enjoyed it."

To his bemused new boss, the man also appeared to be unflappable, in an environment where intense pressure coexists with a general understanding that, on occasion, tempers will flare; that every so often, under the right circumstances, one could expect a childish outburst, a slammed door, even the occasional pot crashing against the kitchen wall.

Yet no matter how many clamoring waiters were tugging at his sleeve, no matter how many extra customers had shown up unexpectedly to empty the buffet, or how many busboys or helpers had called in sick on a Saturday night, Bob just kept his eye on the ball. Unperturbed, Bob got the job done. No fuss, no problem.

Gary was amazed. "The commercial food service industry has to be one of the most high-pressure businesses in the world," he said. "That's because you have these intense peaks during the day. You have a tremendous push to meet a lunch opening, for example. You go like mad and then, immediately, the pressure stops. Lunch is over. But dinner is up ahead. It's an emotional roller coaster, and every single day is built that way. There are very few people who can stand up to the continuous emotional build and always hold their cool."

Nor is losing it necessarily shocking. "The way I was trained, I didn't have to hold my cool," Gary said. "I served my apprenticeship under a super European chef, and part of the makeup of a chef is, if you don't like something, you lose your temper, you blow it off."

At first he was curious. How was Bob really dealing with the frustrations? He couldn't be that controlled. He didn't appear to drink. Like Wetmore, Gary never saw him take more than a beer or two, once in a very great while. He didn't seem to be holding anger inside, festering just below the surface. He obviously wasn't oblivious to his external environment—just the opposite, actually. He didn't seem to miss a single beat of the circus-band rhythm of a kitchen going full tilt.

He just seemed singularly at peace with it and with himself, passive and unaffected.

"I think you find very few people who can withstand

the pressure, especially in a new job, and not crack in front of people," Gary said. "Bob was a person who could take the pressure and change that would go on, on a minute-by-minute basis, and remain in control of his temper. Unless you've lived through a week or two in a good restaurant kitchen, it's very difficult to know how unusual that is."

In the kitchen, Bob also showed a talent he had never before exhibited and never again would: the ability to innovate on short notice. Even the best chefs can lack that. One example came to be known to Gary as the Chicken Capistrano incident.

It was buffet night, a weekly event at the Pinery, where the neat presentation of hot and cold dishes on a long, linen-draped table belied the feverish activity in the kitchen. On this particular night, more than the usual number of early arrivals had shown up, well-dressed but hungry people trying to be discreet as they eyed the offerings on the buffet and waited for the first person to take a dish from the stacked plates. With so many people on hand early, Gary realized that he had miscalculated. More food would be needed, especially one additional hot entree. There was nothing ready in the kitchen in the required quantity.

He banged through the swinging doors and mentioned the dilemma to Bob, who was busy with some pots.

"I don't know what we are going to come up with at this point," Gary muttered as workers bustled around to at least get more salads and condiments onto trays.

Bob seemed unconcerned. "You handle out there," he told his boss, walking over to the double doors of a refrigerator and peering in. "Let me see what I can do."

Gary got busy outside as the first customers began moving along the buffet table. Twenty minutes later, he realized he had been right: there wasn't going to be enough hot food. When he edged nervously back into the kitchen, however, he was astonished to find Bob beaming over a great vat of food he had obviously just prepared. It appeared to be big chunks of braised chicken with a light sauce, on a bed of shiny white rice, with tiny bits of red and green peppers and other things. It looked wonderful.

Gary got a spoon out and tried it. He loved it. It was delicious, the chicken cooked just right, the sauce just tangy enough. What's more, there appeared to be a ton of it.

"What in the world do you call this?" he asked Bob.

His assistant shrugged. "It's just something I put together from the refrigerator."

Gary dipped a clean spoon in and ate some more. "Bob, this is real good," he said, ordering a kitchen helper to move it out onto the buffet. When the food was rushed off, he told Bob, "Usually, you know, you have to experiment with something a few times before you can put it out. But you nailed it the first time. Dead on. Not only is it good, but it fits in with everything else we're serving out there."

Bob smiled and went back to work without a word.

A couple of hours later, he and Gary were finishing up in the kitchen when a regular customer came back, as some diners will do, to ask for a recipe.

She said everybody at her table had raved about the new chicken dish. "What was it called?" she wanted to know.

Bob stepped right up. "Oh, that was chicken . . . Chicken Capistrano," he said affably. It was obvious to Gary that he had just invented the name.

Two weeks later, the woman was back.

"I've gone through every recipe book I can find, and I can't find anything called Chicken Capistrano," she told Gary, who had Bob write out the recipe for her.

Gary later recalled that several years after that, he was eating lunch at a downtown Denver hotel when he noticed something listed as a daily special that made him laugh: "Chicken Capistrano."

Before too long, Bob moved more into public. Gradually, as Gary depended on him more to manage the operation, Bob was emerging from the confines of the kitchen to the dining rooms themselves, where he would greet and socialize with the customers. One night, during a luau buffet at the Pinery, Bob even donned a gaudy Hawaiian shirt and draped a lei around his neck to preside, mingling with the guests—"lawyers like you wouldn't believe," Gary said, "well-known local people who came in week after week and were getting to know him"—carving the pineappled ham and having a grand time of it.

"He was great with people," Gary said. "He wasn't keeping a low profile, he wasn't hiding, and he wasn't shy. If you are responsible, as I was, for a kitchen operation, who do you want out there in public in your place? You can have the best food in the world, and put someone out there with a crappy attitude, and everything goes down the tubes."

Gradually, the ground was firming under Bob's feet. Blurred outlines came into sharper focus as a man, simply by routinely occupying a place and time, acquired a lengthening recent past. Merely by being unchallenged, Bob Clark's identity began acquiring buttresses to support its rising structure.

By 1975, in a city whose attention was directed west, not east, he knew that few people if any would remember a face that, even in 1971, had been only a one-day blip on the national media screen.

He knew the time had come to reclaim his church, not as a haven, for a haven is intrinsically unsafe, but, again, as an abode.

From his earliest days in Denver, he had known which church that would be when the time came. During one foray by bus into downtown Denver, Bob had noticed the tall stone bell tower and the soaring stained-glass windows of St. Paul's Lutheran Church on Grant Street, a few blocks from the bus station and only one block from the gold dome of the Colorado state capitol.

When he was ready, he did not push open the big oak doors and walk boldly in. No, he did what he knew best. He began blending in for a long period, until he was familiar.

St. Paul's was no inbred small-town parish like Zion Lutheran back in Bay City, where generations of a family were baptized, confirmed, educated, wed, and buried, and assessed. St. Paul's was "on a bus line," its pastor, the Reverend Robert A. West, pointed out. In a transient western city in the 1970s, St. Paul's attracted "people starting their lives over, single people, people walking in off the street," the pastor said.

By no means was St. Paul's a church of drifters. Then and now, it was a parish with a proud history and a tradition of practical urban Christianity. But by the 1970s, it had become a church of strangers. When he knew it was safe, Bob Clark found solace there, where he knew that a man's past mattered little, that salvation was waiting to be reclaimed, now that he was born again.

Pastor West had noticed Bob's presence in the congregation for several months before the stranger officially rejoined the Lutheran church on June 29, 1975.

In 1976, with his name in the phone book for the second consecutive year, Bob Clark decided that he was secure enough to pound another major supporting pile deeper down into the earth.

Certain bureaucratic verities needed to be in place. Now it was time to obtain a driver's license.

This was possible because Bob Clark's identity was now established. In a computer at the phone company, for example, there was the kind of ratification of his being that can come only from dealing with a customer who has a history of paying his bills. To accept Bob Clark as a valid person, all the data bank at the motor vehicles office needed to know was that the phone company data bank did. Soon after that, data banks all over the Denver area would be linked in mutual proclamation of his undisputed existence.

So one day in the spring of 1976, Bob Clark, telephone customer, employee, taxpayer, congregant, and, at last, licensed driver, drove proudly back to Columbine Street in a used Volkswagen Beetle, bright orange.

In many residential areas, an eccentric single man pulling up to the curb in an orange Beetle would be a curious sight, but here, with the campus of the University of Denver only a few blocks away and the Greek letters of the Zeta Beta Tau fraternity emblazoned on the big house across the street, Bob Clark knew he wouldn't rate a second glance.

Having wheels meant he was no longer restricted to the bus routes, and Bob acted accordingly. With a car, Bob could become more useful to his church, where he had already established himself as a friendly figure who would stay after services to help prepare the coffee hour and clean up when it ended. Now, with his car, Bob placed himself in the service of his parish, eagerly volunteering to drive the old and infirm people to and from services each week. As John List's had been in college, Bob's name was always there at the top when the volunteer sign-up list was posted. As always, he was known as kind, solicitous but distant, an "ordinary guy," one parishioner said, who didn't seem to leave much of an impression beyond that.

Bob, eager to achieve status in the place where it mattered most to him, conveyed to his pastor that he had an advanced degree in accounting. He was eventually appointed to the parish finance council. Years later, Bob would even serve a two-year term as treasurer of the congregation, a post that many considered second in actual importance only to the pastor's.

As the days grew shorter in the autumm of 1976, Bob Wetmore started to feel restless, as a person accustomed to the open skies will when cooped up in town too long. He knew he was too old to face another winter in the mountains, but he was desperate to get away from the clutter of the city, where someone seemed to be in your face every waking moment, and to smell the timberline pine again, if only for a day. Since he knew that Bob hadn't ever ventured any farther from Denver than Wheatridge, and knew the Rockies only as a decorative border on the horizon, he suggested they make a day trip, for a change of scenery.

They were at work in the noisy kitchen at the Pinery. It was late in October, when the quaking aspen are shimmering in the hills and the skies at the higher elevations are so clear you can see the stars at noon. Both he and Bob were off on Mondays.

"So let's you and me go up that way first thing Monday morning?" Wetmore said. "You'll like the scenery, and we'll be able to be back at a reasonable time."

"Sure," Bob said. "Thanks."

But the next thing Wetmore knew, Bob had hurried out to the gift shop and come back with a map of Colorado and a look of concern. He wanted to know exactly where they would ge going.

"Well, I figure we'd go up to the North Park—along Poudre Park, past Collins, over the Cameron Pass up a ways to Walden," Wetmore said laconically. "Down Fourteen to the old Rabbit Ears's still passable this time of year. Then on to Granby. A full day's trip. I figure we'd stop up there for a couple of minutes to see this old rancher I used to work for that's retired now."

Wetmore didn't need to consult a map. He could envision

the great loop around the Front Range. It wasn't like city
driving: basically, there's one way in and one way out, the
same as it had been since the trails were blazed and the
passes first forged. But Bob, with his brow furrowed, had
spread his map out on the table and was trying to trace
the route with a pencil. He had Wetmore go over it again,
slowly, with estimations of when they would arrive where.
He jotted the information down in a notebook, into which
he finally tucked the map. About 350 miles all told.

"How about you driving?" Bob suggested. "I'll navigate.
That way we won't get lost."

Wetmore shrugged. He didn't mind driving. "It's fine
with me," he said. "That way you'll be able to appreciate
the scenery better, too, Bob. I tell you, you ain't seen the
like of it."

They set off early on Monday with Wetmore behind the
wheel of the orange Volkswagen and Bob alert with his
map and his notebook. They weren't a half-hour out of
Denver on Interstate 87 North before Bob began looking
for landmarks. When he found one, he'd tick it off on his
list.

It was a spectacular day, crisp and fragrant. As they
drove north, the terrain quickly changed from the hamburger joints and car lots on the edge of the city to alpine
meadows dotted with snowberry shrubs curling into the
foothills. Neither man spoke much as the little car climbed
higher.

Bob watched carefully for the turn onto Route 14 just
past Fort Collins. Now the ascent began in earnest. Wetmore was pleased to find that the Volkswagen didn't falter
badly on the ascent as they drove west into the Rockies.
Wetmore could never drive into this country without thinking of early settlers and pioneers who had to hack and bull
their way across these mountains, inching up the crests
of the massive rocks week by week, always to turn another
bend and suddenly behold a vista of supernal beauty that

took your breath away with its visual force, its staggering
assertion of the obstructions that lay ahead, as far as the
eye could see across snow-crusted peaks and icy glacial
summits hoving into a sky that no longer held the assurance
of horizons.

Wetmore parked the car a little off the two-lane highway
just past the Cameron Pass, at ten thousand feet. He shut
the engine off and got out, walking to the side of the road,
where he stood alone for a while, with his arms folded
across his chest and the cold wind tousling his thin white
hair. He was a tiny figure on the edge of a precipice over
a world where waterfalls plunged unheard into canyons
far below, down past the treelines where the spruce and
fir give way to the ponderosa that cover the troughs of the
great granite seaswells of the Continental Divide, where
the courses of rivers are determined, east across the plains
to the Mississippi, west to the Colorado.

Wetmore didn't understand why his companion hadn't
got out to take it in. Bob said it was too cold to get out of
the car. When he walked back to the Volkswagen, Wetmore was surprised and a little disappointed to find Bob
huddled in the passenger seat with the engine on and the
heater running, studying his map with a frown.

"We'd better get going," Bob said.

As they drove on, Wetmore noticed with some annoyance
that Bob's attention was riveted on the map. When he did
look outside, it was to confirm certain landmarks—Bald
Mountain prominent to the north just a thousand feet
above the pass, and Hagues Peak and Mummy Mountain
together at a greater altitude to the south, Richthofen
looming ahead at thirteen thousand feet—as if they were
service stations and traffic lights turning up on a set of
directions someone had drawn up for an address on the
other side of town.

After a while, as the road descended from the highest
elevations, Bob seemed to relax. He looked idly out the

window, watching for road signs giving the distance to Walden, the little ranch town up at the fork of the Michigan and Illinois creeks that was their destination. It wasn't far from the Wyoming border.

"Anybody who's ever been up there and can't get just a little bit shook up is dead," Wetmore muttered peevishly as the rugged high elevations give way to scraggly meadows where the occasional knot of livestock could be seen grazing. Bob didn't say anything.

So Wetmore laughed. "That is, of course, till you feed cows seven days a week in them blizzards, thirty-five degrees below zero," he said. "You got to harness up four work horses, two of them broncs. Take your saddle horse along and he's disgusted, but you need him just in case something happens—you got a way to get back, see. He'll take you back if you get lost. Then it ain't beautiful, of course. There ain't a fucking thing beautiful about it then."

But Bob remained intent on the road signs. A little way up the highway, he saw the one he wanted.

"You go right at this stop sign up ahead," he told Wetmore.

Wetmore knew the way. He had spent a good part of his middle age and beyond here around Walden, winter and summer. He turned right and drove along a dusty two-lane road that led to the ranch that he had considered his headquarters in the years before he came down to Denver. It was early in the afternoon.

"I know this place pretty good," Wetmore told Bob. "This fellow here, Howard, that had backed me in business had a private cow horse, which was named Tony, a damned good cow horse, all business, which was broke out by an old drunk down by Granby, and Howard had later bought him. He had me in to feed him. This horse wouldn't ever let nobody ride him but Howard or me. Me and Tony hit it off."

"Tony who?" Bob asked. "I thought we were going to stop in to see someone named Howard."

"We are. Howard is this rancher," Wetmore said with some consternation. "Tony is the horse that's probably still kept here."

Wetmore made another turn on a road that ran past the outbuildings of the ranch, which appeared deserted. "Over there's the old bunkhouse," he pointed out. "Up ahead is the barns. Over here's the shed. There'll be a wood gate up ahead, just past those trees, by the pasture."

They parked in front of the gate. Both men got out and walked to the fence. Wetmore squinted across the pasture and smiled broadly when he spotted the big red bay dozing with four other horses in a shady dell. He made a little clucking noise. Shaking out its mane, the old bay looked toward the noise, a good 250 feet away. The horse stirred itself and trotted quickly up the pasture, then pulled up short about twenty feet from the two men to take visual measure of the familiar sound with a sidewise look. Wetmore made the noise again. The bay tossed its head and whinnied, and sauntered right up to him.

The cowboy was immensely pleased. "Tony, you miserable old son of a bitch," he cackled, rubbing the bay's face. He looked at Bob's impassive expression and said, "This here is Tony."

Almost as if he was remembering his manners, Bob put out his palm tentatively toward the horse's head, as if to pat it, but then quickly withdrew it, like a child afraid of having to wash its hand in disgust because an animal licked it.

The bay, of course, could have cared less. The horse turned, put up its head and trotted off down the meadow to the shade.

They spent only a few minutes with Wetmore's rancher friend before Bob suggested it was getting late and there was a long way to go. He remained subdued, and seemed chilled despite the bright afternoon sun, even when they stopped for a late afternoon lunch down in Granby.

"I saw that," Bob said over lunch, in a tone that seemed to carry a hint of accusation.

"You seen what?" Wetmore asked as he munched his sandwich.

"The way that horse came to you. That horse knew who you were."

Wetmore made a pained face. "Well of course the god-damn horse knew me! Jesus Christ, a horse ain't like a cow, for Christ's sake."

Bob flinched a little, as he always did when directly confronted with profanity. But he didn't mention the horse again, and he fell into a long silence back in the car.

Wetmore didn't feel like talking either on the long, winding drive south from Granby along Route 40. He had supposed Bob would enjoy the trip—for all he knew, Bob *had* enjoyed it—but by the time they turned onto Interstate 70 for the last leg eastward, back to Denver, it was nightfall. As they pressed on toward the lights of the city, Wetmore decided that Bob Clark was a man he no longer trusted. He didn't seem to have an inner core. "The man was hollow," Wetmore said. From that day onward, Wetmore would remain friendly, but he would have very little more to do with Bob Clark.

Wetmore tried to explain it years later: "You develop a sense of self-preservation living in them hobo jungles, but that's a different thing. I can't say that I got any bad signals from Bob Clark—as a rule, the signals were neutral. But toward the end, especially him not showing any animation up there in them mountains, except some weird kind of suspicion, well, I just didn't care to be around him any longer."

Familiar patterns began to emerge. On their way to work, Gary noticed that Bob seemed to be talking more frequently about his training as an accountant. Before long, Gary, who was extremely proud of his perception in having chosen Bob as his protégé, came to realize that this full-blown natural in the restaurant business was in fact pining for his own true vocation: Accounting. Accounting! The idea was heartbreaking to Gary.

But since the chef was more friend than boss, he understood and acquiesced. A restaurant calling had its joys and remunerations; it was creative; at a certain level, it was certainly a craft, and at its highest peak, some had even claimed for it the status of a minor art. But it did have two very persuasive drawbacks.

One was those awful hours. For two years after graduating from the all-night shift at the Holiday Inn, Bob had worked a split day shift—half of it during the lunch rush and the other half for the dinner period. In between there was little to do but read and wait to begin work again, or dabble with his numbers.

"He'd take a couple of hours off in the afternoon," Gary recalled. "Well, when you're out in the middle of nowhere with no place to go, you'd read or whatever. Bob had a big pad of paper—it must have been twenty-four inches by thirty inches or so, one of those accounting pads. He began developing a system for playing roulette. I have never in my life seen such a conglomeration of numbers."

And worse than a split shift, spending your time off dreaming up roulette combinations, was the work week itself. This was, after all, a business whose employees ate their meals, by definition, when no one else especially wanted to eat. The allure of holidays is lost on those who toil in restaurants; when normal people relaxed, you only worked harder, you worked like a whipped cur at times, you damned well made hay while the New Year's, Mother's Day, Easter, Memorial Day, Fourth of July, Labor Day, Thanksgiving, and Christmas suns shone.

And the other drawback was the intrinsic instability of

a business in which today's trendy new restaurant can very easily become tomorrow's arson investigation.

Gary had sensed that Bob would say no late in 1977 when he told him he had received a better job offer at a country club in Golden and asked him to come along. Accounting, Gary had come to realize, "was just in his personality, which was very thorough, very exact. I realized that his unbelievable ability to work with figures, and the lack of stability in the food service industry, was leading him directly back into accounting, where the hours were more stable, where you weren't looking at working every Saturday and Sunday."

As it turned out, this had become a major consideration for reasons that had nothing to do with Bob's personality. For Bob had begun courting. In the spring of 1977, for only the second time in his life, the man had fallen in love.

Delores H. Miller was a tall, attractive woman in her mid-thirties, recently divorced from a military man. A shy, religious person, she had recently taken a job in the warehouse of the base exchange at Fitzsimmons Army Medical Center in Aurora, just across the Adams County line east of Denver.

They met at a singles social sponsored by area Lutheran churches. It was not a whirlwind romance. Delores would tell friends she barely recalled anything Bob had said during their first conversations. Shy people have a way of identifying each other and gravitating together in social events, and she and Bob did just that. Soon the encounters became regular. Before long, Delores had even prevailed upon Bob to learn how to square dance. He was embarrassed and clumsy at first, and while no one would ever accuse Bob Clark of being a natural dancer, he did develop some poise and with it some enthusiasm. In an informal atmosphere, Bob's coat and tie had always stood out. But with Delores, Bob started showing up in shirts open at the neck. He even bought a pair of jeans.

From the start of their relationship, Delores was attracted by Bob's gentle nature. She decided that he was obviously a man of good character. He wasn't bad looking. While she wasn't prepared to consider marriage again, not by a long shot, and not to a forty-six-year-old widower (Bob had shaved six years off John List's age) who didn't seem to have particularly promising career prospects, Delores kept seeing Bob, who was very persistent and friendly, and in time Delores's friends simply regarded them as one of those couples whose names would usually be uttered together: Delores and Bob.

"He was always sweet to her, it was like he was almost too sweet," one of those friends said. "He would practically trip over himself trying to open the door for her. She seemed to like being with him, but it was obvious he was in a bigger hurry to have a serious relationship than she was. After her divorce, she wanted a little breathing space."

Because she sensed the aura of tragedy around it, Delores didn't ask a lot of questions about Bob's background, and she didn't press the few she did ask, once she had his brief explanation.

"What he told me was, his wife had died of cancer, and she was a very sickly lady," Delores said in 1989. She never was shown, nor did she ask to see, photos of Bob's first wife.

Gary, who maintained his close friendship, first saw Bob and Delores together in the late 1970s, well after they began dating regularly. Then recently divorced, Gary had invited them to join him for dinner at the Mount Vernon Country Club in Golden.

"They weren't members, but I'd made arrangements to get them into the club to have dinner," he said. "We were having a buffet. He had talked about her for quite a while before then, but this was the first time I met her."

He knew right away that Bob was deeply in love. "I had

never seen a man pay so much attention to a woman," Gary said. "It beats what you read about chivalry and everything else. There was a genuine feeling that he was concerned about everything she did, every single little thing she said.

"Later on, we went out for dinner quite often, and it was always clear that Bob's absolutely first order of concern was Delores's well-being."

In the autumn of their first year together, Bob invited Delores for a drive into the mountains. They drove into the high country, to a side road, just a gravel driveway, off Route 40 as it curls south of Sawmill Gulch into sleepy Hot Sulphur Springs. At the end of this road was a general store with two battered gas pumps out front. The store's merchandise ran heavily toward dry goods, clothing for the most part, some of it practical, such as parkas and gloves, some of it frivolous, sweaters and T-shirts for the tourists. But the ranks of tourists who were just passing by had thinned over the years after the opening of Interstate 70, and the general store had fallen on hard times.

Bob Clark and Bob Wetmore had stopped at the same place a year earlier on their own drive into the mountains, for a cold soda before heading into Granby for lunch. Wetmore hadn't realized it then, in his annoyance over his friend's imperviousness to beauty, but Bob had made firm note of at least one impression on that trip: the general store was for sale.

In the early glow of courtship, when so much seems possible to accomplish together, he had come back, with Delores beside him, to look at that store and consider a future as its proprietor. While Bob had almost none, Delores had some money. But it turned out to be only about half of what was required for the down payment on the store, $28,000. Like most pipe dreams, it had been a foolish one. Bob turned back onto the road for Denver, where the safe path would lead into accounting.

Once the fleeting fantasy of being a shopkeeper, as his father had been, was put in its place, Bob was prodded by Delores to move more decisively to regain a foothold in his profession. She strongly approved of his decision to turn down Gary's offer to work at another country club. Though Bob would work part-time for Gary on occasion, making extra money as a prep cook, and take a temporary job as a short-order cook in the tea room of Denver Dry Goods, a department store, it was apparent that Bob was determined to reestablish his career, even if he, an M.B.A. and a former bank vice president, had to start at the bottom.

With Delores's encouragement, Bob enrolled for training courses in income-tax preparation sponsored by H&R Block, the national tax service company. At the same time, he began scouring the want ads. The opportunities were there. Even after the early tremors in the oil business in the middle 1970s, Denver was a city with a viable economy, the center of an area where high-technology manufacturing plants had been drawn by an educated workforce, access to great recreation, and a dearth of labor unions. It was also the center for banking and real estate development for a megalopolis that had sprawled over old frontier towns and now encompassed the apron of the entire front range of the Rockies from Pike's Peak to the Wyoming border.

Delores didn't press Bob much, but she was curious as to why such a well-educated, sober man of obvious ability would have been working in a kitchen for so long.

Bob's explanation made sense. She said he told her he needed the mindless routine of kitchen work "to rest from accounting, to get his life back together because of his wife's illness."

As he looked for a new job, he moved once more, from Columbine Street to an apartment in Wheatridge, an area where there was a lot of new development and new businesses as the suburbs pressed out to Golden.

Finally, late in 1977, Bob was back in the accounting

business. It wasn't an impressive start, not as Ernst &
Ernst had been in Detroit. With new apartments and new
offices going up everywhere, companies such as cabinet
dealers and carpet wholesalers were doing brisk business.
One of them, a firm called Roberto Carpeting, needed
someone to keep its bills in order.

Bob didn't even need a résumé. He had known not to
overreach as he got back into accounting. In fact, he seems
to have gone to some lengths to impress his new employers
with his very lack of status. In his job interview at Roberto
Carpeting, he made no claims to being anything other than
a man with decent accounting credentials who seemed to
have had his own reasons for spending the past five years
of his life working in a kitchen. The employee whose talent
Gary Morrison had so admired, who could efficiently manage a kitchen, run a buffet, make the customers feel as if
they had been royally welcomed, didn't seem to present
himself at Roberto, where his new employers saw only an
apparently decent, well-spoken, and neatly dressed man
who needed a job. He seemed eager to please, and he didn't
have a lot of demands.

"The job didn't pay a hell of a lot," said one former
coworker. "All it was, basically, was making sure the bill-
ings stayed straight. I barely noticed the guy, except that
he seemed to always be watching. You had the impression
he wanted to know where everybody was all the time.
Other than that, the guy's a blank. People come and go,
some of them you hardly notice."

Bob stayed for two years. As usual, he impressed some
coworkers with his good nature, his punctiliousness, his
careful attention to grooming, but little else. The only thing
that caused him to stand out in the minds of several other
coworkers years later was this:

Bob ate lunch at precisely the same time every day, and
almost always in the same manner. He would rise from

his desk, pick up the cassette player he kept on it during working hours, and take it with his bagged lunch out to his orange Volkswagen in the parking lot. There he would put a classical music tape cassette into his player, turn the volume up high, and eat his sandwich and fruit with the windows rolled up, summer and winter, lost in thought.

In September 1978, about a year after he started work at the carpet wholesaler, Bob moved to another apartment, Brentwood on the Park, in Aurora, close to where Delores lived. He would stay there for seven years, paying rent of $175 a month initially and about $300 when he left.

During the time he worked at Roberto, he also did some part-time work at income tax time, both for an H&R Block branch office and on his own, at home, thanks to a small network of friends from the restaurant business who brought their tax forms to him.

In October of 1979, two years after he had reemerged as an accountant, Bob found a better job as office manager at All Packaging Company, a Denver firm that made supermarket wrapping and packages. This job did require a résumé, which Bob managed to produce. It correctly listed his current employment at Roberto Carpeting, and his academic background. From 1972 to 1977, it said, he had worked for R. C. Miller & Co., a firm in Wheatridge, Colorado.

There wasn't any incentive to check the résumé beyond the current employer. If anyone had, it would have been learned that no firm named R. C. Miller & Co. existed in Wheatridge during those years. R. C. were, of course, the initials of Robert Clark, and Miller was Delores's last name.

Delores, who didn't know about Bob's deception on the résumé, was impressed by his steady progress once he decided to throw himself back into accounting full time. Not only that, but the man was no shirker. He had taken courses. When the hours were available, he worked nights and Saturdays. He was a respected man at church. Increasingly, Bob Clark was beginning to look like a solid marriage prospect.

At All Packaging, where his starting pay was $300 a week, he made only a slightly deeper impression than he had at the carpet wholesaler. He had a tiny office, and several coworkers remembered years later that it seemed oddly devoid of personal effects, though no one really remarked upon it at the time. There were no photographs. On his desk, the only item not related to the business of All Packaging was his tape deck, which he kept murmuring at low volume during the work day. As he had at Roberto, he would take it to his car at lunchtime and eat listening to classical music.

When given half a chance, he was relaxed enough now to talk freely about his religion.

"If you gave him an opening, he'd bore you to the point of tears with talk about religion and church," one woman who knew him said. "You had to remember not to bring that subject up. Otherwise, he was just sort of there. No one really had a bad word to say about Bob, but no one really seemed to know him. You just got the impression that he was taking everything in, but who knows why? It was basically a very boring job. He seemed perfect for it."

Gary Morrison also noticed that Bob seemed content. Bob had always been a chess enthusiast, but he went at it with a newfound verve once he was back in his world of numbers and charts. Bob favored a strategy that allowed his opponent to become overly confident. "He would let me get in a couple of moves. Then he'd kill me," Gary said.

Friends who occasionally visited Bob's apartment, Gary among them, also noticed that he had begun acquiring

military strategy board games and playing them avidly with
anyone who could keep up.

Among his favorites were Civil War games, which could
be played at a basic and intermediate level. Other games
were terribly complex. One, called Third Reich, could take
eight hours or longer to complete. It was played on a complicated board the size of a wall map. It had over five
hundred counters representing the military forces of
twenty nations involved in European theater of World War
II. According to its manufacturer, the Avalon Hill Game
Company, a division of Monarch Avalon Incorporated, of
Baltimore, among the various features in the exhaustively
detailed game were strategies on "costs for offensive options, attrition, production, conquests, alliances, intervention, neutrality, breakthrough combat, exploitation,
airborne assaults, amphibious assaults, shore bombard-
ment, sea escort, air and naval bases, convoys, strategic
warfare." The company, which produces dozens of strategy
games for various skill levels, said it put this one "on every
hardcore gamer's list of best games."

It seems to have been Bob's favorite; entire Saturdays
were consumed playing it. He always took the side of the
Axis powers, with Nazi Germany in charge. When en-
grossed in the game, his very personality changed. His face
became blotchy and he brooked no interruption. By the
time the game ended, invariably with the triumph of the
Third Reich late in the day, he would be flushed and
sweating. Only one friend, a business associate in Denver,
had the skill, the time, or the inclination to spend more
than one session at Third Reich with Bob. When this man
moved East, they continued to play by mail.

Bob had begun to acquire his board games when he
worked at the Pinery, Bob Wetmore said. "He'd talk about
the strategy. That was part of his psyche, wasn't it? You'd
see him playing that game, all emotionless at first. Then

you'd realize this was one cold, calculating son of a bitch,"
he said.

Meanwhile, Bob and Delores began seriously envisioning
a future together. He wanted to get married, friends saw.
But Delores resisted, saying she wasn't ready for marriage
yet.

Nevertheless, they were laying plans. In 1981, on St.
Patrick's Day, the two jointly purchased a two-bedroom
condominium in a garden apartment complex on Peoria
Street in Montbello, a part of Denver just east of Stapleton
International Airport. The price was $26,900.

Delores moved in by herself. Bob continued to live in
his apartment, from where he had begun trying to establish
his own business as an accounting and tax consultant. To
friends, he began complaining that Denver's economy was
souring and that going into business for himself, his dream,
was proving more difficult than he had believed. Other
than his feet, it was the first time friends in Denver recall
Bob really complaining about anything.

Bob worked hard to make his own business into something he could do full time, but the economic tide had
turned strongly against him in the 1980s. At one point,
sensing opportunity in Wheatridge, the suburb he knew
well and a place where the newly unleashed savings-and-
loan industry was lending money copiously for the building
of new strip malls, office centers, and apartments, Bob dug
into his small savings and invested several thousand dollars
in the purchase of a franchise for the direct-mail distri-
bution of advertising coupons.

His territory, north of Interstate 70 where the suburban
sprawl had begun to push right up onto the curve of North
Table Mountain, certainly looked promising. New growth,
new shops, new people coming in, lured by proximity to
the interstate and cheap rents. But it didn't have any vi-
tality beneath the surface. Many of the new businesses,

which had been built with loans from brand-new banking institutions that hadn't exercised the caution that had once prevailed in the savings-and-loan business, didn't quite get off the ground. The bank loans were easy—the bill for that tax-supported gold rush wouldn't come due for many years. The physical facilities had sprung up, one after the other. But the demand didn't seem to be so strong for what these businesses were selling. There seemed to be too much business and not enough patronage.

"In his franchise area, there would be a dry cleaners, for example; restaurants, service stations, other shops. You'd get your percentages off when you brought in one of the coupons they issued," Gary explained. "Bob was good at running the franchise, except the economy and the area that was his franchise made it impossible to come out of it with profit.

"The businessmen would tell him, 'I can't pay you this month, but here's my card. Come in with your wife for a free dinner,' and 'I can't pay you this month, but bring your suit in, we'll clean it for you.'"

Bob lost what little savings he had in the failed venture.

Yet, as had been the pattern before, he plunged on as the red ink deepened. He turned his attention to his consulting service, Robert Clark Associates. One former neighbor recalled Bob proudly showing him his business card, but conceding that the business so far didn't have more than a few regular customers like Gary Morrison, who came to Bob for tax work and occasional small jobs like reconciling bank statements.

He was successful in his courting of Delores, however. In the summer of 1985, Delores agreed at last to marry him.

Chapter Eleven

OUT BY THE DENVER AIRPORT, WHERE WIDE RUNWAYS slash through fields that only fifteen years ago were thick with weeds, out in the clutter of new condominium complexes and strip shopping malls, Wanda Flanery was paying attention, as usual, to the nuances of life around her. Nice people had started to move out lately, and a rougher breed of tenant was arriving. Renters, not buyers. Whereas she had once seen vans with the names of well-known moving and storage companies emblazoned on them, now she saw people who hauled their belongings in pickups or rented trailers, people with mattresses strapped to the roofs of their cars and loud radios blasting.

So Wanda was very concerned when she noticed cardboard moving boxes stacked up in the adjacent backyard of her neighbor, Delores Miller, one Saturday late in the summer of 1985.

She hurried outside and found, to her relief, that Delores was bringing boxes in, not taking boxes out. A tall, clumsy man with a red face beneath his receding hairline was with her, sweating under the burden of a cumbersome carton that had knocked his eyeglasses askew. Wanda had never seen the man before, though Delores was such a close friend that she thought of her almost as a surrogate daughter. The couple seemed to be trying not to attract attention as they lugged boxes from the back seat and trunk of Delores's car in the parking lot.

Curious, Wanda went out back when the man was at the car. She gave a short hiss across the fence to get Delores's attention.

"Hey, what's going on?" the older woman asked when Delores looked up.

"Oh," Delores said, blushing. "That's Mr. Robert Clark. We're going to get married in a few months. We're just moving some of Bob's things in."

That Delores even had a boyfriend was a surprise to Wanda, a bright-eyed and normally cheerful woman in her early sixties who prided herself—these days, as a matter of safety and prudence—on not missing much of what was going on around her. In their many conversations together, about work, family, money, weather, and whatever, Delores had never mentioned a Bob, let alone a Bob she was about to marry.

Later, after being formally introduced when the boxes all were unloaded, Wanda realized that Delores had been more concerned about her thinking that Bob was moving in before the wedding, which he was not, than that it might seem odd that she would never have mentioned to a good friend the fact that she was seriously contemplating marriage in the first place.

The wedding was set for the Saturday before Thanksgiving. As the date approached, it occurred to Wanda, who had seen her own daughter married and who loved the trappings of weddings, that Delores seemed more apprehensive than joyful. "Bob wanted to get married something awful, but Delores, you could tell she wasn't as sure," Wanda said. "She had her qualms."

On several occasions, Delores sought assurance from Wanda that marrying Bob was a good idea.

"Well, you know him, honey, I don't," Wanda told her gently. She was uneasy about getting involved in such a situation. She liked Bob well enough, but who could say, except the person who presumably wished to spend the rest of her life with him? "It's up to you," Wanda advised her. "You have to decide for yourself."

"Well, I just don't know," Delores said on one occasion. "What I'd really like to do is run, just get away from it all."

As the wedding date approached, though, Bob became even more affectionate. He always had a bouquet of flowers in his hands when he showed up. Finally, Delores's misgivings gave way to an excitement that was infectious to Wanda, who was thrilled to be taking part once more in the happy preparations for the wedding of someone she loved.

Delores chirped happily that her entire family would be at the wedding, which was to take place back East. Together, the two women went shopping to choose the trousseau, a beige gown with delicate lace and a champagne-colored trailer. The high heels also were beige.

Wanda, whose husband was disabled and confined to bed, cited the prohibitively expensive air fare as the reason she couldn't accept the invitation to the wedding. But she saw Delores and Bob off before their flight.

On November 23, 1985, Delores and Bob were married in a Lutheran church in Reistertown, Maryland, where Delores's mother and several other relatives lived. Only one member of the wedding party could have known at the time that a mere twenty miles away, in another Lutheran church in Baltimore thirty-four years earlier, John and Helen List had exchanged their wedding vows.

After a week-long wedding trip, Bob moved in with Delores. One of the first things Bob did next was to transfer his church enrollment from St. Paul's, where he would be much missed by the pastor and other elders and where he was saddened to have to relinquish his proud post as treasurer, to Delores's parish, St. Mark's Lutheran Church in Aurora.

At St. Mark's, Delores already was a well-liked Bible

class teacher. Enthusiastically, Bob decided to plunge into his new parish life, volunteering to teach a Sunday school class for adolescents. But his skills as a catechistic taskmaster weren't appreciated in Denver. Within a short time, his Sunday school students were dropping out and complaining to their parents. The new teacher was too strict, drilling them in their lessons and insisting on disciplined attention to every detail. He was a tyrant. It was done quietly to save embarrassment, but Bob's new career as a Sunday school teacher came to an end almost as soon as it started.

This failure was soon followed by another. By the time he married Delores, Bob had been promoted to comptroller at All Packaging, where he was now earning $490 a week.

But in April 1986, five months after the wedding, his job at All Packaging also came to an end. Bob was fired.

As usual, no one really had a bad word to say about him. It was simply that he had failed to . . . keep up, company officials would say later. The business world had evolved. Creative responses to new competition required new ways of thinking, of using computer technology and market information as a weapon, not as merely a tool. "Marketplace" was the buzzword, sometimes preceded by the word "global." The structure of the marketplace was changing, even bewildered small businessmen such as the producers of meat wrappers were being told in a flock of avidly read national business publications that were sounding the alarm. No one was quite sure what the new way was, exactly. But as the eighties reached critical mass, people saw clearly that the old way was out. It was a shame to lose a decent man like Bob Clark. But Bob, Bob was old way in spades.

"Bob's job grew, but he didn't," is how his boss, Robert Bassler, a vice president, explained it.

Again, the rules had changed in the middle of the game. Bob Clark walked off the field in silent defeat.

Several years later, when All Packaging officials went to the files out of curiosity to examine Bob Clark's records, they found his folder empty.

Delores had been very proud of Bob's promotion to a job with an important title. Some friends said it was the deciding factor that caused her to agree to marry him in the first place. Neither of the newlyweds had an inkling that he would be thrown out of work like that, days short of his fifty-fifth birthday, just at a time when the man was starting to look like a winner again.

Delores was unhappy not only at the misfortune that had befallen a man she loved, but at the unfair strain it placed on a wife, financially and even socially, who has to go off to work each morning, to a job she loathes, while her spouse stays home and "does the cooking," as she contemptuously put it to a friend.

Not that Bob was sitting around watching television all day. True to form, he threw himself feverishly into the task of finding a new job. Each morning, he would get up with Delores. Just as she dressed in her work clothes, so did he. Attired in a suit or in neatly pressed slacks and a sports coat, with his tie in place and his shoes shined, he sat at the kitchen table and pored over the want ads. He wrote. He would call. Rebuffed again and again, he dusted himself off and trooped to the next interview for a low-paying accounting job.

But Denver's economy was in trouble. Employers weren't so eager anymore to hire just any competent person who walked in the door with a good attitude. They wouldn't say so, of course, but a man in his late fifties was not the most alluring prospect anyway. There was a litany of unspoken prejudices against such an applicant. "Unflexible" and "demanding" were among them, even before the applicant sat down for an interview. Likely to be a drain on the already strained health benefits was another. Many people would give up after a few months of rejection. Bob kept at it, day after day.

Now, with Bob at home so much next door, Wanda got to know him better. She felt sorry for him when she saw him in his best suit, with that look of goofy determination on his face, headed off for another job interview. He never went out on an interview without looking "immaculate," she noted.

"How'd it go today, Bob?" she would ask sympathetically when he got home after being turned down for another job that, thirty years earlier, he would have been insulted even to have been offered.

"Oh, you know. It won't be too long," he would say and crack that mirthless grin.

All day long, even when he was cooking dinner or, as she once was surprised to see, sitting in the kitchen playing checkers alone, Bob would keep on his tie and coat.

When they spoke "I noticed that I would be the one doing most of the talking," Wanda said. "I started to like him real well during that time, the poor guy. He was really trying to succeed. I tried to make him laugh and things, and sometimes he would seem to, but it was hard to say because he was so awfully quiet, too quiet, really, I see now. It was obvious that no one was really close to him."

It was on one of these chats that Wanda picked up her first indication that there might be a darker layer beneath that cordial but opaque exterior. From the first day they had met, she suspected that Bob was older than he claimed to be. Since he had recently celebrated a birthday, she was bold enough to try to pin him down.

"How old did you say you were on your birthday?" she asked.

"Why, fifty-five. Why?" Bob said, raising his eyebrows and tilting his head in that way he had.

"Oh," Wanda replied, her face full of Irish good humor. "Well, you sure don't look fifty-five, Bob."

Bob seemed to take this as a compliment, but that wasn't how Wanda meant it. She meant he looked five or six years older than that, and she thought it very odd that an ordinary man not connected with show business or some similar field would fib about his age.

This was one noticeably tinny echo Wanda got back from Bob from those normal social soundings people send out in the process of evaluating acquaintances. But over time, as Bob and Delores settled into the routine of married life next door, there were others. While Wanda needed little prompting to discuss her grandchildren, whose photographs she kept atop her television, or to talk about growing up in Kansas City, or any of those unremarkable things that make up a normal life, Bob didn't seem to have a past that extended back much before meeting Delores. In fact, he was unnerved and even outright evasive when asked conversational questions about any aspects of his life other than Delores.

"Were you ever married before?" Wanda asked him once during a friendly chat over the waist-high fence that separated their little back patios.

He stiffened. "My first wife died," he replied. "She was very ill." He looked her right in the eye. "It was very tragic."

"I'm awful sorry, Bob. No children?"

"No children," he said, turning away from her with a quick, jerky motion that positioned him for retreat back into his house.

She never brought up that subject again, and Bob never gave her any reason to devote any serious thought to it. Even though she considered Bob oddly rigid and controlled, a little courtesy and kindness went a long way with Wanda; Bob was courteous to her and obviously kind to Delores. The truth is, she was actually fond of the man. She knew she wouldn't ever have considered doing what Delores did, which was to marry him, but she liked him well enough.

As Bob floundered looking for a new job, he kept hoping that he might be able to establish his own business as a consultant. Robert Clark Associates was reborn, but every time Bob spent money on it, for supplies or postage, Wanda said the strain seemed to grow worse. "He would spend money right and left when he was working, and now he was still spending, and that riled Delores, who wasn't a spender," Wanda said. "He had typewriters, computers, you name it."

By the fall of 1986, with Bob still out of work and unemployment benefits exhausted, Delores's tolerance was reaching some limits, and she let Bob know it. "I'm sick and tired of this," she said loudly over the back fence one Saturday. Wanda noticed that Bob was sitting just inside with the door wide open, and could clearly hear his wife. "If he doesn't find a job pretty soon, I'm leaving him."

The tension showed in other ways. "Once, Delores bought him a new pair of pants for his job interviews, and he didn't especially like them. Bob was real particular about his clothes. And she said to him, right there in front of me: "Well, you don't look good in anything.""

Finally, Wanda decided her neighbors desperately needed to get out for a day to forget their troubles. In October, she suggested the three of them take a drive to a German October festival in a little mountain town not far away. She was delighted when they accepted, and happier still when they began making their usual elaborate plans for the outing. For a time, it was the old Delores and Bob, touching each others' hands, murmuring encouragement, acting like newlyweds.

"They seemed to be having a ball," Wanda said. "Bob meticulously, and I mean meticulously, planned every move. He was going to fry some chicken, this many pieces, exactly. She was going to cook this many potatoes. They were going to wear such and such clothes. We would leave exactly at such a time."

It was a glorious fall day, and Wanda had never seen Delores and Bob so at ease. At the festival, brass bands pumped out polkas and Bavarian marches. Beer flowed and frothed over mug handles, sauerkraut spilled from paper plates, mobs of people grew increasingly festive and friendly as the sunny afternoon wore on in the mile-high air. Bob bought Delores a big floppy hat, and she pulled the brim all the way down so that it looked like a bonnet. Two merry Lithuanians across the table who had been drinking all day informed her that since this was exactly how one would wear such a hat in Lithuania, she must then be Lithuanian. They insisted on speaking to her only in that language until she admitted it. Finally she did, though she was nothing of the sort. "We were in stitches," Wanda said. "On our way out, she even stopped to buy her mother the same kind of hat."

The laughter didn't last, of course. As 1987 arrived, nothing was improving. Bob had no job prospects, and Delores was hating her own job more than ever. And as is so often the case with misfortune, when it seemed things couldn't get any worse, they did.

The source of this trouble was the condominium. As the savings-and-loan industry began collapsing from its own cupidity, the house of cards it had constructed in the wild days of free lending also began tumbling down. Entire shopping malls, which never had any business being built in the first place, were deserted. Residents of condominium complexes like the Clarks opened the mail every few months to find a different, unfamiliar bank demanding the mortgage payment. Upkeep of the common property declined. Improvements weren't made. Equity began to disappear. Dreams of retirement in a pleasant community where responsible property owners puttered in well-tended small gardens, smiled at each other in the neat, shrub-lined communal areas, and adhered to the social contract had started to become nightmares.

The first sign of trouble was the official-looking papers that began appearing on the front doors of some of the neighbors who had moved away. "NOTICE OF FORE-CLOSURE," they declared in red letters. "BE IT SO KNOWN . . ." There were only a few at first, but within a couple of years a resident couldn't walk from apartment to car without passing a flurry of them, ragged and torn on the doors, snapping in the wind like warning pennants beside windows covered with sheets of plywood.

So much for equity. Then came the drug dealers and other troublesome characters, lured by cheap rents offered by banks anxious to generate revenue on foreclosed mort-gages. The plastic trash bag was the moving container of choice for the new arrivals, people roaring up with those radios blasting. A siren couldn't have been sounding a more compelling alarm to the property owners who were holding on, like Wanda and the Clarks.

At the Clarks' apartment, classical music often played. But it wouldn't be blasting through the walls. Now there were times that the older tenants couldn't even think straight, with rock music thumping into their conscious-ness like war drums.

"Do you hear that?" Delores would moan when she came over for a cigarette after dinner some nights. "Do you hear that?"

One weekend afternoon, Delores spent hours searching for her dog, a little mutt that had managed to get out through the back gate. She found it dead. It hadn't been run over by a car. It had been beaten to death.

The next major trouble began in the winter of 1987. Wanda later laid the blame for it squarely on what she considered to be a bad but excusable habit: Every week, when she made her regular trip to the supermarket, she would buy several of those weekly newspapers—Wanda herself derided them as "those crazy ones with stories about Elvis working behind the counter of a 7-Eleven"—the so-called supermarket tabloids that clamor for attention at checkout counters with headlines trumpeting not only quirks of the behavior of celebrities, dead or alive, but miraculous weight-loss techniques, oddities of human physique, and, occasionally, unusual crime stories.

For a couple of dollars, and with more assurance of satisfaction than the purchase of a lottery ticket, Wanda would tote home several of these newspapers each week, scooping up the ones with the most outlandish headlines, for the good laugh that increasingly she had come to believe she deserved.

So it was that Bob's next-door neighbor, looking for nothing more than a chuckle or two on one such shopping day in February 1987, came to abrupt attention while she thumbed through the February 17 issue of a tabloid called the *Weekly World News*. She had come upon an article well inside the paper that indicated to her with compelling persuasiveness that Bob Clark bore a startling resemblance, in physical appearance, demeanor, and habits, to a notorious mass murderer who, the paper said, had been on the loose since 1971.

"The Perfect Crime," the headline read over a story that described the most confounding murder case police in New Jersey had worked on since the Lindbergh kidnapping.

Wanda proceeded to read the terrible account of John Emil List and that gruesome day in New Jersey in November 1971. John List, who had murdered his family, those women and those children, and then disappeared into thin air.

In point of fact, Wanda probably would have scanned this particular story just briefly and flipped through the pages to something less depressing if it were not for a remarkable coincidence. As she glanced up idly from the photograph of the wanted man that accompanied the story, she gazed out her back window and encountered an image on the patio that made her blink several times. It was only old Bob, fussing with the lid on his trash can out there. But to Wanda, it appeared to be John List himself.

Her eyes darted from Bob to the newspaper and back. She read the story all the way through.

"Oh my God," she said in amazement.

"Your God, what?" asked her daughter, a young woman named Eva Mitchell, who had taken Wanda shopping and was sitting on the couch watching television.

Wanda passed the newspaper to her, saying, "Look at this paper, Eva. Look at this story about this man who killed his family back East. This man looks just like Bob Clark, I swear it. It's Bob Clark."

Eva took the paper and pretended to read, but she was more interested in the game show. "That's crazy," she told her mother, who had gotten up to peer out the window for another look. But Bob had already gone back inside his house.

Eva dropped the paper onto Wanda's chair. "How can this man be any Bob Clark?" she said dismissively, returning her full attention to the television. "Don't go on being a busybody, now."

Wanda smiled, but her mind was racing. Being a busybody was exactly what she did best. With muggers lurking by the dumpsters after dark, busybody was fine with her.

Wanda read the article all the way through again, this time very carefully, as her initial incredulity gave way into a nagging sense that she might be required to do something more than just remark on it. If this is a coincidence, it's a whopper, she thought, evaluating the uncanny similarities. For starters, John List, the murderer, looked exactly like a younger version of Bob Clark. The description of

John List fit Bob like a glove: polite, formal, distant. That
could be a million other people, but the possibilities nar-
rowed fast: List, like Bob, was an overtly religious man, a
devout Lutheran who took active part in parish affairs and
even taught Sunday school. Wanda knew about Bob's recent fling at Sunday school. List was a pleasant, orderly
man who usually wore a coat and tie even on casual occasions, a man with a twitchy little grin that never seemed
to make it all the way to a smile.

Wanda shuddered when she read in the caption accom-
panying the FBI photo that John List had a mastoidectomy
scar that ran from the base of his right ear right down to
his shirt collar. Bob had exactly such a scar. It was an
ugly old thing. You couldn't miss it.

Furthermore, the ages seemed to dovetail, allowing for
Wanda's suspicion that Bob was a few years older than he
claimed.

Just before dinnertime that afternoon, when Eva left to
pick up her husband from work, Wanda was still silently
fretting over the newspaper article that lay in her lap, with
her cat now asleep on top of it. She didn't even turn on
the television news, as was her habit every night at six.

Around six-thirty, she heard Delores coming home next
door. "Should I tell Delores about this craziness?" Wanda
said in a high little singsong voice to the cat, which, un-
interested, took the opportunity to drop to the floor and
pad away. "Do you want this old lady to start trouble?"
she called sweetly after the animal.

Trouble was the last thing Wanda wanted. And who
would want to cause any more trouble for sweet, meek
Delores, who had enough already? Or even poor old Bob?
What right, Wanda considered, did she have to barge into
Delores's life with some goofy newspaper that seemed to
accuse Bob of being a mass murderer? Why make things
worse for anybody?

She sighed and read through the story one more time,

looking for signs to tell her she was being silly. She looked, but they weren't there. Wanda started to make a mental checklist with each clue that, uncanny physical resemblance aside, seemed to point right next door: The murderer was just over six feet tall, with horn-rimmed glasses, a receding hairline, brown eyes. Bob. Would be about sixty-one years old. That's how she figured Bob. With that long nasty scar behind his right ear. *Bob*. Deeply religious, Lutheran church. *Bob*. Sunday school teacher. *Bob*. Neat dresser. *Bob*. From Michigan. *Bob told her that!* Mirthless. *Bob*. Worked as an accountant. *Bob!* Went from job to job, spent beyond his means, seemed to have chronic money problems. *Bob! Bob! Bob!*

Wanda decided some things, such as the safety of someone she cared about deeply, were more important than friendship. She took the paper over and knocked on her neighbors' back door.

Delores opened it a crack, then unhooked the security chain when she saw who it was.

"Is Bob home?" Wanda asked furtively, glancing around when Delores invited her in.

"No, he's managed to find some night work at least, at H&R Block," Delores said. "It's income tax time, you know."

Wanda sat down at the table, wishing she could light up a cigarette. Because Bob had asthma and disapproved of cigarettes for health reasons, there was no smoking in the Clark apartment. When Delores felt like a smoke, she had to go over to Wanda's to sneak one.

"So what's new with you, Wanda?" Delores asked pleasantly.

"I want you to read something for me, honey," Wanda said. She pushed the newspaper, opened to the page with the article on John List, across the table.

"What's this?"

"Delores, just read this for me."

Delores fiddled with her glasses. With a thin, bewildered smile, she scanned the article, rushing through it for some indication of what Wanda was on about. Blinking, Delores looked up over her eyeglasses and asked, "What does it mean?"

Wanda took a deep breath. "Delores, honey. I'm sorry, honey, but isn't that Bob?" She tapped her finger on the picture of John List. "Your husband, Bob?"

Delores toyed with the edge of her glasses and read a little bit more. "Gosh, Wanda," she said in tone more quizzical than convinced.

"Read what he did," Wanda said.

Delores giggled, but read some more. "Oh my gosh," she muttered. "Isn't that something?"

Wanda wondered if she was getting through. "Delores," she said patiently, "I think this man is Bob. Bob Clark."

Now she had Delores's attention.

"Oh no, Wanda," she protested with a bit of indignation. But then she relaxed and spoke to Wanda as if addressing a child who had just reported seeing monsters in the dark. "This isn't Bob, Wanda," she said. "You know my Bob. He's a wonderful man. My Bob wouldn't even hurt a flea. How could you think this awful man is my Bob?"

Wanda felt her face redden, but she pressed on. "Delores, why don't you show this to Bob and see what he says? Just see, okay?"

"Well, I suppose I could, just for fun," Delores said. "That man does look a little bit like him, but so do a lot of people. He might even enjoy it." She made a face and said in a comic growl: "Mass-murderer Bob."

Both women began laughing. Wanda felt a little foolish, but she was relieved to know her friend didn't seem offended. Delores folded the paper back open to the front page, then creased it across the middle and lay it aside.

"Do you want some coffee?" she said, remembering her manners.

"Oh no, honey. You're just back from work. Let me get out of here and let you get your dinner. You're probably starved." At the door, Wanda made one last try. "Well, you keep that thing and show it to him," she suggested. "You are going to show it to Bob, then?"

"Sure."

"Okay," she said. "I didn't mean any offense. I just thought you would find it awful interesting."

"See you tomorrow?" Delores asked amiably.

She avoided Delores the next day, however. Now, after a fitful night's sleep, Wanda felt plain foolish, an old busybody running over half-cocked to her best friend's house to say her husband was a murderer.

Preposterous.

But what if it was true?

This thought leaped back into Wanda's mind the minute she laid eyes on Bob after church on Sunday. He was out back sweeping the last of autumn's leaves into a neat little mound on the patio. He was still in his church clothes. He caught her staring at him through the window and waved clumsily.

That night, Wanda made up an excuse to go over for matches and took Delores aside while Bob was watching 60 *Minutes* in the living room.

"Did you show it to him?" she asked, making a deliberate attempt to sound amused.

"What? That newspaper article?"

"Yes, did he see it?" Both women noticed they were whispering.

"Oh, that," Delores said, sounding unconcerned. "I threw it out, to tell you the truth. That man wasn't anything like Bob. It wasn't even worth showing him. I'm sorry—you didn't want it back, did you?"

Of course not, Wanda assured her. And she meant it. Without the evidence nagging at her in black and white, she had decided to dismiss the whole thing as a weird

coincidence, just the sort of thing you can expect to get,
paying attention to anything written in some ridiculous
newspaper that prints stories about space aliens in the
Pentagon and men having seven-pound babies.

In fact, Wanda would have been quite content never to
have to give the matter another moment's thought.

But as things would turn out, this would not be the
case.

Chapter Twelve

DURING INCOME TAX SEASON, BOB BROUGHT IN A LITTLE extra money again in the first quarter of 1987, but that trailed off, as usual, after the fifteenth of April.

At the same time, problems mounted at the condominium complex. Owners were complaining that basic maintenance, provided for in their agreement with the company that managed the property, was going undone. Upkeep deteriorated in the kind of self-fulfilling prophesy that causes some owners, convinced they'll never be able to recoup the price they paid, simply to walk away and let the bank have the property. Burglaries, unheard of when the Clarks had bought their place in 1981, became routine. Delores and Bob were distraught. They had begun to realize that, far from making a little profit on the place if they were to sell it, they would probably take a loss.

"All of a sudden, people were selling crack and everything here," Wanda Flanery said. "My children started begging me to get out, but what could I do?"

Twelve of the old-timers, including the Clarks, got together to withhold their mortgage payments until improvements were forthcoming. In response, the management company hired an attorney to begin foreclosure proceedings.

So one day in November, it was with vast relief that Bob opened the mail to find a favorable response back from an employment agency in Richmond, Virginia, that had used the opportunity of Denver's well-known economic troubles to take an ad in the local papers offering jobs at various Richmond firms. One of them was looking for a junior accountant.

Bob used some of the money saved in the mortgage strike to fly to Richmond for an interview. He was delighted to get the job at last. With income tax season coming up again, they wanted him to start right after the first of the year.

He said he'd be there. Delores would join him later.

At Christmas that year, there was at least a muted note of joy, as friends wished the Clarks well in the new life they were eagerly anticipating back East. Gary Morrison took the Clarks out to dinner just before Bob left, and bade farewell to a man he said he would always consider his friend.

Enthusiastic again at the prospect of another fresh beginning, Bob was especially pleased at the location. Richmond, the capital of the old Confederacy, had real allure for a history buff with a special interest in the Civil War. In the distant recesses of time, there were vaguely fond memories of a young lieutenant from the Midwest in 1950, wandering fascinated inside the old Southern White House of Jefferson Davis, staring in wonder at the Confederate flag that had snapped defiantly in the wind above the state capitol, marking the elegance of the Lost Cause from a point just below the U.S. flag itself.

And Richmond seemed vibrant, unlike Denver. The job didn't pay a lot—$25,000 to start—but the firm, Maddrea, Joyner, Kirkham & Woody, seemed to be prospering in an area of the country where the economy was still growing, in metropolitan Richmond, the very model of an area that had moved beyond unwise dependence on one industry, tobacco, and diversified into banking, transportation, and technology. In Richmond, Bob was told, you can still think of a bright future.

Delores agreed to stay in Denver to sort out the condominium problems, and also to make arrangements with the civil service for a job transfer to a military facility in the Richmond area, preferably the Defense General Supply Depot just across the James River in Chesterfield County, southwest of downtown Richmond. By the late spring or summer, Bob figured, he and Delores would be well ensconced in a new life far from smog-ridden Denver.

Delores knew she would miss her church friends in Denver, but she wasn't going to miss working at Fitzsimmons, where she wasn't certain which she despised more, the job itself or her supervisor. And good riddance to the condominium. Besides, Delores's mother and other relatives wouldn't be far away, in Maryland. In fact, her mother, who was turning eighty, had volunteered to come out when the time came, help her pack for the movers, and then drive across the country with her daughter in Delores's Toyota to provide company. Delores told friends she was actually looking forward to the adventure. Not the least of the enticements that lay at journey's end, of course, was having a spouse who would have a job again.

Before Bob left, Paul Miller, the employment agency supervisor who had placed him in the new job, contacted a local realtor, Betty Garter Lane, and explained the situation. Betty, an aggressive saleswoman who also took a special pride in her ability to ease transients into new surroundings—"poor little lost chicks," is what she called them—phoned Bob in Denver and was pleased to encounter a courtly gentleman who seemed to know what he wanted.

First, temporary lodging while he searched for a new home. No problem, Betty said. It was arranged for Bob to rent a room with kitchen privileges in the five-bedroom house of a friend, Wally Parsons, a Richmond-area business consultant who was eager to make new contacts and liked the idea of having an accountant on the premises, especially at income tax time.

From Denver, Bob wrote to Betty as soon as the initial arrangements were in place. "Thank you so much for your help in finding a suitable place to live when I arrive in Richmond," he said in a letter dated January 11, 1988. "Now I'm really looking forward to moving."

About a week later, entertaining the notion of a new beginning, with a future, at a firm that could one day be known as Maddrea, Joyner, Kircham, Woody & Clark, Bob loaded some boxes of books, clothes, and other possessions into the used 1981 Ford Escort he had bought to replace the orange Volkswagen when he still worked at All Packaging. Bob went over his road maps one last time, kissed his wife goodbye and, with a symphony playing on his tape deck, set off across the country on what would happen to be the last leg of his long odyssey.

Right away, Bob felt at home in Richmond. He had always liked the South anyway. His housemate, Wally, a big, smooth-mannered, chain-smoking fifty-year-old with a ready smile, decided that his new tenant was a man of taste and refinement with an appreciation for what Wally called "the finer things in life." Besides, Wally, a fellow history buff, soon realized that Bob was "the only man I ever met in Richmond who could give you a persuasive argument for the positions of either side in the War Between the States."

So impressed was Bob with the reception he received in Richmond that he wrote back to Delores the first night he was there, urging her to expedite the condominium matter and join him as soon as possible, whether or not she was able to arrange a job transfer to a military facility in the Richmond area.

Betty, a dark-haired woman in her fifties, was proud not

only of her business acumen, but also of her heritage as a certified, if somewhat disinherited, daughter of the old Richmond aristocracy. She had been a member of the crusty Richmond Club, the old-money country club, almost since birth, and she didn't hesitate to point out that the *current* initiation fee—she hadn't paid any such thing, of course, since she had been initiated as a little baby—was $25,000.

Betty resolved to do her utmost to help Bob and his wife settle comfortably and happily in Richmond.

But this was a resolve she would later come to regret.

She picked Bob up after work one night toward the end of February, a couple of weeks after he started his job at the accounting firm, to go on the first of what would be many house-hunting expeditions.

"So how do you like it?" Betty asked when he got into her car, a Cadillac Seville, in the parking lot outside the firm, which was located in a suburbanlike office complex across the street from a shopping mall.

"It's a wonderful car, Betty," Bob allowed, stroking the upholstery admiringly.

"Not the car. The job. How do you like the new job?"

"Oh. Oh, the job is fine. They seem like very fine people, intelligent people."

Betty had already wondered why an older man with apparently excellent credentials in his field—the agency had told her he had an M.B.A. and someone had said something about his being a certified public accountant—was starting work as some junior accountant at what she considered a poky little accounting firm. But she decided it was none of her business. Probably he just didn't care for the rat race at the better companies.

At first, as they cruised various sections of the city, Bob seemed eager to please and easy to accommodate. Betty decided that finding the perfect house would be a breeze.

She soon learned otherwise, as one expedition ended and another was set.

The notebook and camera he carried with him on their forays should have been the tip-off. As days stretched into weeks of unsuccessful hunting, Bob took pictures of houses and made copious notes about houses for sale in every section of the sprawling metropolis. On his lunch hour, he would take the photos to a one-hour photo lab in the shopping mall to have them developed. Then, at night, he would send photos of the viable prospects, along with his own notes, back to Delores for her opinion. The tedious process threatened to become a full-time pursuit, but Betty had made a commitment. She decided she would go "above and beyond the call of duty" to fulfill it.

It wasn't as if the Clarks had the financial wherewithal to be fussy. In fact, according to Bob, who became even more taciturn when the discussion came around to finances, there seemed to be only about $6,000 available immediately for a down payment, though he said he was managing to put aside some money from his salary, enough, probably, to cover closing costs when the time came.

Six thousand dollars and a fussy disposition limited one's options considerably, Betty knew. Figuring on the minimum ten percent down, that meant the Clarks were limited to the $60,000 range and below, assuming they could come up with the closing costs. This did not augur for the sort of commission that causes a real estate agent to start thinking of that week in the Caribbean, Betty knew.

Yet she pressed on cheerfully. Townhouses? No, that wouldn't do. He and Delores had had their fill of that in Denver. How about a detached ranch, out by the arsenal? Bob didn't like the looks of the neighborhood. And nothing too far out, either. Delores was very concerned about the commute. He himself didn't mind, of course. But Delores was strict about the amount of time he could spend on the road.

As they prowled the Richmond suburbs over the course of weeks, Betty learned that Bob's M.B.A. was from the University of Michigan. Without prompting, he volunteered the information that he had been married before, to a woman "who died of a brain tumor." There were no children. When his wife died after a long and tragic illness, he said, he went out to Denver to put his life back together.

"Bob was a nice, sweet, conservative gentleman to me," Betty said. "He was certainly all of those things." But, she added in a confidential tone, "He was strange? When he laughed, it was, like, strange? When he smiled, it was like his face would crack? He was, you might say, programmed? I couldn't quite put my finger on it."

Like so many people who would encounter Bob Clark, she tried to describe the misgivings she realized she had felt only in hindsight: "His voice was very deep, very controlled. When you talked to him on the telephone, it was like he was reading something from a script. You know how people have inflections in their voices, they go up, they go down? He didn't have that. It wasn't like he was an automaton or a robot, don't misunderstand me. But he just didn't have those inflections."

By the end of March, Betty decided she had exhausted all of the possibilities. Bob simply wasn't going to make a decision without Delores, she felt. But suddenly Delores was reported on her way. Bob said that plans had changed, Delores had quit her job at Fitzsimmons after being told there was no possibility of a transfer to a military facility near Richmond for the foreseeable future. Delores's mother had flown out to help with the final arrangements, and the two of them were even now driving across country for Richmond, with the furniture en route separately in a moving van. Bob was obviously eagerly awaiting the reunion.

When Delores got there, she moved into the room with

Bob at Wally's house. They put the furniture in storage at the Extra Attic mini-storage facility in the West End of Denver. Then they were ready to go house-hunting together.

For Betty, Delores's arrival brought encouraging news. Not only might a decision be easier to get now, but she learned there was actually more money available, bettering the odds of finding a suitable place. While Bob didn't have "a dime to his name, himself" Delores had some $14,000, in fact. While she wasn't willing to commit all of it to a down payment, some of it would be available.

It was then, however, that the matter of the condominium came to her attention for the first time. A mortgage company considering a loan will tend to raise its eyebrows at one from an applicant whose previous house is still a liability, with six months of past due payments on the mortgage. According to Robert Hatch, a lawyer who represented the condominium management in the foreclosure, Bob had also taken out a second mortgage on the Denver property.

As Betty saw it, the situation was a microcosm of one aspect of the savings-and-loan crisis: "They hadn't paid their mortgage payment on it since the previous October because there was some mixup; the mortgage company that had held the mortgage had gone out of business, and there was another bank, and it went bankrupt, and then some other bank bought out that bank; the place was going downhill, the builder hadn't done what he said was going to do. They withheld their condominium fees. Foreclosure proceedings began. They got a lawyer." The property also was now worth less, not more, than the principal on the mortgage loan. That was the way these things sometimes went. Who ever said life was fair? The buyer didn't always come out on top, especially with the lawyers lined up. "They lost," she said with a shrug.

Shortly after she got to Richmond, Delores wrote to

Wanda Flanery about the condominium, which, she said, "is going to rob us of everything we own."

It was the middle of May, after Delores and Bob came back from a Mother's Day visit to her mother, before the house-hunting resumed, this time with Delores. "If she saw something she liked, Bob would meet us after work and we'd go back," Betty said.

Betty noticed something mildly disagreeable on those occasions, with the three of them frustrated at the lack of success in finding a house: "Right in front of Bob," she recalled, "Delores kept saying what a nice home she and her first husband had, how she had hated to leave it. How she didn't know how long Bob would be able to keep this new job."

Given the problem with the condominium, Betty advised the Clarks that their best hope was to find a house with an assumable mortgage, a transaction that wouldn't require excessive scrutiny from an anxious new lender.

Luckily, such a listing arrived in Betty's office about a week later. It was a three-bedroom, two-bath house in a suburban subdivision she knew fairly well, Brandermill, a new community of homes set back on lots thick with oak and pine, and situated around a 1,700-acre lake below Midlothian. Brandermill was perfect for an older couple who, like Bob and Delores, didn't have children and wanted a secure environment. A $93 million extension of the Powhite Parkway had recently opened to link Brandermill to the commercial hubub of suburban Midlothian less than ten miles away. On the new, uncrowded parkway, it was only a thirty-minute drive, with a seventy-five-cent toll, to downtown Richmond. Brandermill's homes, and there were more than a thousand, in models with prices that ranged from $70,000 to more than $350,000, were all close to the lake. In its slick promotional brochure, illustrated with the smiling happy faces of men, women, and children of all ages (but only one apparent race, Caucasian), the community boasted an eighteen-hole golf course, twenty-four tennis courts, five swimming pools. Brandermill was subdivided into scores of neat, quiet residential "neighborhoods" tied together by loop roads that kept through traffic off the streets where the homes were set back in the trees. Half of Brandermill's residents, the community's statistics show, were newcomers to the Richmond area. So physically well executed was the development that it had garnered a citation as the "Best Planned Community in America" in *Better Homes & Gardens* magazine.

And the new listing on Betty's desk also was priced right. The blue-gray ranch home with a porch, at the end of a cul de sac called Sagewood Trace, was listed for $76,500, with an assumable mortgage because the owners had recently bought a house closer to the city and were anxious to sell.

Betty did some quick arithmetic. Perfect, she decided.

She was proud of herself for being able to find something so well suited for the Clarks. So Betty was flabbergasted when they drove down there and Delores and Bob turned their noses up at it. It was too far from his office, Bob thought. Delores had a problem with the highway tolls, which she thought were excessive. Neither of them seemed to like the house itself. They thought it was overpriced for such a modest place.

The sellers, Carolyn and Richard Merkel, wanted to move from Brandermill to a more convenient location on the West Side, where they had already closed on their new house. They thought the price they were selling their Brandermill house for was on the low side. But, Carolyn Merkel said, by the time they had seen the last of Bob Clark, they were ready to give him the house to get him out of their hair.

After several trips to Brandermill, and almost a month together in the rented room at Wally's house, Bob and Delores decided at last to go with the house in Brandermill.

Bob came by frequently, though, before the formal agreement of sale was signed. "He would walk around with a notebook, and stand there and read to me from a list of questions he'd prepared. Then he carefully write down my response," said Carolyn Merkel, a soft-spoken woman in her thirties who was mystified by Bob's attention to detail. But she overlooked what would have been infuriating in a more aggressive person because he was so diffident and polite, and he seemed so helpless at times.

Once Bob arrived with his camera to take pictures of the house from all angles, inside and out. On another occasion, he questioned her carefully about the neighbors, after seeing some visitors at a nearby house.

"He was very concerned about there being a lot of people in the neighborhood," which in fact is very quiet, Carolyn said. One afternoon, he sat in her living room making a list of each of the ten closest neighbors' names. In a subsequent encounter, it was clear to Carolyn that he had memorized all of those names.

"You can come with me to meet the neighbors," she suggested, trying to be helpful.

"Well, maybe," he said, but that was the last he mentioned the neighbors.

Finally, to Betty's immense relief, the Clarks offered $72,000 for the house, including the existing, assumable mortgage of $63,000. It was accepted.

Betty, aware that almost all of the money for the down payment was Delores's and not Bob's, suggested casually that perhaps the house might be put in Delores's name. Actually, she was acting less out of concern about Bob's credit rating, which didn't matter so much on an assumable mortgage, than for Delores's best interests, which she almost instinctively wished to protect. She was surprised when Bob showed not the slightest trace of hesitation about having the property in his wife's name. The agreement of sale was signed, and the Merkels thought they had seen the last of Bob's earnest, perpetually fretful face until the date of closing.

They were wrong. Bob came by more often than the mailman, it seemed, usually on some mission to make a slight amendment to the existing agreement of sale. Richard Merkel, a wiry man with a sense of humor, found that Bob was so unprepossessing that his initial annoyance was giving way to an amused curiosity about just what he would show up asking for next.

The shelf paper, Bob said sheepishly on the phone one day. Delores was insisting that the shelf paper inside the kitchen cabinets be included in the sale. Carolyn covered the phone and made a face to her husband. "Who in the world asks for the *shelf paper?*" she said with amazement.

The bug whacker, Bob said the very next day. The bug whacker on the porch. Fine, Carolyn said, after checking with Richard, who merely shrugged. The bug whacker was included.

"Thank you," said Bob, who never forgot his manners.

Two days passed without a call from Bob to the Merkels, who were under no legal obligation to amend anything in the sales contract. But it didn't last.

The trash cans? Bob enquired. Could the trash cans be included?

At first, Richard bristled at this triviality when Carolyn told him that night. But finally he agreed. The Merkels' three battered old trash cans would go along with the deal. Surely, that would be the end of it.

It wasn't. A few days before closing on the sale, when the phone rang at lunchtime, Carolyn guessed who was calling. Bob said they would need all of the warranty cards and instruction books for the kitchen and laundry appliances. Carolyn, an organized person, happened to have kept all of these in a file. She made a special trip to Bob's lawyer's office to drop them off in time for settlement.

But then it seemed the deal was off.

Delores called Carolyn the next day and said she had instructed the lawyer to cancel the purchase. Carolyn was virtually speechless and waiting for Richard to come home when the phone rang again. It was Bob, apologizing. "We'll go through with it," Bob said.

Delores had phoned Betty with the same information, however. "She said she wanted to get out of the contract," said Betty, who was now more concerned about her reputation than her commission. So Betty made the Clarks an offer: "I'll tell you what," she said. "If you want to sell that house in a year, I'll sell it for no commission. I'll write the ad for you—you pay for the ad, and you show the people around the house, but if you find somebody who wants to buy the house, I'll draw up the contract, take them by the hand, take them to the loan institution, follow them right through just as if there was a fee involved. I don't want any of my clients ever to say they were unhappy with me."

Bob said that would be fine.

Settlement was the following morning, and Betty used the occasion to reiterate her offer before witnesses.

The sale closed with no further hitch; and the Clarks took their furniture out of storage and moved down to Brandermill.

But Bob didn't disappear from the Merkels' life as expeditiously as they had hoped. Carolyn began getting phone calls at work, even though she had never told Bob where she was employed. He was always cordial and apologetic. First he wanted to know how the air vents worked. She told him. Next he wanted to know the names of the trees in the yard. She said she wasn't sure—some pines, an oak or two. He said he was starting a list of the trees and shrubs on the property. Then he called to report that he had just purchased a kerosene space heater, but his wife

was unhappy because it was too big. Was it? Carolyn didn't
have any idea. Well, should they leave it on all night?

"I wouldn't do that," she replied tentatively.

The next time he called, which would be the last, Bob
was uncharacteristically testy. It was a side of him Carolyn
hadn't seen before, and she was sure that if she had been
exposed to it earlier, her good will would have been considerably less liberally proffered. The utility company had
just come and installed some sort of transformer box on
the edge of the property, Bob complained. "If we had
known this, we would never have moved here!" he snapped.

Before they considered moving out to Brandermill, Delores and Bob ascertained that a Lutheran church was
nearby. Brand-new churches were plentiful in the rural
stretches of Chesterfield County, where both the rapidity
and the nature of the ongoing change could be seen in the
churches built in clearings cut into the woods along two-
lane highways, with signs in front that had lettered on
them shibboleths of modern evangelical and pentacostal
Christianity such as "ministries" and "living word" and
"wings of faith."

The Clarks' new congregation, the Lutheran Church of
Our Savior on Route 360, was more mainstream Protestant
than many of its evangelical neighbors, but not any more
established. It was obvious, looking at the clean right angles
of the oak-hued wooden exterior of the church, which faced
a parking lot whose dividing lines looked as newly painted
as the foul lines on a major league baseball field, that the
building hadn't seen many winters. The church was not
much over a year old when the Clarks joined. Like their
neighbors in the other new little churches in the clearings,
the congregation's 250 members had one thing in common
besides their shared religious beliefs: Only a few years
earlier, virtually all of them had been strangers to one
another.

Delores quickly found a place in the weekly Bible study group. But Bob didn't have time yet for involvement in the parish on days other than Sunday. That would come later, when they were more financially stable. Right now, though, he was a man with a $600 a month mortgage and a job that paid only $480 a week.

Toiling nights and weekends again, he took in free-lance work that often wasn't economically productive. In one project for a friend's long-tottering business venture, Bob assiduously put the badly disorganized accounting books into respectable shape after many weeks of after-hours labor. For his work, Bob received not cash but a number of shares of the stock. But having its books in order wasn't all the business required by the time Bob came into the picture. Within months, it went bankrupt. Bob's stock was worthless.

Yet he did not despair. In fact, Bob seemed virtually indifferent to such setbacks. Instead, he would repair most nights after work to the office he had set up in a spare bedroom and go at it, hunched over his and other people's accounts, a penumbra now framed between tall file cabinets in the fluorescent glare of the desk lamp.

In the early morning, when he didn't have an early appointment at the chiropractor he saw regularly, Bob made time to tend the roses that had bloomed in some profusion in the back yard. Then, on weekdays, he would leave for work exactly at seven-thirty in his Ford, which had on its rear window a sticker that certified the driver as a contributor to the Fraternal Order of Police, the national labor union for police officers. He would always greet his closest neighbors, Joseph and Jacqueline Stefano, an immigrant couple in their thirties who had moved in next door with their three children, nine months before the Clarks arrived.

The Stefanos liked having two quiet, older people living next door. But they had to warn their teenaged daughter to stop taking a shortcut she favored, strolling across one corner of the Clarks' property as she left for school. Bob never complained about it, as such. But the girl's parents noticed that if he happened to be outside when she stepped onto his ground, he would stop what he was doing in his garden and, with his hands on his hips, stand there watching her—it wasn't clear if he was scowling or just squinting—until she got off the property.

It took Bob just over a half hour to make the drive to work at Maddrea, Joyner, Kirkham & Woody. The accounting firm had a small suite of offices in a business complex across from a shopping center a few miles from downtown Richmond. The area was cluttered with strip malls, fast-food restaurants, motels, and heavy traffic that moved, even when it moved slowly, in patterns that didn't change much from day to day. Bob was always at his desk before eight-fifteen A.M., fifteen minutes before starting time. This gave him time to have his coffee and read the morning paper.

The receptionist at Maddrea, Joyner, a woman named Sandra Silbermann, found herself intrigued with the odd new accountant, whose desk job kept him around all day while the other three accountants often were out of the office, doing audits.

For one, he was remarkably nice to Sandra, who had to handle myriad office duties and juggle the incessantly ringing telephone at the same time. Others would let the phone ring and ring when Sandra wasn't at her desk until she scrambled back to get it. Not Bob Clark. Bob would drop what he was doing to come to her assistance.

"He was very helpful to me. He always backed me up on the phone if I couldn't get to it right away," said Sandra, a woman in late middle age whose New York accent stood out in the laconic drawl of Richmond speech. Like many of his friends and associates who stopped later to recall him, Sandra gave a good deal of thought to the positive things about Bob. The man was diligent, solicitous, helpful, courteous. Once, when she had injured her wrist, he volunteered to take the office postage meter down to the post office to have it tabulated and reset, a tedious chore. Like many other mature women who became casual acquaintances of Bob's, she initially liked him immensely. She even wished that her own husband would be as solicitous.

"We had become pretty good friends," Sandra said. "With just the two of us here so often, if we had free time we'd just stand around and talk."

But then, as usual, Bob started losing points. At tax time, when he moonlighted at H&R Block, he worked till ten o'clock at night and on Saturdays as well. Sometimes, when things were slow at the office, he dozed at his desk. Sandra studied his face on several of those occasions and realized that he was several years older than he claimed to be.

As is routine when two people start to become acquainted, there are questions about background—not rude, intimate questions, just normal everyday conversation questions that human beings use to establish natural social reference points with each other. The parameters, invariably politely narrow, include general information about birthplace, family, social interest, likes and dislikes. But in such social interaction with Bob, those little red warning flags always got hoisted. It wouldn't be sufficient to cause a person to remark on the misgivings at the time. Only in retrospect would people give voice to the vague signals that made them remember being slightly uneasy.

"I once asked him if he had any children, and he got this funny look," Sandra said. "He said yes, he had adopted his first wife's child, but he was divorced from the wife." His tense reaction caused her to drop that line of discussion quickly. "I guess he put me off," she said. "I just didn't continue in that vein. I guess what we talked about was current events or gardening, tips on good health, things like that."

There were other instances of behavior that were not quite remarkable, but odd enough to come to mind later. Bob received his personal mail at the office. And on occasion, when Delores would call, Sandra would engage her in friendly conversation for a few minutes before passing her on to her husband. Bob, she said, seemed "pretty nervous, for some reason," when that happened.

Then there was lunch. Bob didn't go out to lunch with the other men. He brought his to work in a brown paper bag and left with it at lunchtime. As she went out for lunch herself, Sandra began noticing Bob eating in his car in the parking lot. Even with the windows rolled up, she could hear the music playing loudly.

Twenty minutes before lunch hour was over, Bob would return to his desk to call his wife. To Sandra, this seemed sweet for a week or so, as he cooed "How was your morning?" and "I love you" into the phone. But after a while, she started wishing she wasn't in the same room. "He would find out how her day was going, and then tell her every little thing that he was doing, every little piece of business that was on his desk," Sandra recalled.

Once he ended his phone conversation with his wife after only a few minutes because, he said, he needed to get a price on mulch for the garden. Sandra wasn't paying much attention as he got out the Yellow Pages and began copying numbers onto a piece of paper. Then he started calling, asking each of the garden-supply stores that answered for its price on a fifty-pound bag of mulch. When he had called them all, Sandra was eavesdropping despite herself as he called two of them back to ask if that—the price was in the range of six dollars—was the best they could do.

Bob then called home to proudly report the price he had

found. Sandra began wondering about the man's priorities in life. Some time later, although she still held to her belief that Bob Clark was a kind and gentle man whom she liked, she read a newspaper story that said that his first wife had had a problem with alcohol. Sandra suspected she had just the tiniest understanding of what might have helped drive the poor woman to drink.

Although the financial strains continued under the burden of the mortgage, Delores found a job working Saturdays at a beauty parlor, and the Clarks, with the troubles of Denver fairly well behind them, seemed at ease within their small circle of new friends.

Wally, like Gary Morrison before him, grew very fond of the couple, who often double-dated with Wally and his girlfriend, Judy. "They acted like newlyweds, holding hands and that," Wally said. Wally took special pride in showing Bob and Delores around his hometown. They took the Clarks to a football game once, but Bob said afterward that he thought football was "too violent," Wally said.

Wally admired Bob for finding what he regarded as a fine wife so late in life, and he let him know it. Besides that, a wife like Delores, a refined and intelligent lady who was never "coarse," who knew how to act in public, would also serve him well in business, once he started moving along on the path to promotion, Wally confided to Bob.

"A wife is either a business asset or a liability," Wally told him in a matter-of-fact manner. "You have an asset."

On the other hand, Delores didn't always seem to relish the role of being a silent asset. In fact, she was beginning to come down on Bob. Among close friends, both Wally and Betty Lane independently mentioned it to her, especially after several minor tiffs sent Bob over to Wally's house to spend the night on a couple of occasions.

As John List had felt with Helen, Bob felt persecuted. "Sometimes Delores just isn't fair," he complained.

"Delores," Wally told her once, "you have got to let up on him occasionally."

Betty recalled, "I had talked to Delores once. I told her back then, I said, you ought to watch some of the things you say to Bob. Nothing's ever right. He's trying hard, he has a job, he's making twenty-five thousand dollars a year. That's not a whole lot, but it's enough for y'all to have a nice life on. He's trying, Delores."

Delores replied, "Well, I know he is, Betty. But, you know, I didn't really want to get married."

"Well, you surely dated him long enough," Betty said.

Later, she took Bob aside and said, "You know, I told Delores how lucky she was to have a man who loved her as much as you do. I don't think it's right the way she puts you down. If I were you, I'd put my foot down."

"Well, Betty," he replied, "I know you're right, but she's just a little insecure. Give her a little time."

But these were minor rough spots on the surface of the new life Bob and Delores had begun creating for themselves in Richmond, where they came into their own socially as a couple in a way they hadn't been able to in Denver.

On the Sunday of Memorial Day weekend 1989, Bob and Delores joined Wally and Judy on an outing to nearby Louisa County to watch a reenactment of a Civil War battle. The next day, a beautiful late-spring holiday Monday, they went into Richmond to attend the annual Heritage Parade in honor of war veterans. Wally was touched to see that Bob's hand went over his heart whenever Old Glory was carried by at the head of a band. Once he noticed that Bob had a tear in his eye as the flag came past.

What a cultured man, Wally reflected afterward in the backyard of his house where a couple of big steaks sizzled on the barbecue. A man of gentle and moderate mien, he thought. Bob, who had seemed happy but distracted throughout the weekend, was on a lawn chair nursing a glass of beer. Here's to new friends, Wally thought, gazing at the reddening coals, the first barbecue coals of the new season. Delores had made her tangy German potato salad for the occasion. The steaks were almost done. Happily, he looked at Delores and, beside her, the alert figure of Bob sitting there in the gauzy twilight of a day that smelled of honeysuckle in the promise of Virginia summer.

Chapter Thirteen

On the Friday before Memorial Day, Kevin N. August, thirty-one years old and an FBI agent for the past three years, was looking forward to the long holiday weekend as the afternoon drifted away lazily in the Richmond office. Everything on his desk was routine: a couple of warrants he had to make some phone calls about before quitting time, some incremental paperwork that needed to be sent to someone else's desk one page bulkier, a batch of bureaucratic flotsam.

August, one of two special agents in the Richmond office who handled the fugitive cases, sifted through the small stack of forms. There was nothing that couldn't wait till Tuesday, after the three-day weekend.

Among the papers he scanned without much interest was a single one-page memo giving information that might lead to the arrest of one of more than ten thousand fugitives from federal felony charges believed to be at large and designated as worth maintaining at least some effort to apprehending.

Attached to this form was the FBI circular with the picture of John Emil List, charged by the state of New Jersey in 1971 with five counts of murder and—this was August's only official interest in the case—by the federal government with a single felony count of unlawful flight across state lines to avoid prosecution.

August looked at the two photos of the murderer, which

certainly stood out in the pantheon of glowering rat-faces who usually showed up on FBI circulars. This guy looked like Dennis the Menace's father. He also noticed that the source of the tip on this eighteen-year-old case was a person who had telephoned a television show, *America's Most Wanted*, the previous Sunday night, May 21. While the program had won grudging admiration in law enforcement circles for the surprising number of fugitives being apprehended as a result of tips from its viewers, you couldn't prove it by Kevin August. In the past year or so, he figured he had checked out fifty of these *America's Most Wanted* television tips, and nothing had ever come of any of them. Like virtually every other fugitive tip, they required tedious checking that consumed hours of time and seldom added anything new to anyone's files except another piece of paper. But you never knew until you checked, that was the point. Thinking no more of the matter, August slid the papers into his in-basket and made some phone calls to wrap up business.

The fugitive tip that sat routinely on Special Agent August's desk over the Memorial Day weekend had arrived at the Richmond FBI office as the result of a serendipitous combination of such disparate factors as Wanda Flanery's reading habits and Frank Marranca's disinclination to take no for an answer.

Wanda made her initial thrust in 1987 after reading a supermarket tabloid. She retreated after being rebuffed. Captain Frank Marranca, in 1988 the recently promoted head of the homicide squad for the Union County, New Jersey, prosecutor's office, made his in 1988. He, too, was rebuffed.

Unlike Wanda, Marranca would not retreat. He would only bide his time.

By the middle of the 1980s, in the Union County prosecutor's office and in the Westfield police department, the

List case had passed on to a second and, in some cases, a third generation of investigators who (considering that absolutely nothing new had been discovered since a policeman writing parking tickets had chanced upon List's old Chevrolet at Kennedy Airport on November 10, 1971) were little more than custodians of the files and warders of the physical evidence—the moldy, blood-stained sleeping bags, the aging Rehwinkle letter, the weapons, the dog-eared crime scene photos and the rest—that was still locked up at the Westfield police station against the unlikely day when John List would be brought to trial.

Which is not to say that John List had been forgotten. No, you could still get a conversation going on the List case, especially in Westfield, where the likes of it still hadn't been seen again, especially among the cops at night after a couple of beers. But the theories were as weary and shopworn now as discussion of the New York Mets choking in the 1973 World Series against Oakland. Everything on the record had been exhaustively analyzed. Only the imponderables remained.

By the middle of the 1980s, even the practical jokes had ceased. For years, every time certain wiseguys in the office went on vacation to some faraway place, there would be postcards—"*Wish you were here. Your good pal, John Emil List.*" or "*Having a ball. Nice to finally have a vacation without the kids! John E. List.*" John List from Disney World. John List from County Mayo. John List from Barbados. John List from Santa Claus Village.

But no one had sent one of those in a long while.

Even the local papers, which for years could be depended upon to run what became known as "Remember John List" stories at regular intervals—the anniversaries of the murders and the discovery of the bodies were the most favored, but sometimes the stories, which faithfully rehashed the facts and added nothing new, seemed to run on an editor's whim—even the papers had found newer anniversaries to commemorate. At irregular intervals, investigators would mail out batches of FBI circulars with a press release to newspapers to try to keep the List case alive, but these had begun to look like a waste of time and postage. The last mailing, late in 1986, was picked up dutifully by the Associated Press, but the bait only got one good bite, by a grubby little supermarket weekly, some poor cousin to the *National Enquirer*, that worked up a story headlined "The Perfect Crime."

It wasn't the perfect crime, of course. Everybody knew who did it. But it seemed abundantly clear that it might have been the perfect escape.

By the time Frank Marranca inherited it, the John List case was just the most famous of officially active, but long dormant, unsolved murder investigations that went back to 1958 in the Union County prosecutor's office. And things had changed dramatically in recent years in the county. Comfortable, well-heeled towns like Westfield, where violent crime was still an anomaly in the late 1980s, stood in stark contrast to deteriorating cities like Elizabeth, the county seat, where drug squabbles and the vileness of poverty had pushed the homicide rate to a level that was greater than New York City's.

So there wasn't a lot of free time to ruminate about John List in the Union County prosecutor's office. But there was one last serious attempt to snare the man who had brazenly walked away from the five bodies of his family.

When they first heard about it from friends, law enforcement authorities tended to scoff at *America's Most Wanted*, a television program that Fox Broadcasting, a subsidiary of the holding company of Australian-born tabloid press baron Rupert Murdoch, began broadcasting in 1988. Each program featured dramatizations of serious crimes whose perpetrators were still at large. These dramatic vignettes were followed by pertinent information about the fugitives, the most critical of which were actual photographs of the criminal, who had just been portrayed by an actor.

The program was a ratings success. It was also generating lively response from viewers, who were invited to phone in with tips on suspects. In its first six months, each weekly broadcast of *America's Most Wanted* was eliciting an average of six thousand telephone calls.

Most of the calls were from the ranks of the perpetually alarmed, people who, for example, are sure that their five-foot-seven mail carrier is in fact the six-foot-five ax murderer who has just been described to them in detail on television. But many were not. Given the odds, an amazing number of the calls coming in were solid tips that were leading directly to arrests. In fact, the program was logging an average of almost one arrest for each broadcast.

Detectives with frustrating unsolved felonies on their hands were starting to take notice. Among them were the investigators in the Union County prosecutor's office.

"When I first saw *America's Most Wanted*, that's the only thing I could think of—getting John List on the air," said Marranca, a trim, dark-haired man in his early forties.

It was obvious by 1988, he said, that "there was no way we were going to find him on our own."

Marranca wasn't the only one who thought about John List and *America's Most Wanted*. After the program started getting a reputation, other investigators in the office began dropping by.

"Listen, can I look at the John List file?" one said. "I want to notify *America's Most Wanted*."

"Hey, it's already been done," Marranca told him. "The letter went out."

The letter went out in the spring of 1988, but the reply came back: No, thanks. The case was too old, and the show was too new to take the chance on a hopeless cause. The show's producers didn't offer a lot of encouragement about the future. Maybe later, they indicated, after the show was more firmly established and could take a chance. Of course, the case wouldn't look any less hopeless then. And it would also be older.

Nine months later, Marranca heard a sergeant in the homicide squad say he was taking a few days off to attend a regional law enforcement conference in Wilmington, Delaware, at which Michael Linder, the executive producer of *America's Most Wanted*, was going to speak.

"I'm going with you," Marranca said. He brought the List files with him.

At the conference, they approached—"collared," was Marranca's word for it—Linder. Politely, the officers invited Linder up to Marranca's room, where photos of the List crime scene were spread out beside several boxes of evidence, as if on display at a sales convention. Carefully, the two cops walked the television producer through the story, not missing any of the weird details.

The details did it. The ballroom, the Sunday school teacher, the confession letter, Patty and the theater. Linder was fascinated. He took down their numbers. When he got back to work, he ordered a segment on List into the works. Even if the case was hopeless, it was good television.

Back in Union County, there was a sense of urgency that none of the investigators now nominally on the List case had ever felt before. *America's Most Wanted* didn't fool around. They insisted on working with the facts. County and municipal detectives, elated at the opportunity for what they all agreed was a long shot, and a last chance at that, scrambled to get their shopworn files in order.

Marranca assigned two detectives just to track down the people who would be witnesses if List were ever captured, Rehwinkle among them, but also school officials, bank tellers, and retired cops like Moran. Everybody was still alive and available, it seemed.

Then the Union County detectives began coordinating with the Westfield department, where the List case was now under the supervision of Bernard Tracy, a detective in his middle thirties who had been one of the teenagers in 1972 who would cruise by the old List house and scurry up the drive on a dare.

"We had to make sure we all had the same paperwork," Marranca said. Once an investigation is as dormant as this one was, agencies jointly working on the case sometimes forget to exchange paperwork. Once the county and municipal files were reconciled, Tracy was designated as liaison to the television program. In Washington, where the show is produced, he spent hours going over the evidence with writers.

But the List segment lacked the one ingredient that the program's producers knew was most directly responsible for the arrest of so many of the felons it featured: a current photograph. The most recent known photographs of List were nineteen years old. Maybe one of those could be retouched, enhanced to show the years, assuming the guy hadn't had plastic surgery.

Linder thought of something that would be more visually dramatic. He knew a commercial photographer and sculptor in Philadelphia, Frank Bender, who was developing a reputation among law enforcement agencies for his ability to reconstruct, in clay, the faces of decomposed bodies that couldn't otherwise be identified. To do this successfully, with no photographic evidence, required intuition as well as artistic skill. Bender had become successful at it. He was commissioned, for $1,500, for do a bust of List for the show.

Bender threw himself into the project enthusiastically. For help, he went to a well-known criminal psychologist, Richard Walter, who works for the state corrections agency in Michigan. Together, the two men debated John List for days—even theorizing about what color socks he might wear. They finally came up with what both agreed was a pretty good guess of how he might look. Essentially, John

List wouldn't have changed much. Always a "meat and potatoes kind of guy," Bender said, he would probably now be a paunchier, older version of the John List who smirked from the FBI flier, with a more pronounced receding hairline. The jowls would sag a bit; that jagged mastoidectomy scar would probably still be behind his right ear because he wasn't likely to have chanced a hospital visit for plastic surgery. As styles changed over the years, he probably wore a different kind of eyeglasses. But they would still be conservative. Nothing with wire frames.

Armed with this armchair psychological profile, Bender enlarged a photograph of List and set to work on the bust. When he was done, he drove to Washington and delivered the ten-pound clay bust, painted lifelike to highlight the facial features, to Linder. If John List was still alive, Bender believed, this was how he looked. Linder and other officials of the program concurred. The segment was ready. Advance publicity went out for newspaper television listings.

The program was broadcast on Sunday night, May 21, 1989, the week before Memorial Day weekend.

The List segment was the first of three. After taking care of some unfinished business—a rapist and jewel thief had been captured thanks to a recent viewer tip—John Walsh, the earnest host of the program, introduced the story:

"Now tonight's first case, the oldest we've ever pursued on *America's Most Wanted*. The suspect, John List, is accused of murdering his family seventeen years ago . . . Tonight, let's try to close the books on the most infamous murder case in the history of New Jersey."

A history buff like Bob Clark would have known that was not exactly the case. The 1932 Lindbergh baby kidnapping and murder in New Jersey mesmerized the nation for years and certainly retained claim to the distinction of most infamous murder in the state's history. Still, the basic outline of the John List case, simplified for its ten-minute run on national television, made for compelling viewing.

An estimated twenty-two million viewers were watching with various degrees of attentiveness as the segment began with the dramatization of the Lists walking up the church steps on a sunny Sunday morning as the church bell tolled and organ music resonated above the chirping of birds.

Among the millions of viewers that night were a handful of people who watched in rapt attention. In silent communion, unaware of each others' presence, they gathered in the lurid glow of television. In Elizabeth, Ed Illiano, aware that the doubts and the guilt would never go away. In Westfield, Jim Moran, who had retired as police chief three years earlier; hopeful and defiant, angry anew at the prim visage of the man who had got away with murder and seemed to mock him through the years. In Oklahoma, Jean Syfert, hurt and still confused, still utterly unable to comprehend the swift and terrible judgment John had pronounced on her family. In Virginia, Bob Clark, alone for the night as his wife went to Bible class; baleful, but serene and unrepentant. In Denver, Wanda Flanery, alert for one more clue that would seal her verdict.

That final clue never came. As the camera circled the bust that Frank Bender had created, the bust of John List, Wanda decided it didn't look a bit like the Bob Clark she knew. And she decided that it didn't matter. For she had known beyond any reasonable doubt over a year earlier when she opened that newspaper. It was up to her now. Kindness was no longer the question. Kindness was easy. Kindness made you feel better. It was more difficult to take an uncertain course that would bring misery to others and no joy to yourself.

Her daughter, Eva, and son-in-law, Randy, were in the living room watching the program with her. When it was over, Wanda scribbled down the phone number given for tips on fugitives. She got up and turned off the set and went into the next room. In a minute, she was back with a letter she had recently received from Delores in which her friend had wondered whether "we did the right thing in coming here." In the letter, Delores had said that Bob had mentioned that he thought Wanda had "such nice" handwriting. She had felt a chill realizing that Bob had scrutinized her handwriting. What was he looking for?

The three of them discussed the matter after the show.

"You know it's him. You know it is," Wanda insisted.

"Why get involved?"

"Because, God forbid, what if something happens to Delores? Could you live with that? Shouldn't he pay for his crimes?"

"Why get involved?"

Finally, Wanda handed the letter to Randy. The cream-colored envelope had the Clarks' return address in the upper-left corner.

"Would you call?" she asked.

Randy made the call, standing in the alcove with the telephone cradled on his shoulder. But it didn't work out right. "Well, is there a reward for this man?" she heard him say insistently. And then, "Well, fine. If you don't want to know where he is, okay." The phone banged down.

Wanda implored him, "Please call back, and just give them the address on that envelope," she said. A reward would be nice. But a reward wasn't really the point.

The young man made the call again. Wanda relaxed a little as she heard him read off the address and carefully spell the name of the town in Virginia.

Chapter Fourteen

ON THE NIGHT OF MAY 21, THE CALL FROM DENVER WAS reasonable enough to make the initial cut. The "live" part of the program—the introduction and setups and the like—had been taped in the afternoon. When the program was broadcast across the country that night, police detectives and FBI agents connected with various fugitive cases were on the set, as usual, taking calls along with the twenty-five operators employed by the program.

The average number of calls came in. A smaller-than-average number, 250 or so, concerned the List case. One of them actually came with an address.

Bernard Tracy, the Westfield detective, was among those taking the calls in the studio that night. But the call from Denver went to someone else. The operator made careful note of the information before picking up on another line.

The next day, it was then sent by mail, along with more than twenty other tips, to the FBI, where the leads were sorted geographically, with each then dispatched to the appropriate field office.

The tip from Denver was the only one from that week's batch that went to the Richmond office, which had a staff of five FBI agents, two of whom were regularly assigned to the fugitive detail. Like much police work, the fugitive detail is a matter of dull routine punctuated by the infrequent flash of danger. The agent doing the fugitive checks first makes a few phone calls in a refining process that further separates the totally baseless from the merely unlikely. No one says "Bingo" just because a couple of numbers come up right or because the initial checks show that such a person exists, happens to exist at such an address, and happens to fit such a description. An agent doesn't go banging on someone's door with that kind of information. But he does start to pay attention. Boredom gives way to the first tantalizing hint of the chase. Like a lion, he'll probably lose interest after the first couple of short sprints don't pay off, but he won't give up if the scent lingers. In this case, the scent was faint, but it was there.

There was no special priority on this tip from a television show, a lead that consisted only of the fact that the man had a name and address and the reputation for being overtly religious. That would narrow the possibilities down to a couple of million American adult males, Billy Graham and the Archbishop of New York among them. But was there something here worth some attention? A lion might tilt its head and sniff the air and gaze motionlessly, seemingly disinterested and bored, at the tall grass beyond, at the faint outlines in the still blades of grass.

A few more phone calls. Motor vehicles had the age. It seemed to be in the ball park. A couple of discreet inquiries, nothing to get anyone aroused. No children. An accountant. Well dressed.

August, a law-enforcement professional, a black man who had risen to the FBI from a small-town police department in Louisiana, studied the old John List wanted flier.

After "Occupation" it said: "Accountant, bank vice president, comptroller, insurance salesman."

After "Remarks" it said: "Reportedly a neat dresser."

After "Caution," it said: "List, who is charged in New Jersey with multiple murders involving members of his

family, may be armed and should be considered dangerous."

The tip had graduated from the category of totally baseless to merely unlikely. It was worth a trip.

Thursday was the day that rounds were made outside
the office on what are called "generic" tips on at-large
felons. There were five to be checked out that particular
Friday. As usual, two agents worked together.

The stops that day were scattered all over the metro-
politan area. It would mean hours of driving. For efficiency,
August always put the farthest-out stop first on the agenda,
followed in turn by the next-farthest and so on. This way,
when you were finished, you were at the point closest to
the office downtown.

The Clark address was easily the most distant, all the
way down in Brandermill, a good twenty-five-mile drive
into the far suburbs.

It was only the first of June, but the day was promising
to be a hot one. Shortly after nine o'clock, August and his
partner got into the car to begin their rounds.

It was a little before ten when they parked the car at
the end of the cul de sac on Sagewood Trace and walked
up the gravel path to the wood porch of the neat little
ranch house. August knocked lightly on the door. Inside,
a vacuum cleaner was turned off. A woman opened the
door a crack and seemed alarmed to see a black man standing there.

"Robert P. Clark?" August asked, displaying his billfold
with his badge and his ID.

"He's at work," the woman replied.

"We're with the FBI, ma'am. Can we come in and speak
with you for a few minutes?"

Delores hesitated for a minute, but then opened the
door. It was apparent that her morning housework had
been interrupted.

August apologized for the intrusion. He asked her if she was familiar with a television program called *America's Most Wanted*.

"We're here because of that program," he said.

When she looked at him blankly, he showed her the FBI flier with John List's picture. He could think of only one way to ask the question. "Could this possibly be your husband?" he said.

Delores looked terrified. The color had drained from her face. She took the flier and tried to read it, but she couldn't. She knew the story. She looked mournfully at the photos on the flier, which had begun to tremble in her long, thin fingers.

Delores did not notice the men inspecting the living room, where a sampler on one wall had the words "Delores 'n Bob" against a blue background. She didn't notice how August's partner eased over to be in a position to survey the hallway leading to the bedrooms. He nodded to August, who then suggested that they all sit down. The agents took positions so that each of them had a different view of the room.

"That looks like it could be my husband," Delores said in a quavering voice in response to the intense interest on the two agents' faces. Yet she was Bob Clark's wife, not this man's, and now her loyalty and her common sense flashed instinctively through the fear that gripped her: "But that can't be my husband," she said quite reasonably. "He's the nicest man in the world."

She started crying.

The agents remained alert, but it was increasingly apparent that this was not a spouse deliberately protecting a violent criminal. They behaved with a solicitude that both men genuinely felt as it became clear that they might be about to introduce her to a tragedy that would forever change her life.

"Well, calm down," August said with as much reassurance as he felt he could honestly offer. "Calm down, calm down. It may be just a coincidence. We do this kind of thing all the time, and they're usually mistakes. It may not be your husband. You understand that we just have to clarify it."

He asked her if she had any photographs of her husband. Delores brought their wedding photo over from the mantel.

August studied it with wonder. There didn't seem to be any doubt now. "Mrs. Clark," he said, "there seems to be an uncanny resemblance here. We need to resolve this problem."

He handed the wedding picture back, but remained hunched forward on the couch. Now he was all business.

"Does your husband have a mastoidectomy scar behind his right ear."

"Yes, he has that scar."

Is he from Michigan?

Yes.

An accountant?

Yes, Bob is an accountant.

And so on. The tone of the conversation had shifted, and all of its participants knew it. The steps were being taken by the book now.

The agents obtained from Delores the address of Bob's office at 1506 Willow Lane Drive in Richmond. August asked for permission to use her phone. In a calm and emotionless tone, August spoke to another agent at the office. They had a suspect, a fugitive avoiding prosecution for murder, an older guy. There was enough to take him.

As a precaution against her alerting her husband, but under the pretext, honestly enough felt, of providing emotional support, the partner stayed behind with Delores as August got into the car and made the drive to the accounting office. Already, two other agents from the office had sped to the location, where they waited quietly in the parking lot.

August pulled into the lot less than thirty minutes later. He found his colleagues just outside the lobby of the three-story office building. They went in. One of the agents had already checked the directory beside the potted tree in the tiny lobby. The accounting firm was listed along with a law office, a painting company office, a psychotherapist, and a personnel office. Two of the agents took the elevator up to the second floor. The other took the stairs.

Sandra Silbermann was on the phone, but she looked up curiously when they came in. At Maddrea Joyner, walk-ins usually didn't arrive in threes.

Peering beyond the reception desk, the men saw one man sitting at a desk, but he was too young to fit the suspect's description. No one was at the other desks. The agents waited patiently for Sandra to get off the phone.

"We're with the FBI," August said, showing his identification. "May we see the office manager?"

"I'm sorry, Mr. Joyner isn't in," Sandra replied, wondering what in the world this was about.

This was not how they had hoped it would go. In this sort of a setting, it is always best to have the suspect isolated, summoned to an office where the arresting officer had control of the immediate space around him.

"Does a Robert Clark work here?" August asked.

"Yes," Sandra said. The words "white-collar crime" leapt to her mind. Embezzlement? But Bob didn't have access to anything to steal! All he did was sort out income taxes and fix snarled bank statements and enter items in the records.

"May we see Mr. Clark?" August said.

Sandra leaned back in her chair and turned to look for Bob. He wasn't at his desk, but she knew he hadn't gone out to his car yet for lunch.

She figured he was in the bathroom. "I guess he's just stepped away from his desk," she said.

The agents looked worried.

"He hasn't gone out," she told them. "Why in the world do you want Bob?"

"We're here to arrest Robert Clark."

Now why would you arrest some poor old accountant like Bob? Sandra thought. Maybe he had embezzled at his previous job.

"For what?" Sandra said, and the reply nearly caused her to fall off the chair she was leaning back in.

"Homicide."

Her mouth was agape as the agents brushed past and headed into the office. She quickly joined them. Bob was just down the hallway, coming back from the Xerox machine with some papers in his hand. He practically collided with August as the agents turned the corner into the hall.

When his past finally caught up with him, Bob Clark was wearing a white short-sleeved shirt and a necktie that was loosened. He had on tan pants. His suit jacket hung on a rack near his desk. Two of the agents moved into position at his side, just past the reach of peripheral vision. August stood facing him. Bob's face didn't show surprise or fear. It showed contempt.

"Mr. Clark," he said, his badge flashing in the light. "We're with the FBI, and we need to confirm your identification."

The badge could have belonged to a meter reader for the electric company for all the scrutiny Bob gave it. He just stood there with the papers in his hand as the agents sized him up and relaxed a little when they realized that this aging suspect didn't pose much of a physical threat to three trained cops in fairly good shape. There was no sign of aggression about to spring. His attitude was more that of a schoolteacher awaiting a student's explanation of himself.

August began, according to the book.

"Would you tell us your name please?"

"Robert Clark."

"We need to ask you a few questions, Mr. Clark. Do

you have a scar behind your right ear?" August could see very well that he did.

Bob turned his head slightly to show it.

"Have you ever had an operation for a hernia?"

"Yes."

"Were you born in Michigan?"

"Yes."

"And you're an accountant?"

"Yes, I am."

There was a pause.

"Are you John Emil List?" August said.

"No."

The agent was surprised. There had been no hesitation in the response, that was one thing. But there wasn't a hint of surprise. And most interesting, there wasn't any sign of annoyance. August figured that his own response, whether he was or was not the man in question, would have been an angry, "Who in hell is John List?"

The three agents had closed in past the physical space borders of incidental conversation.

"Do you mind if we search you for weapons?" August said. It wasn't a request.

Bob shrugged. "Okay."

August told him to place his arms out at full length and lean against the wall. He complied without any objection whatsoever.

When the pat-down was finished, August addressed him: "You're John List, aren't you?"

"I know who I am," the man said, seeming to force indignance into his voice. "I'm Robert Clark."

Standing off to the side watching this unfold, Sandra had to move away when Bob gave her the mournful look of a man who believes he has been betrayed. Red blotches, she noticed, had broken out on his face.

The officers were prepared for any sudden move, but

Bob just stood there impassively, waiting for the external world to act on him.

"Then you won't mind coming down to the police station for fingerprints?" August asked. He had the cuffs out. Passively, Bob held out his hands and let August lock them on. August read him his Miranda rights.

Sandra jumped at the clank of the cuffs being snapped shut. She and the other accountant in the office, Les Wingfield, were standing off to the side and they both looked at the clock at the same time when they heard the cuffs go on. It was eleven-ten A.M.

"Uh-oh," Les said in a low voice to Sandra, as if he had just finally figured out what was going on. "Looks like Bob's going to jail." He gave a soft whistle. Les had never liked Bob, who had impressed him as one very cold fish.

Bob, unprotesting, head bowed, was hustled out without further ceremony, and, Sandra noticed, without his suit coat.

The federal agents helped Bob into the back seat of August's car. One man got in beside him. In the driver's seat, August was mildly perplexed. He had arrested literally hundreds of people, and never encountered one like this. This guy hadn't even asked what the *charge* was. Forget about the innocent ones. Even the guilty suspects asked that! It was a little nerve-wracking, in fact. Before he started the car, August looked over his shoulder directly at Bob, who hadn't said a word since being handcuffed.

August felt a little silly as soon as he'd said it: "If you are John List," he told the suspect sternly, "you did a terrible thing by killing your entire family."

The suspect didn't reply. But as he started the car, August did think he had seen a tear faintly glistening in Bob's eye.

They took him first to Richmond police headquarters for fingerprints. A few blocks away, the magnolias were in bloom on the neatly groomed grounds of the state capitol.

Young men and women on their lunch hours from state offices relaxed and mingled in the cool shade.

At police headquarters, it took a while for the fingerprint expert to finish taking Bob's prints and making the comparisons. When he did, he walked out to where the agents were waiting and gave the thumbs-up sign.

"That clinches it," August said.

After almost eighteen years, the authorities had at last made an arrest in the murders of Helen, Alma, Patricia, John, and Frederick List. The suspect was booked on the federal charge of being a fugitive from prosecution for homicide. He was booked under the name John Emil List.

At two o'clock, after a brief wait in the lockup at the federal courthouse, the suspect, handcuffed again, was readied for his first hearing.

Among the affidavits and other statements he had signed was one swearing that his name was Robert P. Clark; another was a financial disclosure statement to make application for a court-appointed attorney.

The suspect walked into the courtroom from the lockup area accompanied by two federal marshals. They took off the cuffs and seated him alone at a table. The marshals withdrew to the sidelines.

As a standard safeguard against a suicide attempt, his tie and belt had been taken from him. So had his eyeglasses, and this made him appear slightly disoriented. He squinted toward the blur as U.S. Magistrate David G. Lowe strode in and took the bench.

The government was represented by Assistant U.S. Attorney N. George Metcalf, who explained the charge to Lowe and asked that the suspect be held in custody without bail pending arraignment and further hearings.

The judge addressed the suspect. "Mr. List?" he began.

"Yes, sir?" the suspect responded.

This was not taken as an admission of anything but an

obsequiousness in the face of authority, however. The magistrate elicited from the suspect the concession that he had been informed of his rights, and then took a few minutes to review those rights for him. The magistrate then asked the suspect if he could afford a lawyer.

"No, I cannot."

"Would you like court-appointed counsel?" the magistrate asked.

"I would appreciate it, yes."

Lowe, who had in front of him the application the suspect had already filled out, had him go over his personal finances for the record.

The suspect said he earned about $2,000 a month in salary at the accounting firm. He said he had recently received a check of $3,000 from H&R Block for part-time work during tax season. He said his wife was unemployed.

Was there any additional income?

"Well, interest on a savings account," said the suspect. "Maybe $50." He declared that the balance in that account was about $1,000.

"Anything else?" the magistrate asked.

The only other assets the suspect could think of were a 1981 Ford Escort, estimated value $800, and the $20 he recalled having in his wallet when he was arrested that morning. "We are purchasing a home," he said helpfully, "but it is in my wife's name."

Monthly fixed bills were $650 for mortgage and taxes and about $200 for utilities. "Various credit cards debts," the suspect added, totaled about $5,000. "I pay about $150 a month on those."

Clearly, the man was living close to the edge of his income if not beyond it. But close isn't enough under federal guidelines. His application for a court-appointed lawyer was denied.

Lowe then ordered the suspect held without bail and

scheduled a bond hearing for Monday, with a preliminary hearing to follow a week later.

"You will be given every opportunity to contact a lawyer to represent you at those proceedings," the magistrate said.

Later, when he was led outside in handcuffs for the drive to the Henrico County Jail, the suspect had his first taste of what was to come. Reporters and photographers were waiting to pounce, pressing in from all angles with their microphones and flashing cameras, demanding, again and again until he was inside the car and it pulled away: "Are you John List? Are you John List?"

Early that same afternoon, Wally Parsons got the most shocking phone call of his life.

"Wally!" a distraught Delores Clark was crying. She sounded desperate for help.

"What's the matter, for God's sake?" he asked.

"Bob has done been arrested."

"What for?"

"Murder," she wailed.

When he recovered from his shock, Wally moved fast to help. The reporters were already calling Delores's house, so he had her come to his place, where she took refuge in the room that Bob and she had shared. First, they arranged for a local lawyer, David P. Baugh, to represent her husband.

At the lawyer's suggestion, they began drafting a statement to respond to the clamor from the press, which was growing louder as the story broke in New York, where it generated big headlines in the daily tabloids and even made the front page of *The New York Times*. By the dozens, reporters and television crews were scrambling onto planes for Richmond and looking for people to interview. Already, photographers and camera crews had set up a virtual camp outside the Clarks' house in Brandermill.

Wally and Delores consulted with Delores's pastor and several of her relatives, and then stayed up long into the night composing the statement, which Wally suggested they give first to the Richmond *News Leader*, in an attempt to take some wind out of the sails of the out-of-town press. When he spoke with a reporter for the local paper, he prefaced the statement with this personal assurance: "You can be a hundred percent absolutely sure that this lady knows absolutely nothing about anything in Bob's past."

In the written statement, Delores asked the press to "respect my right to my personal privacy during this very dramatic and uncertain time." Delores said she was making the statement "reluctantly," and that it would be her final comment on the matter.

"I was shocked to hear about Bob's arrest and what he is charged with," her statement said. "This is not the man I know. The man I know is kind, loving. A devoted husband and dear friend. He is a quiet yet friendly man who loves his work and people he works with.

"He loves our new home and loves working in and out of it and around it. We both enjoy going to church. Bob is a man of devotion and faith. I find this hard to believe. I hope somehow this is not true, and if it is, he was so stressed out that something snapped.

"I am devoted to him. I hope that somehow God will see us through this."

Delores had been turned away when she tried to visit her husband on the afternoon of his arrest. The next day, Friday, she and her pastor from the Church of Our Savior, the Reverend Joseph M. Vought, came back at noon and were allowed in.

Bob was being kept by himself in a two-man cell in the isolation area of the county jail. The cell had frosted reinforced glass windows, not bars. There was a toilet, a sink, and two bunks. The minister was allowed into the cell itself with the prisoner. Delores had to peer through the glass and speak with her husband on a telephone. She could hear that Bob was crying, too.

The minister realized that Bob hadn't slept. He looked shaken and exhausted. "There seemed to be some relief about him," Vought told reporters outside the jail. "Whether that was reflective of the fact that he didn't have to put up the front anymore, I don't know."

Delores went back alone to visit her husband the next day, Saturday. When she got back to Wally's, she told him they had "a very pleasant conversation, reminiscing about our life together." They did not discuss specifics of what he had been charged with, she said.

Bob Clark had been less well known than Delores at the Church of Our Savior, where Sunday services were dominated by buzzing about the arrest. A large number of reporters showed up at the church, but they couldn't find many people who had any but the most general impressions of the quiet, well-mannered man. The minister had warned congregants from the pulpit to be wary of speaking about Bob Clark publicly, because, Vought said, "people's lives are hanging in the balance here."

Speaking himself to reporters, Vought said before services, "The man police say is John List is not the man we know.

"We are continuing to minister to Bob and Delores Clark," the minister lectured the news media, whose interest was in a mass murderer, not a congregant. "We pray that falsehood and sensationalism will be replaced by truth and compassion."

After a weekend in Henrico County Jail, the suspect didn't forget his manners. Sandra Silbermann was at the office on Monday morning when she picked up the phone and the operator asked if she would accept a collect call from a Bob Clark.

She did. "Bob? Bob?" she said, wondering if someone was playing a mean joke.

But it was him, all right. She recognized the deep monotone.

"I'm sorry I was picked up at the office," he said. "I'm sorry if I caused any inconvenience."

"Bob?" she said, "are you all right?"

He said he was fine. He asked if she would gather his suit coat and the few personal belongings from his desk. He had hired a lawyer, who was sending someone by to pick them up, along with his car, which was still parked in the lot outside. Sandra told him that his things, mostly mail and little personal effects like a letter opener, were packed in a box. A large container hadn't been needed. He kept no pictures in the office, and on the wall behind his desk, some certificates belonging to a former employee still were hanging.

The conversation didn't last much more than a minute.

The defendant waived the Monday hearing. The next court appearance came on Thursday, a week after the arrest. The defendant entered a plea of not guilty. Magistrate Lowe took note of that before setting bond at $1 million.

The suspect allowed himself a small, tight smile when he heard how much bail he was worth.

The suspect appeared surprised as the federal prosecutor then moved to drop the fugitive charge. But any sense of good fortune was quickly dispelled when he realized that this was merely a way to expedite allowing him to be taken into custody by the state of Virginia to await extradition to New Jersey on the five counts of first-degree homicide. U.S. marshals escorted the suspect out of the federal courtroom and turned him over to a Virginia state police officer and a Henrico county detective, who accompanied him back to the county jail. That afternoon he was taken before a county district judge and remanded into state custody pending an extradition hearing to show cause why he should not be returned to New Jersey for trial.

In the courtroom as observers during that proceeding were Captain Marranca and an assistant county prosecutor from Union County who had flown to Virginia the night before to begin preparing for the trial.

As the suspect was led in and out of court during the day, reporters noticed that he was carrying with him a paperback book. He wore the same suit—now reunited with its jacket—that he had on when he was arrested. He kept his head down and ignored the question that was still being shouted at him: "Are you John List?"

The same afternoon, in another attempt to put an end to the clamor for information about her life with Bob Clark, Delores held a news conference outside her lawyer's office on Oregon Hill, a part of town that overlooks a bend in the James River.

Looking frantic, Delores repeated her belief that her husband was not John List. "I do not believe it. I love my husband very deeply," she said. "I do not believe this is the same man." As the reporters and photographers pressed in, she began weeping. But she stayed with it for twenty more minutes.

"People who know Robert would agree he has a great desire to do well and to maintain good relationships with others," she said in a halting, frail voice, reading from a prepared statement which trembled in her hands. "My husband has many sincere and dedicated friends. He has always been very helpful and kind to those in need. Robert is an exceptional man. He has great faith and loves God.

"I have never known Robert to be anything but a sweet and gentle man of good character. We have had a happy marriage filled with mutual respect and love."

After she read her prepared statement, the questions were shouted at her. She seemed to recoil from each one as she answered waveringly.

Didn't he show you any pictures of his previous wife who died? Weren't you curious?

"Well, no," Delores said uncomfortably.

Did that lady in Denver show you the newspaper article about John List and say she thought it was your husband?

"She did come over and show me the paper. I dismissed it because I felt it was not true."

Are your finances sound?

"No. I would not say so."

How can you continue to believe in your husband in face of all of the evidence that he is in fact John List?

"I do not know. I have not seen that report or anything. I do not know."

Baugh leaned near to her and said in a stage whisper, "How much longer do you want this to continue?"

"Whatever it will take to get them away."

What Delores Clark did not understand, and would not comprehend for some time, was that they were not going to go away, and not because of any vendetta against her privacy. Most reporters, in fact, tried to respect that as best they could under the circumstances. With prosecutors assuring them that there was not a single doubt that Bob Clark was John List—the fingerprints matched, the mastoidectomy and hernia scars matched, every physical characteristic matched, and had Bob Clark even tried to come up with a shred of evidence that he had existed before November 1971, when he arrived full-grown in Denver?— the interest was virtually uncontrollable. With the suspect out of touch in jail, his wife was the next closest news source available. She was not as much a victim of the news media as, like so many others, another victim of John List.

But in this kind of ugly situation, someone usually goes beyond the already liberal boundaries in cynical quest of the victim. The *New York Post* proved to be the one.

One afternoon not long after the arrest, Delores was driving with a friend from Richmond out to Midlothian when her maroon Toyota was cut off at an intersection by a car with a man who craned precariously out of the passenger window and fired off picture after picture of the terrified woman trapped in her car.

"They almost caused us to have a terrible accident," said Delores, who didn't know who was in the car or what they wanted. "I got hysterical."

The next day, the *New York Post* carried photographs of Delores in sunglasses, with a scarf pulled over her head, looking as frantic as a trapped bird.

Four months later, in *Manhattan inc.* magazine, an admiring article about the management of the *New York Post* incidentally mentioned this feat. Bill Hoffman, a reporter who had been in the car with the photographer, bragged: "We were so whipped up, we pursued her on a high-speed chase through the suburbs of Richmond and got her trapped at a traffic light. And we got pictures of her. We got her. No one else got her."

The attention faded, of course. There were always new things to pursue. The suspect was in jail, protected by warders and lawyers from outside reach. Delores went home alone and began the process of putting her life back together.

The house would have to be sold, of course. She put it on the market, listing it with a real estate agent she knew from church. Delores never told Betty.

Betty understood. The church provided solace. The church did not give betrayal. The house in Brandermill, once a symbol of a new life, was now a monument to deceit, with a mortgage of $650 a month. It was sold quickly, without profit.

Late in August, Betty decided to make a farewell call on Delores before she moved to Maryland, where her relatives were. Delores had obtained an unlisted phone number, so Betty drove out to Brandermill unannounced. She was heartened to see Delores's car in the drive. Someone's dog had dragged a gnarled old beef bone onto the wooden front porch of the house and left it there. The front windows were open. A breeze rustled the sheer white curtains.

Betty rang the bell and waited with a friendly smile.

"It's me," she called into the window. "It's Betty!" she called cheerfully. As she waited, she noticed that the paint on the outside of the house was cracked and peeling. It was long overdue for a paint job.

Delores unlocked the door and looked out. Betty was shocked by how thin she had become. There was an almost feral look in her eyes.

"I'm sorry, Betty. It's sold," Delores said. Then she slammed the door shut and snapped the lock in place, as if afraid Betty would storm in.

Betty was dumbfounded to be treated like a door-to-door salesperson. She bent to call in the window, "What? Delores? Delores!"

"It's sold!" came the defiant cry from within.

"Hey, that's not what I came here to talk to you about," Betty said in a clipped, stern tone. "Delores, we'll talk through the window if you want to."

"No, Betty! We wouldn't have been here if it wasn't for you. This is all your fault."

Betty figured that someone had to get the blame, and it was to be expected that it wouldn't be Bob yet. "Delores, I don't know why you're so mad at me," she said through the window screen. "I never did anything to you. I helped you."

"Oh yeah?"

So Betty gave up. "Well, I wish you lots of luck," she said. "Tell Bob hello for me." There was no sound from inside the house. She waited a few minutes, but only the curtains stirred. With her head down, Betty, who had only wanted to be a friend, went back to her car across the street and drove away.

Chapter Fifteen

"WE ARE NOT GOING TO ACQUIESCE ON ANYTHING," DAVID Baugh, the suspect's lawyer, said after the governor of New Jersey made a formal request on June 22 to the state of Virginia for the extradition of "John Emil List, also known as Robert P. Clark."

"We are not putting up any resistance; we are only requiring the commonwealth to prove everything," he said. "He has these rights and we're not going to give them away."

After the initial rude shocks of prison routine, the suspect had adjusted quite well to his new life in jail. Here was a prisoner who did what he was told, when he was told, and the other times kept his nose buried in a book. If there were promotions in prison, as there are in the army, this buck private would be in line for his stripes already. As it was, the guards bestowed what they could: Within days, the term "model prisoner" was pinned on him like a campaign medal.

Bereft, finally, of options, he was also released of expectations; free, for the first time, to submerge himself in what deMolinos had called "a confidence in God's sovereignty, a detachment from all things." A prison is a place obsessively devoted to the promulgation of the very virtues that were the bedrock of John List's life: control, order, obedience, separation from the external. What to one man might be a horrible cage, to one so inwardly directed might be a monk's cell in which to cleanse the soul in quietude.

In letters from prison to his friends, the suspect began to refer frequently, and at length, to the "Spiritual Guide" of the persecuted deMolinos, who had written:

The valley of our outward being is filled with suffering, darkness, desolation. On the lofty mountains of our inmost being, the pure sun casts its rays, inflames and enlightens. The believer is clear, peaceful, resplendent, serene.

This place of which I speak is the rich and hidden treasure, the lost pearl. Pray:

> *You are poor to look upon.*
> *But inwardly you are full of wealth.*
> *You seem low,*
> *But you are exceedingly high.*
> *You are that which makes men live*
> *A divine life here below.*
> *Give to me, O highest Lord*
> *A generous share*
> *Of this heavenly happiness.*
> *And true peace,*
> *Which the world of the senses*
> *Is capable neither of understanding*
> *Nor receiving.*

When he was not reading or praying alone, the suspect occasionally was permitted to spend some time in the day room with the general population, but he usually brought a book there, too. Twice a week, Delores came to visit.

Early in the morning of June 29, just before the extradition proceedings were scheduled to begin, Baugh made a surprise announcement that his client had agreed to be extradited on the condition, granted by the Union County prosecutor in an effort to speed things along, that he could go to New Jersey still stipulating that his name was Robert P. Clark.

New Jersey lost no time. The Union County sheriff, Ralph Froehlich, immediately took custody of the prisoner. Froehlich and a deputy accompanied the prisoner back to the Henrico County Jail, where he picked up some books and other personal belongings he had accumulated since the arrest. Froelich then hustled his prisoner off to the airport, where a Piedmont Airlines flight waited. Froelich removed the man's handcuffs so he could read comfortably. The prisoner was in the middle of a Michener novel when he was extradited. During the flight, he also chatted amiably with his two captors, primarily about the Civil War and the Confederacy. Three hours later, handcuffed, wearing a light gray suit that was set off incongruously by new white sneakers, John List was taken off the plane at Newark Airport. For the first time since November 10, 1971, he was back in New Jersey.

On the flight, the prisoner did not object to being called John List. However, the sheriff cautioned those to whom he relayed this information not to make too much of it, for the prisoner was a most extraordinarily accommodating fellow. "I could have called him Mandrake the Magician," Sheriff Froelich said.

The well-behaved Union County prisoner who maintained for so long that he was Robert P. Clark started to come to terms again with John List late in 1989, with the summer gone and the initial burst of media attention spent, with the certain knowledge that, legally at least, he was now just another inmate stashed in an overcrowded jail waiting for trial.

The Union County Jail, in the back of the Greek Revival courthouse in downtown Elizabeth, housed a good many accused murderers in 1989, none of them as famous as John List, each of them crammed in among seven hundred prisoners, in cells with double and even triple bunks. Outside, on the sidewalk below the barred windows, prisoners' girlfriends loitered during the daytime and held shouted conversations with their incarcerated lovers.

But John was lucky. While any common poor wretch who had merely murdered another poor wretch in a mutual drug-crazed rage on a bad Saturday night would find himself sharing a cell with two or three equally hapless villains, John List, by virtue of the heinous scope of his crime—five murders, women and children, all in one day—was accommodated in what was in effect a private room, a cell in the jail's isolation unit, a room that had not bars but Plexiglas windows, situated in a section of the jail usually reserved for those with communicable diseases, informants, or others whom jailors wanted to separate from the general population.

John had little to fear from his jailmates. It is no longer true that inmates are hardest on those fellow prisoners who commit atrocities against the weak and vulnerable, such as children. All that is needed today to achieve respect is celebrity, and celebrity is measured in exposure on television minutes. To the inmates in Union County Jail, and some of the warders as well, John was a superstar. He was even accorded the deference of being referred to by his alias instead of the name stamped on his paperwork.

"Hey, Bob, you going to watch *America's Most Wanted* Sunday night? Maybe you'll see somebody you know," was the sort of good-natured gibe that followed Bob into the game room, where fellow inmates usually made room for him near the television.

In New Jersey, John List, his meager savings now gone, qualified for a court-appointed attorney. Elijah Miller, the assistant public defender for Union County, took the case and, despite the fact that he also had five other active murder cases at the time, threw himself energetically into it. By the time pretrial hearings began in March 1990, Miller and his staff investigator, William Henderson, had retraced the steps of John List's life, interviewing everyone they could identify who had known him either as John List or as Robert Clark. For a public defense, it was an enormous effort, designed to buttress a two-pronged defense strategy: One, to show that the defendant was an otherwise law-abiding citizen who could have committed the crimes he was charged with only under extreme mental anguish; and, two, to battle fiercely to hamper the prosecution's case by preventing the admission of the state's most important piece of evidence, the confession letter to his pastor that John List had left, locked in a file cabinet, on the crime scene. The defense would contend that the Westfield police, by their hasty and imprudent actions at the crime scene, had illegally obtained a privileged letter written by a congregant to his minister.

Miller, a young black attorney who had left private practice for the more stimulating legal challenges of a public defender, was vehement in his insistence that maintaining "an orderly society" dictates that "we touch all of the bases" in providing a fair trial, no matter how guilty the defendant appears to be in advance. "If it is done properly and fairly," he said, "then all of us will be able to live with the results."

Through preparations for the trial, the inmate spent his days in quiet study of the Bible or other reading, religious and secular. He spent many hours with a deck of cards and a notepad, calculating statistical odds. A Lutheran minister was a regular visitor. Several times he spoke on the phone with Delores, although she did not visit the jail.

And he kept up a lively correspondence with the little network of friends who remained loyal to Bob Clark.

It must have been difficult for a proud, self-aware man who so craved status to have to address his friends on stationery with the address "Union County Jail" printed at the top. But he wrote frequently, invariably beginning with an apology of one sort or another, in a hand that appeared cramped by the confines of the lined jailhouse stationery.

To Betty Lane, he wrote a note that showed he was aware of Delores's rebuff: "I am truly sorry for how you were treated when you went to see Delores. She has been under a great deal of stress during this period. Which is certainly understandable. Then she had further trauma in selling the house. She has since moved out of there and seems a great deal calmer . . ."

He didn't neglect friends' birthdays. Bob Wetmore got one letter in January 1990 that apologized for sending a belated birthday greeting and thanked his old friend for talking to the public defender's aide, Henderson, who, he wrote, had been doing "a fair amount of traveling to talk to people who know me, to help in our defense posture." A month later, Bob wrote again, stating that pretrial hearings were about to get under way and then, "the real action begins." To an amazed Wetmore, it seemed that Bob was looking forward enthusiastically to the trial.

Wally Parsons in Richmond and Gary Morrison in Denver also received regular letters, which they came to eagerly anticipate. "The last letter I got from Bob," said Gary, "you know he's got a lot of time on his hands, so he plays a lot of solitaire, plus a little chess too. Well, he had developed a massive amount of figures for playing solitaire—how many times out of a hundred times through the deck would a king come up, the ace of spades come up, how many times out of a hundred tries would you make it all the way through the deck without having to back out? All kinds of variables. I got cross-eyed just looking at those figures."

At no time did the prisoner concede in writing what even his most steadfast friends knew well, that he was

John List. It was as if the rules of this game forbad conceding it.

But there were no protestations of innocence, at least, and a hint of self-righteousness began creeping into his correspondence. Early in the fall, a group of friends, including some of those he had played war-strategy games with by mail from Denver and Richmond, received a packet from Bob that contained photocopied pages from the religious manifesto of deMolinos, who had written:

"It is the nature of each of us to be rather base, proud, ambitious, full of a great deal of appetite, judgments, rationalizations and opinions," one passage said. "If something does not come into our lives to humiliate us, then surely all these things will undo us.

"So, what does your Lord do? He allows your faith to be assaulted, even with suggestions of pride, gluttony, rage . . . even despair . . .

"Your Lord desires to purify your soul, and He can use a very rough file. Yes, He may even assault the purer and nobler things of your life!"

Yet for a long time after the arrest, the prisoner had had to actually confront the past only in the private fortress of his own mind. But on November 7, 1989, two days before the eighteenth anniversary of the murders of Helen, Alma, Patricia, John, and Frederick List, he came face to face with that past.

At the invitation of Elijah Miller, Jean and Gene Syfert flew from Oklahoma to New Jersey. From the day of the arrest, Jean had been determined to confront John one day and demand to know, "Why?" She readily took the opportunity when it was offered.

She was very nervous. Sleepless the night before the flight from Oklahoma City, she fortified herself with ten milligrams of Valium before she and Gene made their way from the hotel at Newark Airport to the jail in Elizabeth.

"What if I see him and pass out?" she asked weakly after they arrived at the courthouse.

"We'll pick you up," he replied.

The lampposts on the streets in downtown Elizabeth were already festooned with Christmas decorations. The Syferts arrived at the jail around seven P.M. It was an unusually cold night for early November, a day not unlike the one on which the List family died.

Jean had no idea of what she would say to John after she asked him why.

Her pulse was racing when she and her husband were ushered into a brightly lighted reception area, where they waited nervously for the prisoner to be brought in. Elijah Miller waited with them. In a few minutes, John came in. He hesitated, but then crossed the room in his familiar bouncy, awkward gait. In the harsh glare of the jailhouse light, the tall, straight-backed form of John List came into sharp focus at last across the haze of the years. Jean recognized him instantly, that slightly lopsided face, more jowly now, those almost girlish lips, and that odd way he tilted his head when standing before someone. He hadn't changed all that much, really, from being the skinny, gawky young soldier she and her sister had met at the bowling alley near the army base, a lifetime ago. Now that he had come into her sight once more in tangible form, with substance and human dimensions again, she felt immediately at ease.

"How are you, John?" Jean said.

He nodded stiffly. She had forgotten how big a man he was, and was surprised by how haggard he looked. Standing there in his tan jail coveralls, he didn't know what to do with the papers he carried. Finally, he lay them on the table and stared at the floor.

"John?" Jean said.

She took a step toward him, and as she did he looked up with an odd, nervous grin. Then Jean did something that surprised herself almost as much as it did John. Impulsively she hugged him.

In that instant she offered what he had never asked for, forgiveness. The hatred was gone. There was still injury. But the bitterness and resentment dissipated as he put his arms around her and lay his head on her shoulder.

The top of her blouse was wet from his tears when he raised his head. He seemed mortified and frightened as he saw Gene Syfert, but then Gene reached out. Wordlessly, the two men shook hands. And then Gene hugged him.

"I think that gave John the shock of his life," Jean said afterward. "Gene grabbed him and hugged him. He really cried. I don't think he was ever expecting that from Gene."

They were allowed to use a private room on the third floor of the jailhouse to talk. It was a small, windowless space, about six feet by eight feet, with a table and a few chairs, one of the rooms used for private conferences between inmates and their attorneys. Elijah monitored the conversation, which went on for over three hours.

Not that it was a happy family reunion. The Syferts believed in mercy, but accountability was important, too.

"Why, John?" Jean said, posing the question she had waited eighteen years to ask.

He looked at her without emotion. "Because there was no other way," he said.

That was what he had written to her in 1971, nothing more.

"Why wasn't there another way?" Jean insisted. Why, instead of having to argue the matter in criminal court, hadn't it been argued in its appropriate venue, divorce court, for God's sake?

But he was impenetrable. The arrogance hadn't abated one bit. "It just had to be that way," he said. Clearly, the subject was closed, and had been since 1971.

Gene had memorized a short list of specific questions,

and after a while he wasn't gentle in asking them. But John didn't want to talk about matters pertaining directly to the crime, and John still had a way of controlling any conversation he engaged in.

Jean kept at it for a little while. "Did you know about Patty and the drugs?" asked Jean, who had found a small bag of marijuana when she searched Patty's room.

He seemed surprised by the question. "No, there were no drugs," he said.

That surprised her in turn. "Well, I think you're wrong," she said.

He didn't argue. It was clear to Jean, however, that concerns about drugs hadn't been a factor in his determination to kill Patty. Nor, the wagging tongues of Westfield aside, had her dabbling in witchcraft been a factor. Hearing about that, John was surprised, but not particularly interested.

"No, I never heard about anything like that," he said matter-of-factly.

Jean was astonished. Could this man really believe he murdered those people merely to do them the favor of saving them? She had never believed that he was insane, not for one minute. If not insanity, what was it, then? Was she looking into the abyss of an arrogance, at the cold depths of which lay the very definition of evil?

Why hadn't he killed himself that night, then?

Why could he live, but not the others?

She wanted to demand an answer to that—*Why didn't you kill yourself, too, John?*. But she was too polite to ask such a question to a man's face.

John was more at ease discussing things like D. B. Cooper. There was a palpable lessening of tension in the tiny room when the conversation turned to that, probably because it flattered his ego, Jean thought. While Jean had always dismissed as totally ridiculous the notion that John List was D. B. Cooper, Gene had believed that it was extremely unlikely, but just barely inside the limits of the possible. If a man has the audacity to dispassionately murder his family, one by one, what kind of a small leap of faith would it take to consider the possibility that he might be capable of hijacking an airplane fifteen days later?

Asked directly about it, John laughed heartily for the first time. No, D. B. Cooper was definitely someone else, he said. In fact, he found the idea as amusing as Jean did.

From that point, the conversation flowed more easily onto the subject of family. John asked about Brenda, and was happy to hear that he now even had step-great-grandchildren. He spoke happily of his own life with Delores in Denver. He asked about the Syfert family, about Eva Morris, Jean's mother, who had died with her nightmares two years earlier, about the Syferts' children. He didn't, however, recall the Syferts' oldest boy. That struck Jean as odd, since the boy had been the one closest to the List children. Like him, Jean thought, Patty and John and Fred they would be in their middle thirties now.

The encounter had a tinge of the surreal. On one side of the table sat the accused mass murderer, who still hadn't yet conceded outside that room that he was anyone other than Robert P. Clark, innocent victim of mistaken identity. Chatting affably with him were two of the three closest living relatives of John List. Shortly before they left, the defendant handed Jean a ten-page letter. She noticed that sections of it had been blacked out by his lawyer. She also saw that it was signed "Bob Clark."

At no time was the word "murder" uttered that night at the table in the jailhouse. But when it wasn't about family, the conversation was about murder. As they spoke, hampered by this awkward, unstated politeness that permitted only oblique references to the crime, Jean realized that she couldn't decide at all just where John List ended and Bob Clark began. Afterward, comparing notes at their hotel room, she and Gene agreed that the man with whom they had just spoken with couldn't either.

"I still saw a deep arrogance in him, and there is so much that I don't understand about why," Jean said later, trying to explain that strange encounter. "But I have compassion, and I think you really have to know John and his life to understand fully why. As far as I know, he would never threaten those children and he never hurt them . . ." Her voice trailed off as she realized the irony of this. "I don't think he really did think he hurt them, when you get down to the real nitty-gritty of it.

"In many ways, Helen's behavior contributed to the situation. How far can a person be pushed? If you didn't have any money, if you didn't have any way of making any more money, and you had all of these terrible problems staring you in the face, what would you do? Could you walk away?"

The question hung in the air before Jean answered it herself. "Of course, I would," she said softly. "I think I would just say, this is it, I can't take this any more, and I would leave."

Months earlier, the Westfield police chief, James Moran, had posed almost the same sort of question, having himself been bewildered by the swift death sentence John List had carried out on his family: "I know about husband and wife fights, long-standing things. I've seen them time and again. They happen. Bang. She gets him, running off. Bang. He gets her. And the mother? That was something else, but maybe he was doing it with some twisted reasoning that he was sparing her. Sparing her. But when I saw those three kids? If he was that desperate, that destitute, he could have just simply got in the car and driven off. Left them there. All of them! They wouldn't have starved to death. They wouldn't have died. He decided to have them die."

Another cop, Tracy, who headed the nearly abandoned investigation in its last years at the Westfield department, was more blunt. "Helen List was seriously ill and heavily medicated," Tracy said. "She had cerebral atrophy. Where was his Christian compassion when he shot her to death? He didn't show her Christian compassion, he showed her contempt."

Tracy added this personal assessment of the John List he had known about all of his adult life: "The guy is a mean, arrogant, selfish, hypocritical piece of shit."

Bob Wetmore said: "Some say Bob Clark was a wimp, but I never thought that. After a while I did begin to realize that he had a devious mind and was a cold, calculating son of a bitch. He was intelligent. But I guess he wasn't as intelligent as he thought he was."

But Gary Morrison said: "The man that I know is not capable of the atrocities that John List is accused of. As a friend, Bob helped see me through many rough times. He was a gentle man—he *is* a gentle man. If the legal system were to convict Bob Clark of being John List and there were ever a chance of a parole, my home is open to Bob. I would feel completely comfortable. The man has a home. There is just nothing that is going to come out and convince me other than that the man I knew was a gentle and kind friend, and my door will always be open to him."

Jean had heard all of the sentiments; indeed, she had subscribed to every one of them at various times. In one conversation in Oklahoma long before she saw John at the jail, she had scoffed at his presenting himself as "this religious person." She wondered, "If John had been the person he said he was, why didn't he just walk away? Nobody made him stay there. If there were problems or whatever the deal why didn't he just walk away? He must have liked the way things were most of the time."

Hadn't John etched pain and grief into eighteen years of her life? Hadn't John List assaulted her family's psyche with the force of a tossed bomb? Why had she forgiven him?

Jean wished she could be unequivocal. She was certainly aware, and quite satisfied, that John was likely to spend the rest of his life in state prison or a mental institution. He would die with his Bible and his arrogance to comfort him. That was more justice than he gave those children and her sister.

In time, Jean was, in fact, embarrassed to admit to the compassion she had felt and the forgiveness she had offered. For hadn't even the all-forgiving Jesus Christ insisted that repentance must come first? John List had been anything but repentant. Still, Jean had made her peace with the person who mattered, with herself. Unto Caesar would be rendered that which was indisputably Caesar's— John List would likely draw his last worldly breath in a New Jersey prison—and unto God would be rendered the final, personal, eternally unassailable judgment that she believed was the preserve of God alone.

"Gene and I both feel there was reason why everything happened," Jean said, apologizing for not being able to make herself more clear. "Not justification. But reason."

The day after she saw John, on a gray late afternoon, Jean went to Fairview Cemetery in Westfield for the first time in eighteen years. Oddly, after so many years, the tombstone still looked freshly chiseled. A clump of impatiens, the tenacious blossom of summer, had begun to wither in its well-tended bed at the base of the stone.

She read the inscriptions for what she knew would be the last time. She had no reason ever to come back, nor would there be any further point in considering moving the bodies of Helen and the children to North Carolina. She knew they were now as immutable a part of Westfield as the stream that burbled deep and everflowing under Elm Street and the hills that rippled to the Watchung range out past the land where Breeze Knoll once stood.

LIST
Patricia M. 1955–1971. Mother Helen L.
1924–1971.
Frederick M. 1958–1971. John F. 1956–1971.
There is peace in the eternal valley. Psalm 23.

The wind was brisk. A few lingering sparrows twittered in the trees in the meadow where the police had cordoned off spectators during the funeral. The birds and the wind and the leaves blowing on the road were the only sounds Jean heard as she read the names cut into the stone and tried to summon their memories to life.

There is peace in the eternal valley. The absence of emotion troubled her at first, until she recognized it for a kind of peace she hadn't known since before the phone call in the middle of the night in 1971.

The memories wouldn't come. *This is just an old grave marker*, she told herself. *Nobody that I know is here.*

Resentment, anger, and fear all were gone. Only sadness remained. She gathered her collar against the wind and returned to her car in the waning light of the November day.

Epilogue

ON APRIL 12, 1990, AFTER HEARING SEVEN DAYS OF TESTI-mony, a Union County jury found John List guilty of five counts of murder in the first degree. Since there was no capital punishment statute in effect in New Jersey in 1971, John was spared the death sentence he had summarily decreed for his wife, three children, and mother.

On May 1, Superior Court Judge William L. Werth-eimer imposed the maximum sentence, five consecutive life terms, thus ensuring that John would never be eligible for parole. "The name of John Emil List will be eternally synonymous with concepts of selfishness, horror, and evil," the judge said with contempt as John stood at attention before him. "John Emil List is without remorse and with-out honor. After eighteen years, five months, and twenty-two days, it is now time for the voices of Helen, Alma, Patricia, Frederick, and John F. List to rise from the grave."

Well before the trial began, the defense dropped its insistence that the state would have to prove that Bob Clark was John List. Robert P. Clark disappeared unceremoni-ously in a flurry of defense motions that could only be made on behalf of John Emil List, among them unsuc-cessful petitions for a change of venue and suppression of evidence. And in his opening statement to the jury, defense lawyer Elijah Miller promptly conceded one other obvious fact—that John List had indeed done what the indictment said he had. After nine months of exhaustive work that had consumed a significant portion of the county public defender's office budget and time, Miller told the jury that "John List's long odyssey has come to an end.

"Let there be no mistake," the tall, thin lawyer declared. "John Emil List on November 9, 1971, killed his family."

During pretrial hearings a week earlier, Judge Wertheimer had rejected Miller's impassioned arguments for suppressing the confession letter to Rehwinkle, which Miller contended had been obtained as the result of an illegal police search and was furthermore protected under "priest-penitent" confidentiality. With the confession letter in evidence and the jurors in place, Miller now had only a few avenues of defense left. While he long ago had decided against trying to argue that John was insane, Miller would attempt to show that John was hampered by a "fragmented" personality. He described his client, who sat calmly at the defense table, as a "tragedy of immense proportion" who was "not programmed to deal with overwhelming problems.

"My client was clearly out of step with the times," Miller said. On November 9, 1971, steeped in "Old World values," aghast at the social upheavals roiling America, battered by severe personal troubles, fearful of what the future held for his children, "his whole world was crumbling," Miller insisted. "On that fateful day, he slipped from despair into oblivion, and entered hell with his eyes open. For the salvation of his family, he acted as he did."

In the opening statement for the prosecution, Assistant Union County Prosecutor Brian Gillet read the Rehwinkle letter to the jury in a tone that was cold, with a trace of mockery. He went over John's request for his minister's prayers: "I will need them whether or not the government does its duty as it sees it."

Gillet paused and gazed from face to face among the

nine men and three women on the jury. This day, he said, the government intended to "do its duty."

He described John as "cruel, evil, and calculating," a failure at marriage, fatherhood, and career who "literally closed the books and blanced out the accounts before taking on a new life" after slaughtering his loved ones on "a day of horror."

On the first day of testimony, the prosecution called seventeen witnesses, among them bank tellers and even the milkman who had come to the house on the day of the murders. Slowly, layer after layer of evidence piled up to persuade the jury that John had committed the murders with full knowledge of the difference between right and wrong, with premeditation, deliberation, willfulness, and malice—the definition of first-degree murder. The most indisputable evidence came in fingerprints, ballistics reports, and autopsies. But the most persuasive, as the defense had known, was the letter to Rehwinkle, which depicted in such grotesque precision a crime that met every condition for first-degree murder.

The defense used one last tactic to deflect the jury from the severest verdicts and perhaps lead it to the conclusion that John was guilty of manslaughter, at least as regarded Helen. Over objections of the prosecution, which deemed the information irrelevant and inflammatory, Miller managed to have entered into evidence the nature of the illness that was destroying Helen List: syphilis.

This was what had sent her home from Korea as a medical emergency in 1947. She had gotten it from Marvin, her first husband, who was so fond of carousing with Seoul bar girls while his wife stayed home with Brenda. After an initial period of severe sickness—the only time it is contagious—syphilis typically lies deceptively dormant, sometimes for twenty years or more, before rising again to torture its victim to a painful death riddled with delusions and fever. Helen had managed to hide the disease from

John until the late 1960s, when the deadly tertiary phase of the disease finally manifested itself, incapacitating her and driving her slowly mad. She had guarded her secret closely, even on occasions such as childbirth and other hospitalizations. In 1951, she had insisted to John that they be married in Maryland, where a blood test was not then required. Over the years, as the initial onslaught of the sickness faded into memory, she had even managed to convince herself that she was cured of it.

When he learned the truth in 1969 after her last hospitalization, John was devastated. But he knew he could not have contracted the disease himself, and he knew the children had not. He told a minister at the time that he understood it "isn't her fault," and that Helen had been unknowingly infected by someone she loved and trusted.

The testimony about Helen's disease had no effect on the outcome of the trial. After the verdict was returned, it seemed clear that all the defense had accomplished was to underscore the tragedy of her life. Helen List, physically abused as a child by her mother, fled into two successive marriages. Her first husband, who died a war hero, gave her syphilis. Her second husband murdered her and three of her children.

After the defense rested on the seventh day of the trial, the prosecution called a psychiatrist, Dr. Steven Simring, to rebut the testimony of a defense psychological expert who had declared John to be an "obsessive-compulsive" person who could not always make reasonable decisions when faced with a variety of options.

In late March, Simring had interviewed John for four hours. In his trial testimony Simring disputed the defense contention that John was suffering from a clinical personality disorder. In fact, Simring asserted, John was suffering from nothing more than a situational depression of the sort that is usually referred to in lay terms as a midlife crisis.

As courtroom spectators listened spellbound, the doctor

went on to describe, often in the murderer's own words, the utter banality of John List's rationalization for murder:

"My mother was a kind woman, overly concerned about my health," John had said. "She always made sure I was overly warm . . . wearing my rubbers, my galoshes."

He remembered being spanked twice as a boy, once by his mother for a forgotten reason and once by his father, with a leather strap, for misbehaving in church. Otherwise, John described a childhood that was remarkably uneventful. "I've always been somewhat anxious about pleasing and not disrupting. I was well behaved in school, in the army, with my wife, and with my mother," he said, describing both women as "strong-willed, domineering people" whom he strove mightily to please.

Without emotion he discussed his marriage to Helen in 1951 after she had told him, apparently falsely, that she was pregnant. "I was always taught not to have intercourse before marriage. I slipped into it," he said. On the eve of their wedding, "Helen told me she was very happy she wasn't actually pregnant. I'm not sure to this day whether she was pregnant or not pregnant."

He recalled the years in Kalamazoo, which soon became clouded with marital and career problems. John resented what he regarded as Helen's flirting with other men. "I once hit this guy for overdoing it," he boasted. "Yes, for kissing my wife. There were other occasions when she overstepped her bounds."

Over the years, Helen complained often about their sex life, which even John conceded "wasn't too good." In their later years together, "she suggested erotic movies—porno. It helped our sex life." But the films were nothing kinky, he added quickly.

About his job problems, he at last seemed to have a glint of understanding. "I couldn't delegate authority well," he admitted. "I couldn't supervise men and women who worked for me."

He recalled how his troubles intensified in Westfield. "I was unemployed," he said. "I couldn't do well at a job. I was borrowing from my mother. Helen was getting worse. I was praying something would happen. The pressure was building up. I couldn't function. I was concerned at the way I was raised. I was always told to handle my own problems. My mother and Helen knew there were problems. I didn't let them know how bad they were."

He said he was worried about Patty's friends' use of marijuana (he was not aware, however, that Patty smoked pot herself on occasion, or that she had become fascinated with the theatrical trappings of witchcraft). "I was concerned that she and the boys would drift away from the church," he explained once again. "I couldn't support them. . . . Finally, I broke and killed them."

Simring testified that before making his final decision, John had carefully "weighed his various options—killing himself, running away, which was an option. Unfortunately, he never considered the option of getting a job."

John told him, "I thought if I [killed them all], my family would all go to heaven and, at least later on, I would have a chance to go to heaven. However, if I committed suicide, there would be a hundred percent, automatically, that I would go to hell.

"I kept praying. There was no income. There was no other solution. Finally, I decided it was the only way. It was a horrible thing, but once I started, I was like on autodrive. I killed them all so that no one would survive. It's like I had no control all the while I was doing it. It's like some force, something that made me move, something beyond my control, and it just got started."

After shooting Helen and Alma, John recalled, "I cleaned up the mess. I don't know what I did the rest of the morning, exactly."

Discussing how he had killed his eldest son later in the day, the murderer said, "John was different. His body had some jerky motions." After shooting the boy nine times, he turned him over to finish him off. "I shot him in the heart, because I didn't want to see him suffer," John said.

In leaving no survivors, John reasoned, "no one would have to think about what happened. That would be worse. It was almost with a sigh of relief that I killed them all and there weren't one or two survivors. Looking back on such a horrible thing, if I had to do it over again, I'd find some other way. I'd try to get help."

Dispassionately, in what the psychiatrist called a businesslike voice, John discussed his escape:

"I didn't really think I would get away with it for more than a week or two," he said. "When I got away with it for so long I was surprised. . . . I decided to stay free as long as I could. I might have had it in my mind to turn myself in, but I never gave it serious consideration. I was afraid of the consequences. I was afraid I would go to jail for a long time."

During his nearly eighteen years as a fugitive, John never gave the slightest hint to anyone about his crimes. "I was enjoying my life," he explained. "I didn't want anything to disrupt my life. I didn't want to burden anybody else."

Indeed, by the time he was starting to prosper in his new career in the restaurant business in Denver, he had already managed to come to terms with the horror of what he had done. "I prayed for forgiveness," John said. "After a while I only thought about it on the anniversary of their deaths."

Why had he left behind a detailed confession letter?

"I had to tell somebody about what had occurred," he told the psychiatrist.

Why had he chosen Denver to hide?

"I knew I wanted to head west. I always wanted to see the mountains. You know, Doc, this is a big country. It's easy to lose yourself."

The jury and spectators sat in stunned silence as Simring

finished recounting what John had told him. Simring then
added his own assessment. In describing the murders, John
"did not feel the enormity of guilt and remorse and sadness
at the loss of his family. I think he's a rather cold-blooded
individual," Simring said as the defendant stared at him
impassively, one eyebrow slightly raised. The doctor found
it remarkable that John had seen fit to lie in his confession
letter about shooting the victims from behind. Nor did he
give credence to John's professed religious motivation. Actually, he suggested, John seemed to switch back and forth
among various excuses "to suit his convenience."

Simring concluded, "He wanted grace in the hereafter,
but he didn't want arrest yet. There's religious belief and
there's religious hypocrisy. I think there's a fair amount
of hypocrisy here."

Fittingly, John ultimately managed to find no support
from the religion whose name he had so shamelessly in-
voked. Even ministers who had known him and sympathized with his problems over the years offered scant
comfort when they were called by Miller to attest to John's
good character and to bolster a defense contention that
suicide—the only unforgivable sin, in John's eyes—had
not been an option. By this stage of the trial, well aware
that a verdict of second-degree murder was the best he
could hope for, Miller realized that it was crucial to defuse
a question that was certainly going to be asked in the jury
room: If John had really, in some twisted sense, believed
that he had legitimate religious reasons for killing his family, why had he not also then killed himself? Why had he
instead chosen to lead a new life free from the liabilities
of that family, and enjoyed that life of freedom for almost
eighteen years? Why was he still alive?

But the clerical witnesses declined to lend support to
the notion that John had managed to enjoy life after killing
only because suicide was the single greatest sin. Reverend

Edward Saresky, the List family pastor in Rochester, agreed that John had encountered serious difficulties managing his career at Xerox in the early 1960s, and said that Helen had made matters worse. "She made a comment to me that was very painful," Saresky testified. "She said that if John was half the man her former husband was, they wouldn't have all the troubles they were having." Yet Saresky wouldn't be drawn into speculation about John's excuses for murder. "Sin is still sin," the minister insisted. "Grace is available for the sinner, but sin is never justified." Saresky, though a key defense witness, helped Miller's case not at all when he added his belief that John's view of religion was inherently corrupt. "John's problem is he knew doctrine, but he didn't know faith. I think John did not trust God."

Reverend Alfred Scheips, who had been the Lutheran chaplain for the youth group John belonged to at the University of Michigan, also failed to come to the rescue. "Thou shalt not kill," the minister intoned in response to Miller's questioning on sin. "Taking a life is certainly wrong." On cross-examination, Scheips described John as "a religious person, but not a fanatic."

Finally, it was the prosecution that framed the theological answer for the jury on cross-examination of Scheips, when he was asked whether there was a greatest sin, a sin for which there could be no forgiveness.

The minister considered his reply for a few seconds before quoting C. S. Lewis: "Pride is the greatest sin."

By the year 2000, 2 out of 3 Americans could be illiterate.

It's true.

Today, 75 million adults...about one American in three, can't read adequately. And by the year 2000, U.S. News & World Report envisions an America with a literacy rate of only 30%.

Before that America comes to be, you can stop it...by joining the fight against illiteracy today.

Call the Coalition for Literacy at toll-free **1-800-228-8813** and volunteer.

Volunteer Against Illiteracy. The only degree you need is a degree of caring.